GOD
Meets the World

BATYA SHEMESH

Copyright © Batya Shemesh

All rights reserved. No part of this book may be reproduced in any form or by any electronic or mechanical means, including information storage and retrieval systems, without permission in writing from the publisher, except by reviewers, who may quote brief passages in a review.

ISBN: 978-1-64606-730-5   (Paperback Edition)
ISBN: 978-1-64606-731-2   (Hardcover Edition)
ISBN: 978-1-64606-729-9   (E-book Edition)

Some characters and events in this book are fictitious. Any similarity to real persons, living or dead, is coincidental and not intended by the author.

Book Ordering Information

Phone Number: 347-901-4929 or 347-901-4920
Email: info@globalsummithouse.com
Global Summit House
www.globalsummithouse.com

Printed in the United States of America

ACKNOWLEDGEMENTS

I wish to thank the Lord our God, King of the universe, for giving us the Torah and the Ten Commandments, so that we may be guided on the right path. Thank you for choosing me to be your emissary to teach the Ten Commandments and spread out your wisdom, through my work.

Thank you David, my dear husband for working days and nights editing and perfecting my work. Thank you for your encouragement, praise and scholarly additions throughout this very important project.

Let's give a big applause to my son Jonathan who is constantly helping with the cooking and housework, so that I have free time to delve into the Bible and write.

Contents

Acknowledgements v
Introduction ix

Chapter 1:   The Laws of Noah 1
Chapter 2:   The Covenant.. 20
Chapter 3:   God Meets the World............................... 39
Chapter 4:   "I Am the Lord Your God" 52
Chapter 5:   Idol Worship 68
Chapter 6:   Do Not Take God's Name in Vain........... 117
Chapter 7:   The Sabbath 132
Chapter 8:   Honor Your Father and Mother 177
Chapter 9:   Do Not Murder....................................... 198
Chapter 10: Do Not Commit Adultery or Incest 223
Chapter 11: Do Not Steal 255
Chapter 12: Do Not Bear False Witness..................... 287
Chapter 13: Do Not Covet.. 303
Chapter 14: The Eternal Laws 313

Epilogue: God's Way 317
Glossary 321
Index 335

Introduction

A robust argument was once occurred in a fifth-grade classroom in New York. The girls stayed late after school as they debated with rising emotions. Over what subject did these eleven-year-old youngsters bicker with each other? What was so important to these girls that they were willing to spend their time after school engaged in a heated argument? Boys? Clothing? Gossip? No, nothing like that. These eleven-year-old girls were arguing about the observance of the Sabbath.

I started the contention in that classroom. I was so zealous for God that I became overwhelmingly upset by the thought that a Jewish girl's father worked on Saturday. I remember speaking with a tremendous passion, as if I were a politician having a public debate.

I came from a world of Orthodox Jewry where the words of the Torah and the whole Bible are observed in detail. Orthodox Jews not only obey the physical commandments, they fulfill the emotional and spiritual decrees like, "You must love your God with all your heart, all your soul and all your strength." (Deuteronomy 6:5) I was very devout and ahead of my years in terms of maturity.

****

In my first book "Who is God?" I tell the story of my first encounter with God and the nature of my conversations with Him. I also present many basic questions of faith like reward, punishment, free choice, justice and even the afterlife.

In this book I offer new insights that shed a light on very practical questions. What does God really think about our world? What are God's rules of justice? How should they be implemented?

The most important part of the Bible is the Ten Commandments. When I was in the sixth grade my teacher taught us that the Ten Commandments are the basis for all the laws in the Torah. I said to myself, *"One day I would like to study the Ten Commandments in depth to figure out how this can be true."* I believe that this day has come.

I am very excited to present this project to my readers. The day that God uttered these Commandments on Mount Sinai was the day that "God met the world." God entered the physical realm by uttering the Commandments out loud for all to hear. This was the greatest prophecy ever. Millions of people heard God's voice emanating from Mount Sinai and lived to tell the story.

In the following pages, I will strive to answer various questions you may have about the Ten Commandments. For example: When did God decide to write ten main laws? How were they given to the world? How are they meant to be implemented? To whom are these Commandments addressed? And the most important question of all: Are they still applicable today?

The American government prides itself for separation between church and state. It's a wonderful ideology and made America a place of refuge for numerous people from many different nations. The flaw of this ideology is that the new generation, the children, are not given a fair choice. The public schools teach the theory of evolution as if it were factual without teaching the Bible or even the possibility of a world created by God. The majority of Americans are not familiar with even the most basic Bible stories. If the establishment wants to be fair, then they should not teach evolution or Bible. The children can go to Sunday schools or after school programs and even their parents can give them some heritage. By teaching evolution on one hand and avoiding any talk about God, the new generation is biased. They get the unsaid message that God is the opium of the masses but the science of evolution is fact. Today there are archeologists and scientists that are proving otherwise.

The belief in God is so basic to the human instinct that public education and media must persistently work hard to constantly keep faith from oozing into the minds of the young and the old. The television, the Internet and our daily struggle to earn a living all distract us from thinking about God, all the more so, talking to Him.

Questions about God and spirituality are left unanswered because the public schools are prohibited from mentioning His name. These children cannot further their understanding of life and faith beyond the sanctity of their own household or religious classes. By the time youngsters complete their secular high school education, they have settled on their ideology in life with almost no room for change. They believe in the American dream of individual financial success and other secular values, including sexual mores which violate the seventh of the Ten Commandments.

You might argue that if you want your children exposed to an education which includes religious ideology, you can send your kids to private school. I feel that the simple people that can't afford private school also deserve a chance for their children to know who God is. If the population at large had faith instilled in them, the crime rate, gambling, alcohol and drug abuse as well as sexual abuse would drop and the respect for their elders would rise. Kids would learn how to behave. Many adults first learn of a Creator in prison or addiction programs such as A.A. Today's ever increasing heroin addiction and other substance abuse is directly related to the lack of spirituality in the school and work places.

The Supreme Laws

The picture of Moses holding the Ten Commandments appears on the façade of the Supreme Court Building. Many states have built monuments of the Ten Commandments in front of their own supreme courts. Some states have ordered the monument removed because it is a violation of separation between church and state.

The states that allowed the public display of The Ten Commandments voted that they are part of history. I would say that they are not only a part of world history but they are respected worldwide.

The Texas State Capital has a beautiful monument of the Ten Commandments illustrated below. The U.S. Supreme Court in a 5-4 ruling established that displays of the Ten Commandments in Kentucky violated the first Amendment of separation of church and state but did not do so in Texas. Even though the Ten Commandments are not the basis for American jurisprudence, people all over the world feel an attachment and respect for these tablets.

I am sorry to say that today in America, there is more respect for the doctors' tablets than the tablets of Moses. However, these Ten Commandments have more ability to save our youth and our future than any doctor's prescriptions.

The Ten Commandments represent and promote a way of life. The way of life that the Bible dictates is a major improvement on man-made judicial systems. It is fascinating to learn about how God would run the world if He did it "His way." This book is an eye opener.

What good does it do to imagine a perfect world? We certainly can't change the whole judicial system. Nevertheless, every person should know God's opinion of what's right and what's wrong, what is forgivable and what is not. It will boost your own sense of justice, free you from obsessive guilt and clarify your mistakes. It will also help you forgive the forgivable and distance yourself from those that have done unforgivable harm.

After the Israelites entered the Land of Israel they forgot all the miracles that God made in Egypt and in the Desert. They sinned by worshipping other gods and forsaking the Holy Torah and the Ten Commandments. When Moses gave his last speech to the Israelites he knew that they would sin and the observance of the Ten Commandments and the Torah would be postponed for a future date.

That day has come. Today we are wise enough to learn the Bible and study God's commandments. This book will show that the Ten Commandments were given to the Israelites in order to teach them to the world. Even without anyone telling them, the gentiles of the world are so attached to the Ten Commandments they fight in court to erect monuments of the Tablets of Moses in and around major state and federal institutions of justice. They feel connected to these laws because as humans created in God's Image we were born with a will to do God's will. The Ten Commandments are a concise summary of His will.

This book gives good solid advice that can be applied to daily living and real problems. I have addressed numerous complex situations that may prevent a person from being able to fulfil the Ten Commandments and have given you God's opinions and ideas. You will get the feeling from this book that God is not so much of a fundamentalist. He is wise and reasonable and most of all He really cares.

A Few Guidelines

Before we begin, I would like to establish a few guidelines to help you understand some of the Hebrew words that I used extensively in this book.

From very early childhood we call God *"Hashem,"* which means the Name. We use it in order to avoid saying God's name in vain. It has become like a nickname, full of love and fond memories.

We also use three other words very frequently:

1) The word *Torah* means the Five Books of Moses, or what is called in English the Pentateuch. The *Torah* can also mean the entire Bible and even the whole Jewish tradition. Many Orthodox Jews consider themselves part of the "Torah World." They also say that they are "Torah observant Jews." In this book when I say Torah, I usually mean the Five

Books of Moses but not always. Sometimes I mean the whole Bible and sometimes I say "Torah Law," meaning God's law as explained in the Torah. It will be apparent from the context.
2) The word Mitzvah means an obligation that the Torah demands from us, whether it's a prohibition, a positive command or just a good deed. The plural of Mitzvah is Mitzvot or Mitzvoth. The Ten Commandments are Mitzvot but so are all the other laws in the Torah.
3) Shabbat: Sabbath in Hebrew. In Israel the colloquial name for Saturday is *Shabbat*. The Eastern European Jews call the Sabbath *Shabbos*. I use the word *Shabbos* in a song about the Sabbath but mostly I use the name Shabbat.

Other words that I used, I translated or explained when I employ them for the first time. They are also in the glossary at the end of the book. I didn't put words in the glossary if they are just a transliteration of a specific Biblical word that is used only once in the whole book.

The Torah gives us background history and detailed explanation of what Hashem really wants us to do. There are many laws in the Torah that are directly connected to the Ten Commandments, some of which I mention in these coming chapters. Many laws in the Torah are special for the Israelites, like the holidays and holy days. While the dietary laws in Bible are stricter for Jews than for non-Jews, Hashem told me that the Ten Commandments were meant for the entire world.

The accuracy of the words of the whole Bible is extremely important. I did some of my own translating of the Bible quotes in all of my books because I couldn't always find scriptural translations that bring out the precise Hebrew meaning. I usually quote the NIV translation before I give my own.

Sometimes translators and interpreters skip words or make grammatical corrections to the Hebrew text. The Bible must be explained without any additions or subtractions. The correct translation may change the entire meaning of words and verses.

For example, Isaiah 58:3 in the NIV translation says, "'Why have we fasted,' they say, 'and you have not seen it?' 'Why have we humbled ourselves, and you have not noticed?' Yet on the day of your fasting, you do as you please and exploit all your workers."

The King James translation says, "Wherefore have we fasted, say they, and thou seest not? Wherefore have we afflicted our soul, and thou takest no knowledge? Behold, in the day of your fast ye find pleasure, and exact all your labours."

There is no reference to workers or labors in the original text. The word is 'Atzabachem,' which means your idols. When the same word is used in Psalms 115, 4 it is translated as idols in the NIV and the KJV translations.

The true meaning of the above verse in Isaiah 58:3 is that Isaiah was angry with those who fast for God and still worship their idols. Just like Elijah said on Mount Carmel, 1 Kings, 18:21, "Until when will you be standing on two thresholds?" At the time the nation of Israel was accustomed to the "changing of the gods."

The complaint of worshiping idols and God at the same time is much more serious grievance than just exploiting workers. If someone worships other gods, Hashem won't answer his prayers. However, if someone isn't perfect and he tries to fast but he hasn't been a good and caring boss, Hashem will still answer him and help him change his ways. You don't have to be perfect to get Hashem's mercy, but you cannot worship other gods. That makes the Almighty distant. Thus, the above are imperfect translations, which lead to an imperfect understanding of what the prophet truly meant. Hashem has helped me give many accurate translations and a much better understanding of the Bible.

I hope and pray that my books will be a source of wisdom in every household that treasures the Bible. It is my dream to continue writing and spreading true meaning of the Bible to the world.

The ideas that I explain here are not all known to mainstream Judaism. I have had many questions about God ever since I was very young. I was also curious about what really happened in Jewish history. In my next book *God's Hidden Treasure,* I will reveal new insights on ancient Jewish History that have never been told before. I thank Hashem for giving me insights that are so convincing and clear that anyone who studies my books with a clear objective mindset, will never perceive the Bible any other way.

I hope and pray that you learn and grow from this book and share your experience with others. It is fascinating to learn what God really meant when He wrote the Torah. You will also begin to understand who God is and what He expects from his most profound creations: Humans.

Permission to Speak

Religious people have God all figured out. He is what religion dictates Him to be. All the Monotheistic religions differ in their definition of God. From the Dark Ages until our modern society, God has been placed as a distant deity only accessible to clergymen with whom He doesn't speak. God was not given permission to speak. He has been quite obedient to the precepts of the religions, but in this generation, He doesn't want to stay quiet any more. Many people, young and old, have heard the voice of God while they are sleeping or awake. Many people have met the Almighty in near death experiences, and are respected.

If someone tells people that God speaks to him or her, their reactions vary. Believe it or not, the first thing that many people ask me is what their personal future will be. The future is not set in stone. It's up to us, determined by our efforts, our deeds, and our prayers.

Maimonides, a famous Torah scholar and doctor who lived in the thirteenth century, wrote the following in his book on prophecy:

> "If a prophet says that something bad is going to happen and it doesn't come true, the prophet is not necessarily a false prophet. The Holy one blessed be He is merciful and maybe the people will repent like the nation of Nineveh, or Hashem decided to postpone his decree like he did with Hezekiah. However, if a prophet foresees a positive future and it doesn't come true, he is a false prophet and should be ostracized. If Hashem tells a prophet His plans for punishments, there is always room for repentance that can change His plans. However, if Hashem promises a good

future, He will surely keep His promise. If it doesn't come true he is a false prophet" (Maimonides, "The Laws of the Principles of the Torah" Chapter 10, Rule number 4.)

Maimonides teachings are widely accepted in Jewish circles. What he is saying in the above passage is: If a prophet foresees a good future it should come true, otherwise you have a false prophet. However, if a prophet sees a bad future pray that it should turn around.

Are You Crazy?

The reaction of many hearing that God speaks to a simple person could be, "This person is insane." Let me give you the words of my husband, David Shemesh, a clinical psychologist who gave his professional opinion:

> *"People who claim that God speaks with them should be judged sane or not, by indices of sanity. Productive, healthy people with good judgment who are rational in their behaviors should not be deemed insane for simply claiming God speaks with them."*

If a person functions normally, has friends, makes a living, lives in a neat functional home and does not need psychiatric medication, but claims that God speaks to him or her, there are only two possibilities. It may be true, or the person may be lying. The possibility that a person functions normally most of the time but is also mentally ill due to an abnormality, in only one important aspect, such as hearing voices, is not medically possible.

That doesn't mean you have to believe every person who claims he or she has a special gift. Many people have all kinds of psychic powers. For example, there are those who possess the ability to speak with the dead or tell the future. There have been many fortune tellers as well as false prophets and false Messiahs throughout the ages. Some of these people really do have psychic abilities, but they are not necessarily messengers of God.

The Torah warns us about a prophet who will give signs and make miracles and then tells you to worship other gods:

> Deuteronomy 13:1–4
> If a prophet, or one who foretells by dreams, appears among you and announces to you a sign or wonder, and if the sign or wonder spoken of takes place, and the prophet says, "Let us follow other gods" (gods you have not known) "and let us worship them," you must not listen to the words of that prophet or dreamer. The Lord your God is testing you to find out whether you love him with all your heart and with all your soul. It is the Lord your God you must follow, and Him you must revere. Keep His commands and obey Him; serve Him and hold fast to Him.

The above verses convey that God is testing you. He wants to see if you really love Him with all your heart and soul. Even if someone produces wonders or miracles, it does not prove that he is a prophet. A prophet is a true prophet when he or she does not add or subtract anything from the original laws of the Torah, the first five books of the Bible. The job of a prophet isn't to create new laws but to teach the original ones and to bring people closer to Hashem.

Even if you are not a prophet and you don't hear Hashem's voice do not be discouraged from having intuition or psychic feelings. Hashem created this world with energies that are not all tangible and he gave some people a talent to tune in. If you too have this talent it is important to say that what you feel is just a feeling and not necessarily the absolute truth. You can say what you feel but it can always change. Like Maimonides said, "Hashem has mercy."

However, if a prophet is not speaking about the future but is just reiterating God's will, His words cannot be changed. The biggest prophecy of all times was a prophecy delivered before millions of men, women and children.

When a prophet hears God's voice he doesn't hear it with his ears. Hashem mixes into his mind, he hears the words in his head. When the Israelites heard God's voice it was out loud in full voice. This level of prophecy was just like Moses who spoke to God face to face. At Mount Sinai God spoke to millions of people at the same time, face to face. Hashem's magnanimous message was not short; it was rewritten in Exodus chapter twenty, word for word. We call this prophecy, The Ten Commandments.

The entire Ten Commandments are directives that cannot be denied or cancelled. God made a covenant between Himself and the People of Israel to keep those Commandments and teach them to the world. They are a covenant that even God Himself cannot retract.

There are many religions in the world, but there is no religion and no other claim, aside from this one, that God addressed millions. It is not conceivable that anyone would tell a story and say that there were millions of witnesses unless it were true. In order to withdraw a prophecy on that scale, we would have to receive another directive on the same enormity.

The goal of this book is to emphasize the importance of these Commandments. Adhering to The Ten Commandments will bring you blessings from heaven. In order to properly fulfil them, you have to learn and understand what they are and how they apply in different situations. In *God Meets the World*, I present you with evidence from the Bible that what I am saying is really God's will and God's way.

The Bible was written three thousand five hundred years ago and it is still fascinating and a contemporary best seller. That alone is enough to prove how special it is. The more you learn the more you will believe that the Old Testament was written by a loving God. This book will help you understand the Bible and learn more about Hashem's opinion in different life situations.

Chapter 1

The Laws of Noah

Before I delve into the specifics of the Ten Commandments, I will tell the story about how God thought of the idea to give ten commandments to the world. He started with Noah.

After the first days of creation, Hashem was really proud of the world that He created. He didn't want to plan the future for this world. He wanted to see what would happen if He let people live and make choices on their own.

At the time of Noah, the people were so wicked that God regretted creating the world. Genesis 6:8 reads: "And God regretted that He created man in the land and He was sad in His heart." Not only did man fail to advance his character, but he also sinned. Mankind learned to cheat, steal, and kill with the superior intelligence that God gave them. The failure of Noah's generation to use this wonderful world properly made Hashem realize that mankind needed guidance and rules.

What Went Wrong in Noah's Generation?

Our current world is thousands of years old. He created this world on the planet earth after many, many failures. The discoveries of archeology that establish that the age of the earth is hundreds of millions of years old are findings from previous worlds on the same earth. The earth is ancient but what we call "Our World," is only what we have since Adam. The world of dinosaurs, for example, was destroyed, and so were many others.

What happened before Genesis, on an earth that existed for untold millions of years is not the topic of the Bible. Genesis 1:1 "In the beginning God created the heavens and the earth." That is about all the Torah says about the years before Genesis. In my first book *Who is God?* I explain fascinating details about the years before creation and about the six days of creation that are written in the Bible.

When Hashem created this world, He thought He did a good job. "And God saw that it was good" is mentioned in Genesis chapter 1, after each day of creation. Hashem was very excited to create a human being who could communicate with others and with Him. This is the first world that has a talking man—the creation of a mortal in the "image of God."

Hashem is just like us; we were created in His image. He gets upset and even angry, when people are corrupt. Ten generations after Adam, people became so evil and corrupt that Hashem regretted creating the world.

One man calmed Hashem down, Noah. (Noah means calm in Hebrew.) Noah was so good that it gave Hashem hope that maybe the world could still be successful. After the flood, Hashem started to think about a new plan and thought to Himself:

> Genesis 8:21, "Never again will I curse the ground because of humans, even though every inclination of the human heart is evil from childhood. And never again will I destroy all living creatures, as I have done."

This verse is evidence that there is an evil inclination. God created us with a conscience for good and one for bad. It's not the devil or Satan who makes us do bad things; it's our conscience. When children are only two years old, they already know what they want. They are already capable of making decisions. But the decisions they make are based on their own experiences, which are very limited. In order to be able to make wise decisions, we need more knowledge than can be acquired just by observation. Without any knowledge, we don't know what to choose. We follow our instincts or inclination which is "evil from our youth."

Hashem realized that giving humankind the gift of free choice was risky. The choices we make can be bad. Nevertheless, He gave us free choice in order to reward us with the pleasure of self-accomplishment. No matter how many presents we receive, the feeling of pride and joy we acquire from having accomplished success on our own, with or without assistance, provides a much more superior inner state of satisfaction and wellbeing.

Originally, Hashem wanted humans to figure out how to build a good and just world on their own. That didn't work, so He decided to help us by giving mankind basic rules to follow. The more we know and understand, the better we will be at making the right choice. Hashem gave Noah a few guidelines to begin.

The Seven Laws of Noah

Rabbinical Judaism teaches that God gave Noah seven laws. These laws are very basic. Many Jews believe that it is our duty to teach these laws to the nations of the world, as follows:

1) Belief in only one God.
2) Do not curse God.
3) Do not kill.
4) Do not commit incest or adultery.
5) Do not steal.
6) Do not eat a limb of any animal while the animal is still alive.
7) It is mandatory to build a system of justice.

There is an American movement called "The Sons of Noah." They follow these rules religiously and are loyal to the God of Israel and the Jewish people even though they do not convert to Judaism.

Ten Commandments for Noah

I would like to make some variations on the traditional Seven Laws of Noah. The following are the laws that God gave to Noah as they are written clearly or encoded in scripture:

1) Belief in one Creator.
2) Do not worship other creations.
3) Be fruitful and multiply.
4) Do not commit adultery or incest.
5) Do not murder other humans or yourself.
6) Do not abort a human fetus.
7) Do not shame others or do them any harm.
8) Do not eat meat with its blood.
9) Build a justice system.
10) Remember the covenant of the rainbow.

****

In the following pages I will explain each of these laws in detail as described in Scripture.

1) Believe in one God who created the world.

Noah already believed in one God. Hashem didn't have to preach to him. What Hashem did ask of Noah was to keep a covenant with Him. The sign of the covenant was the rainbow.

> Genesis 9:17 says, "So God said to Noah, 'This is the sign of the covenant I have established between me and all life on the earth.'"

Hashem is on one side and all life on earth is on the other. This symbolizes the oneness of God, who is the Creator of the whole world. In order to believe in the Covenant you have to believe that Hashem has the possibility to fulfill it. Only a god that has full reign over the whole world can make such a promise.

Before we teach our children about God as a law giver we should teach them about God as the Creator of the world and the universe.

2) Do not worship other creations.

> Genesis 9:2, "Your fear and dread will be on all the animals, the birds in the sky and all those who crawl on the land."

The word *dread* is not an exact translation; it's should be translated as awe and respect. The animals are to respect and fear you, not the other way around.

This is a blessing and a commandment. We are commanded to rule over the earth. We should not worship other animals or trees or even people. We should use them for our benefit. That doesn't mean that we have the right to abuse them any more than your boss has a right to abuse you. The world is ours. We must take care of it.

God gave us the power to rule over animal and plant life. He gave us an innate self confidence that we are the superior species. When you worship God, you feel self-confident. When you worship idols you become subservient to them. An idol worshipper is worried that he must appease his god and give him donations and sacrifices.

Even today there are people in the world that still worship animals and even bugs. Animal worshipping civilizations are not able to advance because of their innate lack of self-confidence that results from a religion that gives animals or other creatures superiority above the level of mankind. Any faith that puts anyone or anything between mankind and God, stymies creative cognitive thinking.

Hashem does not want us to be meek. He wants us to have self-esteem in order to perfect the world. Hashem gave us wisdom above all other creatures and still humankind has worshipped animals and idols from the beginning of history.

God told Noah that He granted man talent above and beyond the capabilities of any other creature. He gave Noah the understanding that it is below his dignity to worship a creature or thing that is less than him, let alone a stone image. When people worship anything that is lower than God they forsake the image of God that was instilled in them.

When we use the power that God gave us, to reign over animals, in order to lord over people, we can even stoop to the level of enslaving human beings. Hashem doesn't want us to intimidate others. This commandment also tells us that humans should have dominion over animals but not over each other.

3) Be fruitful and multiply.

> Genesis 9:1 says, "Then God blessed Noah and his sons, saying to them, 'Be fruitful and increase in number and fill the earth.'"

When we have children, we are called upon to educate them to have a family life for themselves when they mature. When children grow up in a home that is full of anger, with an accompanying tense atmosphere, when they mature, they might not want to marry and have their own families. When you speak to your children with patience and love, you are encouraging them to be happy and excited to build their own family and develop the world. Even after your children have grown, when your grandchildren enjoy visiting you and they see how much you enjoy them, they are further encouraged to start their own families to continue to rear their own children and grandchildren.

Does Hashem still want people to have children nowadays? Don't we have enough people on earth?

Hashem doesn't care so much about quantity as much as He cares about quality. He destroyed a whole generation during Noah's lifetime. Hashem wants more good people. He wanted Noah to rear more descendants because Noah was a good father. If you know that you can be special parents and nurture your children to become decent and honorable adults, then go for it. If you adopt children, then you might be creating virtuous people, by giving them a better upbringing than they would have had otherwise.

4) Do not commit adultery or incest

The blessing to be fruitful and multiply includes prohibitions against promiscuity, infidelity and other sexual crimes. Any type of behavior that violates traditional family living, doesn't promote being fruitful. Noah understood this. Later Hashem had to spell it out in the Ten Commandments and in the Torah so there would be no questions about it. See more in the chapter entitled, "Do Not Commit Adultery."

5) Do not murder other humans or yourself.

> Genesis 9:5, "And for your lifeblood I will surely demand an accounting. I will demand an accounting from every animal and from each human being, too, I will demand an accounting for the life of another human being."

Along with the prohibition against murder, there is the prohibition against suicide. If anyone kills a man or even if someone kills an animal just for sport, Hashem will punish them. This includes killing yourself. If you suicide, there will be an accounting for that action in heaven.

Sometimes people are so angry that they want to hurt their enemies or even slay them. Out of fear, aggravation and surrender, they can blame themselves, hurt themselves and even suicide. This prohibition is saying that this is not your way out. If you suicide, you will be prosecuted as a murderer in the next world. Read more in the chapter entitled, "Do Not Murder."

6) Do not abort a human fetus.

> Genesis 9:6 says, "Whoever sheds human blood, by humans shall their blood be shed; for in the image of God has God made mankind."

The text in Hebrew literally says, "whoever spills the blood of human inside a human his blood will be spilled." "A human inside a human" means an embryo in its mother's womb.

Our sages consider an embryo to be a viable human being from forty days after conception. Thus Jewish law allows for an early abortion. Of course if the pregnancy endangers the mother, we are allowed to abort at any time. Jewish law chooses the mother's life over her baby's.

Hashem loves babies. He wouldn't create an embryo so it should be killed. The only consideration for abortion is the physical and emotional welfare of the mother. If the pregnancy is within the first forty days from conception you can be much more lenient and allow for abortion if there is any risk to the mother, even a risk of emotional trauma. After that time period we do not allow abortion unless the mother's life is in danger.

On the other hand, an embryo that is not implanted in the womb is not considered to be alive. Therefore, Jewish law allows to dispose of extra embryos from in-vitro fertility treatments or to donate embryos for stem-cell research.

Every man was made in God's image. Just because you can't see the baby doesn't mean he or she isn't made in God's image. If an embryo is made in God's image, how much more so, a child.

Some parents treat their children with aggressiveness. They feel that children need to be disciplined. A child has a pure soul. We must talk to children as if we are speaking to angels. If they do something wrong, explain calmly that what they are doing is not good. If they don't understand, read Bible stories to them that they can understand. You can even write your own stories in order to customize them for the child's particular struggle. Speaking to children aggressively just teaches them to be aggressive too!

In my work as a healer I have helped many hyperactive and tense children by diet alone. Children need good nutrition in order to learn and grow properly. In my book called *Choose Life* I elaborate on the special nutritional needs of children.

It is also important to do extensive blood tests on children that are out of control. I had a seven-year-old client whose behavior was so bad that she was on her way to be kicked out of school before she came to me. I had her take regular blood tests and we found that her thyroid was totally out of the normal range. If this had not been caught, the child would have gone from school to school and her life would be ruined. Her behavior had a metabolic cause and was not her fault. We treated it naturally. The little girl stayed in the same school and excelled. She graduated and went to a good high school of her choice.

Why don't doctors check the thyroid of children? Simply because they know that the medicine for thyroid may not be not safe for little children, so they would rather not find out. Natural supplements for the thyroid are easy to find and are safe and effective.

This is just one example of how a child could be judged unfairly. Never rush to conclusions, even with adults. Blaming people is not with is the spirit of accepting that they were created in the image of God. Blaming a child or yelling at them is so much worse.

7) Do not shame others or do them any harm.

If the verse, "Whoever spills the blood of a human inside a human his blood shall be spilled" is only a prohibition against abortions, then why not say, "Whoever kills a human in a woman, his blood shall be spilled"?

This verse was written in for all genders, in order to add another important meaning: When you are embarrassed, you blush. Your blood runs up to your face. The verse says if you cause a person's blood to spill while the blood is still inside him, you too will have your blood spilled. In another words, if you embarrass someone else so badly that they blush, then you too will have to suffer a similar embarrassment. This is a prohibition against shaming another human being or hurting someone emotionally. If we do hurt someone physically or emotionally, we must ask them for forgiveness.

Those who shame others with lies in court or in any public setting, violate two of the Ten Commandments: Not to bear false witness and not to murder.

Judaism considers shaming another person in public, a type of murder. Doing so is akin to character assassination. Inflicting hurt on someone in their soul and heart with words causes the person to "go through hell." It is worse than physically injuring someone without embarrassment as that damage may heal more quickly. An emotionally wounded heart might not even be healed in a lifetime. That is why rape of minors, especially incest, is so egregious.

Hurting a child is considered even worse than hurting an adult. A child is too innocent for their pardon to be accepted by the heavenly court. In other words, if you ask a child to forgive you he or she doesn't have the authority to forgive until after they are twelve or thirteen years old. If you hurt someone who is mentally handicapped, it may not be possible to be forgiven at all, so be careful. If you did hurt a handicapped person in any way, try to reconcile with him or her through payment, or a by giving a special gift.

8) Do not eat meat with its blood.

> Genesis 9:4 already states, "But you must not eat meat that has its lifeblood still in it. And for your lifeblood I will surely demand an accounting. I will demand an accounting from every animal. And from each human being, too, I will demand an accounting for the life of another human being."

Can an animal give an accounting for killing a human? Even if animals could talk, they don't really have the free will to choose to kill or not to kill. They can however, be a witness of their own killing.

The only reason to kill another animal would be to save your life in self-defense, or for your own sustenance and nutrition. Even then it has to be without blood. You certainly cannot eat fatty meat that is unhealthy!

Genesis 9:5 says "But you must not eat meat that has its lifeblood still in it." The rabbis translate this to mean that it is prohibited to eat a limb of an animal and let the animal live. Of course you are not allowed to do that. To take a limb of an animal and allow the animal to live is cruel and unusual punishment. However, the simple, straight understanding of the scripture is not to eat bloody meat. That was the main intention of this prohibition.

Eating of blood in any form is forbidden to Jews and non-Jews alike, as it says in Leviticus 17:12: "Therefore I say to the Israelites, 'None of you may eat blood, nor may any foreigner residing among you eat blood.'"

The only kind of meat I can think of that has no blood in it at all, is boneless poultry and even that should be washed and checked. Jewish authorities say that it's acceptable to eat meat if it's barbeque or if it's soaked and salted in order to get all the blood out completely.

Hashem doesn't want us to eat unhealthy foods. He would be happy if we all ate only whole grains and whole grain products instead of white flour and white rice. In His opinion we should all eliminate white sugar from our diet. In my book *Choose Life* you can learn all about what God wants us to eat for the health of our bodies and souls.

In Genesis 8:20 Noah gives a sacrifice of kosher animals:

> Then Noah built an altar to the LORD and, taking some of all the clean animals and clean birds, he sacrificed burnt offerings on it. The LORD smelled the pleasing aroma and said in his heart: "Never again will I curse the ground because of humans, even though every inclination of the human heart is evil from childhood. And never again will I destroy all living creatures, as I have done.

This is an interesting passage. It means that Noah was already taught by Hashem what animals are pure and therefore kosher for sacrifice. Even before the flood, Noah was commanded to take seven pairs of the pure animals onto the ark.

The scripture says that Noah gave a burnt offering, which was entirely burnt on an altar. As opposed to a sacrifice of which the meat is eaten, Noah did not eat the meat of the animal offered as a burnt offering. Noah knew that a sacrifice must be made of kosher animals. However even if he wanted to eat meat that was not through a sacrifice Noah was forbidden to eat the blood.

> "The LORD smelled the pleasing aroma."

The reason that the aroma was pleasing to Hashem is because Noah trusted Hashem so much that he was willing to sacrifice some of the few animals that he had. In those days, sacrificing an animal was the way to pray. Only after the Holy Temple was destroyed, and the Jews started returning to the Land of Israel around the year 538 BCE, did the prophet Hosea institute the concept of prayer in place of sacrifices.

> Hosea 14:1,
> "Return, Israel, to the Lord your God.
> Your sins have been your downfall!
> Take words with you and return to the Lord.
> Say to him: Forgive all our sins and receive us graciously,
> that we may offer the fruit of our lips."

The Torah allows the sacrifice of certain mammals on the altar. Hashem only decided to allow this as a reaction to the sin of the golden calf. Hashem saw that the Israelites were not able to worship God without a Tabernacle and holy ceremonies, so he commanded Moses accordingly. Nowadays we don't need animal sacrifices. All we need is our prayers and our Bible.

The true reason we are not allowed to eat blood is because eating blood makes us aggressive. In the following translation it says, "the blood is the life," but in the Hebrew, it literally says, "the blood is the soul."

Ingesting blood is not healthy for our bodies or our souls.

> Deuteronomy 12: 23-25
> But be sure you do not eat the blood, because the blood is the life, and you must not eat the life with the meat. You must not eat the blood; pour it out on the ground like water. Do not eat it, so that it may go well with you and your children after you, because you will be doing what is right in the eyes of the Lord.

Kosher meat and poultry is slaughtered in a way that is painless to the animal and the blood is spilled into a hole in the ground and covered as if it were being buried. Without the blood the meat is much less damaging. Nevertheless, the quantity of meat that is consumed in the American diet is not healthy even if it is kosher.

There is no problem with fish, it's blood is not damaging to our soul and its flesh is not damaging to our body. The Torah only allows seafood that has fins and scales. The scavengers in fresh and salt water that live on dead and decaying aquatic life matter, are not kosher by Jewish law.

> Leviticus 11:9
> Of all the creatures living in the water of the seas and the streams you may eat any that have fins and scales.

Noah was originally permitted to eat all different kinds of animals. Just the sacrifices had to be kosher. Genesis 9:3, "Everything that lives and moves about will be food for you. Just as I gave you the green plants, I now give you everything."

Only later in the Torah do we learn that the animals that were originally designated for sacrifice are the ones that are pure for the Israelites to eat.

9) To build a justice system.

The reason our sages assert that Noah was commanded to build a justice system is because it says in Genesis 9:5,

> "And for your lifeblood I will surely demand an accounting. I will demand an accounting from every animal and from each human being, too, I will demand an accounting for the life of another human being."

The word "accounting" hints that there should be a formal court of law where the exact details can be described and analyzed.

If the people of Noah's town had a good justice system, Hashem may not have had to destroy them. The world that Hashem wants Noah to build is a world with courts of justice and a system for enforcing the law, so evil people will not be free to do what they want.

10) To remember the covenant.

When you see a rainbow, you should say a prayer and give thanks to Hashem for the world in which we live.

> Genesis 9:9-11, "I now establish my covenant with you and with your descendants after you and with every living creature that was with you—the birds, the livestock and all the wild animals, all those that came out of the ark with you—every living creature on earth. I establish my covenant with you: Never again will all life be destroyed by the waters of a flood; never again will there be a flood to destroy the earth."

Hashem made a covenant with Noah, his descendants and all the animals. He will never destroy all life again through a flood. Noah has to keep his side of the covenant. He cannot destroy animals or people and must obey the laws that Hashem gave him. When mankind promotes the extinction of species through any means, humans violate the covenant made with Noah. We are called upon to treat others, both humans and animals, humanely. Human and animal rights groups promote the safeguarding of the covenant with Noah. There was even an organization called National Rainbow Coalition, founded in 1984 for civil rights and social justice.

The inhabitants of Noah's town were murdering people for whatever differences they had between them. God showed Noah a rainbow to tell him that just like there are many colors in a rainbow, people are also different from each other.

God made a covenant with Noah that He would not destroy the earth again. Instead, He would teach the human inhabitants of the earth rules by which to abide by in order to have people get along with each other and make this world a better place in which to live. It was at this time that Hashem decided that in the future he would write basic laws and give them to the whole world.

Hashem realized that if in the corrupt world of Noah, He found a good man, then in every generation there will be good people like Noah. If He would give the world laws to follow, the good people of each generation would become better and better. There was a time when Hashem couldn't find enough good people to merit the existence of their cities. Those cities were called Sodom and Gomorrah and they were destroyed because their inhabitants did not keep the covenant of Noah.

This last law of Noah is a commandment to remember that Hashem made a covenant with humankind that if man keeps the laws of Noah, God will never destroy the world again. The best time to remember this is when we see a rainbow. This beautiful sight should remind us of our covenant with God.

A Double Rainbow

We were visiting a very special tourist site in Northern Israel. It's a pond where hundreds of thousands of cranes stop to rest from their migration. The cranes were attacking plantations in the area so the government decided to feed them, thus helping troubled farmers and encouraging many more birds to flock to the area.

Even though it was raining on and off, we were really enjoying the site. We were in a covered tractor, as close to the birds as possible, when we saw a rainbow emerge. Everyone got excited, and I led the group with the Jewish blessing, "Blessed art Thou the Lord our God who remembers the covenant, is loyal to His covenant, and is forever existing as the day He spoke."

Suddenly I saw another rainbow coming out aside from the first one. The vision was the most beautiful sight we ever saw! It was a clear, vivid double rainbow.

We were in the midst of a long, drawn-out civil court case at the time. We were living with fear and anxiety for years. This double rainbow took away all my fears. A few months later we had a miraculous settlement of our case, but the real double rainbow was yet to come. Two years later we celebrated the birth of our adorable new twins, a baby boy and a baby girl.

Chapter 2

The Covenant

Moses gave the Torah to the Israelites on Mount Sinai. What part of the Torah was it? It couldn't have been the whole Torah because more than half of the Pentateuch relates to episodes that happened after the Ten Commandments were given.

Moses didn't take his laptop to the desert. He didn't have a feather pen and ink either. Our great prophet had to chisel out every letter on a slab of stone. When did Moses have a chance to do this? When were the stories of Genesis written down? Were the Genesis stories known before they were written down?

In order to answer these questions, we have start from the beginning; from Abraham.

Abraham Our Father

The people of Abraham's generation believed in gods who needed gifts and sacrifices to be appeased, but they did not believe that their gods observed the actions of people. Sacrifices were made for rain, birth of children, food, livestock, safety from enemies and success in battle.

Abraham had lots of questions about these gods, ever since he was a young boy. Just by thinking and searching for answers he discovered that there is one invisible God that created the world. God was very impressed with Abraham, and He spoke to him. He taught Abraham that the one God that created the world is a loving God and wants man to succeed in making a good world. He told Abraham about the big flood and about the laws He gave Noah.

God loved Abraham because he was a thinker. He didn't just follow the teachings of his generation. Ever since Noah died, Hashem waited for someone to be born, who would be able to understand, learn, and teach His statutes. Abraham would be the one.

> Genesis 18:19
> For I know him, that he will command his children and his household after him, and they shall keep the way of Hashem, to do justice and judgment; that God may bring upon Abraham that which he hath spoken of him.

Abraham found favor in the eyes of the Lord. He loved him like a best friend. Genesis 18:17–20 quotes Hashem thinking to Himself about Abraham:

> Then God said, "Shall I hide from Abraham what I am about to do? Abraham will surely become a great and powerful nation, and all nations on earth will be blessed through him. For I made myself known to him, so that he will direct his children and his household after him to keep the way of God by doing

> what is right and just, so that God will bring about for Abraham what he has promised him."

God taught Abraham what is right and what is wrong. He also wanted to share His secrets with him. He told Abraham about the people of Sodom and Gomorrah and Abraham prayed for them. He asked that they be saved in the merit of the righteous people in the cities.

> Genesis 18:32
> Then he said, "May the Lord not be angry, but let me speak just once more. What if only ten can be found there?"

He answered, "For the sake of ten, I will not destroy it."

There were not even ten righteous people in Sodom and Gomorrah so Hashem had to destroy them. Abraham did not continue asking Hashem to save Sodom and Gomorrah for even less than ten people. That's because there were actually five wicked cities in the same area that Hashem wanted to destroy. If there wasn't even one couple in each city, Abraham knew that there was no hope.

Genesis 19:24, "Then the Lord rained down burning sulfur on Sodom and Gomorrah—from the Lord out of the heavens."

The remnants of five cities are found in Israel near the Dead sea. You can read the book *Exodus Case* by Dr. Lennart Moller to learn more about the remnants of these cities including pictures of balls of sulfur leftover from the fire and sulfur that Hashem brought on those cities. The book has photographs of thousands of archeological findings. It is amazing to see the evidence and learn that the account in the Bible is accurate.

The Laws of Abraham

After Abraham's death when God spoke to Isaac, the scripture distinctly mentions that God taught Abraham His laws:

> Genesis 26:4–5
> "I will make your descendants as numerous as the stars in the sky and will give them all these lands, and through your offspring all nations on earth will be blessed, because Abraham obeyed me and kept my safeguards, my commands, my rules and my fundamentals."

Abraham was given four types of rules: safeguards, commands, rules and fundamentals.

1) "Safeguards"

The Hebrew text says *Mishmarti*. The root of this word is *shamor* which means guard. That is most precious thing for us to guard is the Sabbath. The Sabbath is called a special present.

> Exodus 16:29
> "Bear in mind that the LORD has given you the Sabbath; that is why on the sixth day he gives you bread for two days. Everyone is to stay where they are on the seventh day; no one is to go out." So the people rested on the seventh day.

This is the only law that Hashem considers a gift—something He gave us. When we observe Shabbat, the Sabbath, the day gives a special feeling and sense of holiness.

Hashem taught Abraham that He created the world in six days and rested on the seventh. He added the Sabbath to His group of laws. Abraham observed the Sabbath in Hashem's honor. The word observe in Hebrew is also *shamor*. It comes from the same root as *mishmarti*. Literally, *mishmarti* could also mean, "the one that I observe." The word *shamor* is the first word in the fourth of the Ten Commandments when the commandments were given a second time before Moses' death.

> Deuteronomy 5:12-14
> Observe the Sabbath day by keeping it holy, as the LORD your God has commanded you. Six days you shall labor and do all your work, but the seventh day is a Sabbath to the LORD your God.

We find the word *mishmarti* in another place in the Torah:

> Leviticus 18:30, "Keep my requirements and do not follow any of the detestable customs that were practiced before you came and do not defile yourselves with them. I am the LORD your God."

In the above verse the NIV translates *mishmarti* as requirements. This verse comes at the end of a long list of sexual prohibitions.

Hashem is giving advice in order to help a person avoid the sexual transgressions: Observe the Sabbath. Sabbath adds such a feeling of holiness to our soul so that we will not even be able to even think of defiling it with sexual abominations.

The Sabbath is a special day for family time. It is also a day for romance with your spouse. When you have one day a week to look forward to for real quality time with your beloved, you will be focused on that day. Once a week we have a festive meal with candles, no phone calls, computers or TV, the perfect background for a romantic evening with your spouse. When you have real quality time with your spouse every week, you will have no desire for anyone else.

2) "My commands"

These are the commandments that were given to Noah that are clearly stated, for example, in Genesis 9:6, "Whoever sheds human blood, by humans shall their blood be shed." Or Genesis 9:4, "But you must not eat meat that has its lifeblood still in it."

Hashem taught these laws word for word to Abraham and he taught it to Isaac.

3) "My rules"

Hashem built His world according to specific laws of nature. Some of these laws He told Noah. For example,

> "The fear and dread of you will fall on all the beasts of the earth, and on all the birds in the sky, on every creature that moves along the ground, and on all the fish in the sea; they are given into your hands." (Genesis 9:2)

Hashem taught Abraham that nature and God are one. We don't have a god for rain and a god for sustenance. When we follow God's laws of nature, we are following God. Therefore, it is a mitzvah to eat natural healthy food, use herbal remedies and protect the ecology.

Ecclesiastes 3:1 states: "There is a time for everything, and a season for every activity under the heavens." Spiritual healing, alternative medicine and conventional medicine can all have their time and place. I believe that prayer to Hashem is always appropriate and beneficial in any crisis. We must pray that we find the correct treatment that may best be effective.

To reiterate, even conventional medicine is part of our natural world. Mainstream medicine isn't esoteric or supernatural. Scientists use the laws of nature to create medications and surgery to help mankind. Alternative medicine cannot take the place of conventional medicine and vice-versa. Both have their advantages and disadvantages.

I propose that the intertwining of both disciplines produces the most effective short, medium- and long-term reductions and cures for illnesses. In all cases, the diagnoses based on conventional medical methods such as blood work, MRI, CT scans, and X-rays are essential for both the traditional and holistic medical practitioners. Natural health professionals have their own tools to diagnose that are useful and very complimentary to the above traditional ones. What is of paramount importance is that the correct diagnosis is reached, no matter the type of medical approach. Without the proper diagnosis, no proper treatment can be achieved.

In sum, Hashem wants us to call out to Him for healing and especially use the nature He created in our treatments. The Torah and the nature Hashem created are equally holy. To be blessed by Hashem, we are to use His nature and not abuse it, especially in the treatment of our ills.

4) "My fundamentals"

These are the morals that can be learned from the laws of Noah. For example, "Be fruitful and multiply." Abraham understood that this meant also not to commit adultery, and he explained it that way to Isaac. Hashem was pleased with Abraham because he understood more than just the simple meaning of the word. Abraham gave his son these fundamentals and Hashem told Isaac how proud He was of his father for doing so.

Another example of a fundamental is that Abraham understood that if a man is made in God's image we cannot steal from him or hurt him in any way.

The Covenant of the Pieces

Hashem made a covenant with Abraham. Abraham would keep the laws of God and God would give him and his offspring the Land of Israel as an inheritance. As a sign of this covenant, God commanded Abraham to circumcise himself and his thirteen-year-old son, Ishmael. This is why Moslems circumcise their boys at age thirteen. Isaac, who was born a year later, was circumcised when he was eight days old.

The covenant between God and Abraham is called, "The Covenant of the Pieces".

> Genesis 15:12-21
> As the sun was setting, Abram fell into a deep sleep, and a thick and dreadful darkness came over him. Then the LORD said to him, "Know for certain

that for four hundred years your descendants will be strangers in a country not their own and that they will be enslaved and mistreated there. But I will punish the nation they serve as slaves, and afterward they will come out with great possessions. You, however, will go to your ancestors in peace and be buried at a good old age. In the fourth generation your descendants will come back here, for the sin of the Amorites has not yet reached its full measure. When the sun had set and darkness had fallen, a smoking firepot with a blazing torch appeared and passed between the pieces. On that day the LORD made a covenant with Abram and said, "To your descendants I give this land, from the Wadi of Egypt to the great river, the Euphrates—the land of the Kenites, Kenizzites, Kadmonites, Hittites, Perizzites, Rephaites, Amorites, Canaanites, Girgashites and Jebusites."

Hashem taught Abraham laws to teach his sons and grandchildren. As a reward for this, his offspring would inherit the land of Israel. Abraham lived before there was a written alphabet for the Hebrew language. Therefore, everything God taught him was oral. Circumcision was their way of signing a contract, sealing the deal.

In Hebrew circumcision is called *"Brit Milah,"* which means covenant of the word. The circumcision means, "You have my word."

Hashem was observing man in order to plan the future Commandments. Since His covenant with Noah, Hashem planned to give the world commandments. He waited for a time when the descendants of Abraham would be able to read and write. Oral Law is not enough. Hashem wanted to make sure that no one would change His words. He already was planning a big showing at Mount Sinai to announce the laws and He wanted them to be written on tablets.

In the Covenant of the Pieces there was a blazing torch that fell from the sky. When Hashem spoke on Mount Sinai, there were blazing torches on the mountain to symbolize the covenant with Abraham that He would never betray, even until today.

Kidnapped

Abraham was the father of Isaac and Isaac was the father of Jacob. Jacob had twelve sons. They were jealous of their brother Joseph because he was very beloved by his father. They were so jealous that they actually kidnapped him and sold him into slavery.

In order to understand fully the story of Joseph's kidnapping, it is worth reading Genesis chapters 37 through 43. At the time of the story of Joseph and his brothers, Hashem realized He would have to make a new law. The brothers were not evil people. They learned the precepts of Abraham from their father, Jacob. They worshiped God and they learned not to kill, but Judah didn't understand that selling his brother into slavery is not allowed either.

Hashem realized that the laws of Noah, even with the added law of the Sabbath, were not going to be enough. The law to remember that we are created in the image of God is vague. Hashem decided that when He will present these laws in writing, they had to be clear cut.

At first Hashem didn't want to put "Do not steal" in the Ten Commandments. He saw that in Sodom and

Gomorrah people were punished for stealing in cruel and unusual ways. For example, they would chop the hand off of someone who got caught taking a fruit off a tree. They put someone in a torture chamber for stealing a loaf of bread. Hashem saw that this was unjust and planned to write a book of laws, in it the punishment for stealing would be financial compensation.

However, when Joseph was kidnapped, Hashem realized that stealing a person is not to be tolerated; it had to be one of the top ten laws. Therefore, He added the law "Do not steal" to his list. The worst form of stealing is kidnapping. Kidnapping is the only form of stealing that has a death penalty.

> Exodus 21:16, "Anyone who kidnaps someone is to be put to death, whether the victim has been sold or is still in the kidnapper's possession."

This kidnapping was caused by jealousy. Hashem saw the jealousy of Joseph's brothers. They lied to their father for years, making him believe that Joseph was viciously torn apart by an animal. Jacob lost all hope and became depressed. This whole incident made Hashem decide to add more commandments to His list as follows:

1) "Do not Covet" because he saw how bad jealousy is and to what it could lead. The brothers started off with jealousy and ended up with lying and kidnapping. In the case of Cain and Abel, jealousy led to murder.
2) The brothers not only lied to their father but they falsified evidence. They took Josephs coat and dipped

it in the blood of a sheep that they slaughtered in order to make Jacob believe that his son was eaten by a wild animal. Hashem added, "Do not bear false witness" because he saw how the consequences of false witnessing were so grave.

3) The kidnapping of Joseph was a serious violation to Jacob's feelings. His sons did not respect him enough. Otherwise they would have never taken Joseph away. They had so much contempt for their father's favoritism that they sold Joseph as a slave. That is when Hashem decided that the commandment to "Honor you father and mother" would be part of the top ten.

There were two tablets. The first one had the commandments between God and humankind, and the second tablet contained the laws between man and his fellow man. Hashem added, "Honor thy father and mother" to the Ten Commandments on the first tablet together with the transgressions against God. By honoring your parents, you are honoring God's partners in bringing you into the world.

4) When Jacob went down to Egypt, he was so happy that Joseph was alive that he didn't want to return to Canaan before his death. The children of Israel stayed in Egypt, a land that was drenched with promiscuity and idol worship, so Hashem added the laws, "Do not commit adultery and incest," and "Do not have other gods before me."

5) Because the Egyptians gave so much importance to the beauty and artwork of their idols, the second commandment was lengthened. In addition to the

law not to worship other gods, there is a verse in it that says not to make any idols or any figurines.

The Covenant of the Word

In all those years of slavery, the people of Israel always remembered to keep the covenant of Abraham by performing circumcision. That's how the daughter of Pharaoh knew baby Moses was a Hebrew (Exodus 2:6).

To this day, Jews from all walks of life keep the covenant of Abraham by circumcising their sons. Little do they know but this mitzvah is a covenant. As mentioned above, circumcision in Hebrew is called *Brit Milah*, meaning the covenant of the word. The act of circumcision is a promise to keep the Ten Commandments and accept the Land of Israel as the inheritance from their forefather Abraham.

It was not enough that God gave His word to Abraham. In order to fulfill His promise, Hashem anticipated the day that his descendants would call out to Him in desperation, with full knowledge that only God could save them. After many years of hard labor, the Israelites screamed out to God, and He answered their prayers:

> Exodus 2:23, "During that long period, the king of Egypt died. The Israelites groaned in their slavery and cried out, and their cry for help because of their slavery went up to God."

The Burning Bush

In answer to their prayers the Israelites would need a leader. This leader would have to be prepared emotionally and spiritually for what was about to occur.

Moses, who was brought up in Pharaoh's palace, was much more merciful than your average Egyptian. His mother Johebed, gave him the love and caring nature that he would need in order to have compassion for the Children of Israel. Because of his compassionate nature, Moses went out to see the suffering of his people. When Moses saw an Egyptian strike a Hebrew, he was enraged. He struck the Egyptian dead and then ran from the authorities, for he knew Pharaoh would surely punish him severely. Moses ran so far that he reached Midian, which was a settlement in today's northwest Saudi Arabia.

In Midian, Moses met a beautiful woman named Zipporah and her family. He married her and worked for her father as a shepherd for his flock. His father-in-law, Jethro, was a very special man. He, like Abraham, found God and taught Moses all about Him.

One day when he was out in the pasture, he saw a light at the top of a mountain. Moses climbed the mountain, and there he saw the burning bush—a bush that burned but was not consumed. (Exodus 3:2-3)

God revealed himself to Moses at the site of the burning bush. He told Moses the whole story of his forefathers. Exodus 3:6 says, "I am the God of your father, the God of Abraham, the God of Isaac and the God of Jacob."

Hashem told Moses the stories of Genesis from creation until his own personal story as baby Moses in the basket.

Moses was an educated prince and knew how to read and write. He wrote down everything that Hashem said on tablets and put them in a cave on the side of the mountain.

Elijah stayed overnight in that same cave, as told in the book of 1 Kings 19:8–9. This cave was found on the real Mount Sinai that was discovered in Saudi Arabia. There are many stone tablets found there, that look just like the shape of the tablets in pictures of the Ten Commandments that we see in pictures. Many people saw those tablets and told their children and their children's children for many generations. Otherwise how would we know what they looked like?

This is a photograph of that mountain top. Aside from the large rounded rocks there are also flat rounded tablets all over the mountain. You can see a picture of them in the book *Exodus Case* by Lennart Muller.

Near the bottom of the picture you can see an opening of the cave that Elijah hid in. There is a lot to learn about the amazing archeological findings that prove the truth of the Bible. You can learn details of these discoveries in the books *The Gold of Exodus* by Howard Blum, *The Exodus Case* by Lennart Muller, and *Exodus, Myth or History* by David Rohl. A few other DVDs have been produced on the discovery of the true Mount Sinai and the amazing findings on the bottom of the Red Sea.

When the children of Israel arrived at Mount Sinai, Moses was very excited. He was worried about his book, The Book of the Covenant. It contained the words of the Book of Genesis and the beginning of Exodus. He ran to the mountain, and found his untampered tablets in the cave. He also took some time to write the story of the Exodus from Egypt. Moses then notified the Israelites that they had a covenant with God.

> Exodus 19:5-6, "Now if you obey me fully and keep my covenant, then out of all nations you will be my treasured possession. Although the whole earth is mine, you will be for me a kingdom of priests and a holy nation. These are the words you are to speak to the Israelites."

This connects to the first covenant God ever made—the covenant between God and Noah, the rainbow. Hashem promised that He would not destroy the world, if the inhabitants of the world keep the laws that Hashem taught him.

When Moses read the Book of the Covenant to the Children of Israel, they promised to do whatever Hashem asks of them:

> Exodus 24:7, "Then he took the Book of the Covenant and read it to the people. They responded, 'We will do everything the LORD has said; we will obey.'"

A Special Nation

Exodus 19:6 says, "You will be a nation of priests and a holy people." How can we be a nation of priests if we don't have a congregation?

The above statement was said just before the Ten Commandments were uttered from the Creator of the world. The Ten Commandments were meant for the whole world. The Israelites were commanded to teach them to the nations of the world, the Torah would be the "teacher's edition."

Before God came out to meet the children of Israel, Moses spoke to the people, saying:

> Exodus 10:5-6, "And now if you listen to me and observe my covenant then you will be the most special people of all the nations, for the whole world is mine. You will be a kingdom of Priests, a Holy Nation, these are the things you should tell the Children of Israel."

God told Moses that if the people of Israel keep the Ten Commandments, they would be special. They would be able to be the teachers of the whole world. The Torah teaches that the nation of Israel is "The Chosen People." We are chosen to educate the world. If we don't do our job, then we let God down and lose our status.

Deuteronomy 7:6-8,
> For you are a people holy to the LORD your God. The LORD your God has chosen you out of all the peoples on the face of the earth to be his people, his treasured possession. The LORD did not set his affection on you and choose you because you were more numerous than other peoples, for you were the fewest of all peoples. But it was because the LORD loved you and kept the oath he swore to your ancestors that he brought you out with a mighty hand and redeemed you from the land of slavery, from the power of Pharaoh king of Egypt.

At the time that Moses said the above statement the Israelites were not the "fewest of all people". There were 600,000 men between ages 20 to 60. That means that there was the same number of woman between 20 and 60 years old. There were also at least three times the amount of children and plenty of people over 60. In total there were millions of people at Mount Sinai.

> Numbers 10:36, "Whenever it came to rest, he said, 'Return, LORD, to the countless thousands of Israel.'"

In those days, nations were very small. In the small land of Canaan there were seven different nations. Therefore, when Moses says that we are the smallest of all nations, he was foreseeing our present day situation. After years of assimilation, pogroms and the dreadful Holocaust that plagued our nation, the Jews are certainly the smallest of all well-known religions and nations in the world today.

Moses was giving the message to our generation. Just sixty-eight years ago Hashem has kept the oath that he gave to Abraham, and the nation of Israel entered the Land of Israel and settled it as a proper country, ruled by its own people and accepted by the UN.

The topic of the Holocaust is very complex. However I did attempt to explain why it happened. In my book *Who is God?* I devoted an entire chapter on the topic called, "Why a Holocaust?"

The reason that Hashem chose the Israelites to be a light unto the nations is, that aside from the oath between God and Abraham, the Israelites were the first nation to turn to God as a whole in unison. When they were being oppressed as slaves in Egypt they screamed out to Hashem:

> Exodus 2:23-25
> The Israelites groaned in their slavery and cried out, and their cry for help because of their slavery went up to God. God heard their groaning and he remembered his covenant with Abraham, with Isaac and with Jacob. So God looked on the Israelites and was concerned about them.

Crying out to Hashem in full voice will bring you Hashem's compassion. That is why Hashem uttered the Ten Commandments in full voice. He wanted to tell the world that it's OK to scream, if you must.

Chapter 3

God Meets the World

Exodus 19:16–19
On the morning of the third day there was thunder and lightning, with a thick cloud over the mountain, and a very loud trumpet blast. Everyone in the camp trembled. Then Moses led the people out of the camp to meet with God, and they stood at the foot of the mountain. Mount Sinai was covered with smoke, because the LORD descended on it in fire. The smoke billowed up from it like smoke from a furnace, and the whole mountain trembled violently. As the sound of the trumpet grew louder and louder, Moses spoke and the voice of God answered him.

The people of Israel prepared for the upcoming event for three days. Moses had to encourage them and lead them outside of their tents because they were hiding from the divine thunder. God made a grandiose introduction in order to prepare the people for the next step: His voice.

When a prophet hears God's voice, he doesn't hear Him with his ears. It's a voice that is in his head, as if someone is entering his thoughts. Until then, God spoke to Moses in his mind like with any other prophet. On this day, God spoke aloud to the entire nation. Together with Moses the people heard Hashem's voice with their ears. After that revelation Moses' prophecies were all "face to face".

By appearing in public with a full voice, God set a precedent that can't be beat. This is the only claim of a unified mass prophecy that has been passed down from father to son for generations. There is a beautiful skit on this topic on YouTube by Lawrence Keleman called Rational Approach to Divine Origin of Judaism. If someone was going to make up a story, why would he say that millions of people witnessed it. It would be too easy to check out its validity. We know about the revelation at Mount Sinai not only because it says so in the Bible, but because the story was passed down through the families who were eyewitnesses.

Accompanied by thunder and fire, God announced ten rules that would make this world a better place. His voice was heard for miles. The nation saw, they trembled and stood afar on that fateful day when God met the world. His presence was undeniable.

The Presentation of the Ten Commandments

>Exodus 20:18–21
>
>The whole nation saw the thunder and lightning and heard the sound of a *shofar*, and saw the mountain in smoke. They trembled with fear and said to Moses, "Speak to us yourself and we will listen. But do not have God speak to us or we will die." Moses said to the people, "Do not be afraid. God has come to test you, so that the fear of God will be with you to keep you from sinning." The people remained at a distance, while Moses approached the thick darkness where God was.

The Big Event

> Exodus 20:18, "When the people saw the thunder and lightning and heard the trumpet and saw the mountain in smoke, they trembled with fear. They stayed at a distance."

The exact translation of this verse from the Hebrew is:

> "And the whole nation saw the sounds and the flames, the sound of the shofar and the mountain smoking. The nation saw, they trembled and stood afar."

The Hebrew scripture doesn't say lightning it says *"lapidim"* which means flaming torches. The same word is used in the Covenant of the pieces:

> Genesis 15:17, "When the sun had set and darkness had fallen, a smoking firepot with a blazing torch appeared and passed between the pieces."

Hashem brought down blazing torches on Mount Sinai in order to connect this covenant to the covenant that He made with Abraham. The mountain was smoking from the fire of these torches.

So why does the NIV translation say lightning? Simply because in Exodus 18:16 it says that there was thunder and lightning.

> "On the morning of the third day there was thunder and lightning, with a thick cloud over the mountain, and a very loud trumpet blast. Everyone in the camp trembled."

In the above verse the word lightning is *birakim* which has no other interpretation but lightning. The lightning came down strongly and ignited fires which produced smoke. So at first there was lightning and then there was fire.

"The nation saw the sounds." The sounds were so powerful that they were above the decibel of a human's ability to hear. The sound was so loud that the sound waves made waves in the air. That is why they saw the sounds instead of hearing them.

"The nation stood from afar." The sound was so tremendous that the Israelites trembled and ran away. Hashem wanted them to back up. They moved far enough away so that they would begin to hear the sounds and also be able to hear Hashem's voice.

If the nation was crowded around the mountain, then those who were close to the mountain would block the view of those further away. Hashem wanted everyone to see and hear equally. In order to achieve this goal, He made the nation of Israel distance themselves far enough so that they could all be part of a big semi-circle to listen and watch together.

Next, Hashem told Moses to bring Aaron with him on the slope of the mountain and the elders would be below. Then Hashem spoke. His voice emanated from a cloud on the mountain as He announced the Ten Commandments.

The Ten Commandments are the Pillars of the civilized world. They should be taught to children as soon as they learn how to read. The following song is a summary of the Ten Commandments to the tune of *Doe a Deer*. It's a great song to teach your children.

The Ten Commandments

Let's start from the very beginning
A very good place to start
Hashem created the world
In six days
On the sixth day a man
He made
A speaking man
Who can understand

The first two people just happen to be
Adam and Eve
By Hashem conceived
They had an offspring who really believed …

Abraham, was the very first one
That made known the one and only God
He taught this to Isaac his son
But Jacob from Esau had to run
So his children had to stay
In Egypt till they learned to pray
The Almighty heard his people cry
And brought them to Sinai
Oh Oh Oh …
Hashem commanded us that day
To remember that we were merely slaves
Only to Him we have to pray
They're no other gods in any way

So His name we must respect
The Sabbath we must remember and protect
Our parents are our treasures too
Because of them I am with You
Oh Oh Oh …
We're not allowed to steal
Not allowed to kill
Family is a sacred thing
And if to court you have to go
Tell them only truth you know

So if, you're jealous of your friend
Remember, what you have is from Hashem
Through your troubles He'll help you too
Just believe that He loves you
Those are the commandments of Hashem
All ten!

All Ten

Exodus 20:15-18
When the people saw the thunder and lightning and heard the trumpet and saw the mountain in smoke, they trembled with fear. They stayed at a distance and said to Moses, "Speak to us yourself and we will listen. But do not have God speak to us or we will die." Moses said to the people, "Do not be afraid. God has come to test you, so that the fear of God will be with you to keep you from sinning." The people remained at a distance, while Moses approached the thick darkness where God was.

The revelation of God on Mount Sinai was magnanimous. God announced the Ten Commandments on Mount Sinai in full voice to a congregation of millions of Israelites. After God finished saying all Ten Commandments, the Israelites called out to Moses. They were too afraid to continue listening to Hashem, so after the Ten Commandments were delivered, Hashem continued to speak to Moses in a thick cloud.

Another Opinion

The traditional Orthodox Jewish elementary school curriculum teaches that only the first two commandments were heard from God and after the first two the Israelites trembled and couldn't continue to listen, so Moses told the Israelites the rest of the commandments himself.

This teaching is based on the commentary of Rashi, a famous commentator from the 11th century. He is the only commentary to go forward with this explanation, which is not backed up by Biblical sources.

According to the scripture only after the Israelites were shaken from Hashem's magnanimous voice, did they plead with Moses to speak for God. Hashem had already finished saying all the Ten Commandments, otherwise how could the Israelites possible interrupt God?! If they did, do you think that they could be heard. The Israelites were dumbfounded when they heard Hashem's voice. There is no way that they possibly would have called out to Moses, or said anything while God was speaking.

In the scripture there is no interruption after the first two commandments. The verse stating that the Israelites want Moses to speak instead of God is after the Ten Commandments were completed. Rabbi Moses Nachmanides, a famous commentator, who lived around the year 1200, also believed this to be true. As a matter of fact, Rashi is the sole commentator that says that Hashem only said two of the Commandments.

Why was Rashi's commentary chosen? The simplest answer is, the printing press. The Torah was first printed on a printing press with Rashi's commentary. School teachers had these books and couldn't afford a full commentary volume that included Nachmanides' interpretation.

Today all the commentaries are available, let alone the simple meaning of the text, so why are the rabbis still teaching that God only said the first two commandments out loud?

Orthodox Jewish children know many prayers and portions of the Bible by heart but not the Ten Commandments. The Ten Commandments are not really given that much importance. They are not discounted, but they aren't given the full status they deserve.

Even the holiday of Shavuot or Pentecost, a celebration of the revelation at Sinai, is called the holiday of the giving of the Torah, when in reality it is the commemoration of receiving of the Ten Commandments. The Israelites got a portion of the Torah on the same day as the revelation on Mount Sinai. This part was called *"The Book of the Covenant,"* but the grandiose occasion at Mount Sinai was the giving of the Ten Commandments.

Hashem's Priorities

Why is it so important to know how many Commandments God said in His voice?

Let's make a juxtaposition. If God announced all Ten Commandments in full voice, then every Israelite present and for all future generations could reliably teach his or her children and grandchildren that The Ten Commandments came straight from God with no intermediaries. If Moses announced the last eight of the commandments, then we are trusting Moses that they are from Hashem, just like we trust Moses that the rest of the Torah is from Hashem.

If every Israelite heard every single one of the Ten Commandments from Hashem, each is a witness that God spoke. It gives so much more importance to the Ten Commandments than to the rest of the Torah. The rabbis were afraid of that. They wanted the Jews to learn the entire Bible and not give more importance to any one part of it.

Today's Rabbis are followers of the Pharisees. Pharisees is a Roman version of their Hebrew name, *perushim* which means commentators. The Pharisees main theme was to make commentaries on the Torah and the whole Old Testament. If the Ten Commandments are the main theme it limits the scope of their commentaries. Furthermore, if the Jewish people must primarily concentrate on only ten rules, Torah Law becomes essentially simplified. On the other hand, if you have to learn the entire Torah with all the commentaries and rabbinical literature in order to be a good Jew, then you will have to go to your rabbi to help you learn.

Hashem purposely gave importance to one part of the Torah. He wrote what He considered the most important words and ideas on special tablets after a very dramatic ceremony.

God knew it would be very hard for the whole nation to keep the entire Torah. Therefore, he specified the ten most important laws. Hashem says, "This is not an all-or-nothing deal. I'll tell you what's most important, and from that point on, it's all extra credit." If the Jewish people would have taught this to their children, millions of Jews might not have left their religion and their God.

We cannot make too many commentaries on the Ten Commandments. They are the words of God, axioms. The Torah itself is also from Hashem but it has many meanings. We are allowed to discuss the scriptures and have our own insights. However, we may not make any interpretations that can possibly contradict one of the ten axioms of God.

Just like in geometry, every new postulate has to pass the scrutiny of the axioms. We cannot interpret a verse from the Bible to mean that you are allowed to steal or that you are allowed to lie in a court of law. Even if a prophet says that God is telling him to transgress one of the Ten Commandments, he himself may not obey what he hears. If a prophet preaches anything that contradicts one of the Ten Commandments, he is a false prophet.

That is why Hashem spoke in full voice at Mount Sinai. The level of prophecy of the simple Israelite at Mount Sinai was far superior than any prophet who lived before or after that time. Not only did they hear God's voice, they also saw the divine thunder and lightning.

Millions of people saw the mountain aflame and heard the voice of God. The Ten Commandments were meant for all humankind and they will never change. No prophet can ever change these laws or detract from their importance. Hashem had millions of people watch Hashem announcing these laws. They can never be cancelled unless millions of people heard God in full voice cancelling any one of them.

When we learn Bible we always must keep the Ten Commandments in mind. If a Biblical verse seems like it may oppose any one of these commandments, it may be a mistake in the translation, interpretation, or commentary.

I would like to take the opportunity here to give a little advice. If someone makes you upset, your spouse, your child or even your friend, check out if they transgressed one of the Ten Commandments. If so, you have a right to be angry and take this transgression seriously. However, if your son walks into the house with mud on your clean carpet, did he break a commandment? I don't think so, unless he did it deliberately.

I know that it may be frustrating but you shouldn't yell. Save the yelling for things that are really bad or dangerous. You will learn more about what is included in the Ten Commandments in the following chapters. Learn them well and you will be able to judge the seriousness of people's actions properly.

The Book of the Covenant

After God gave the Ten Commandments at the revelation of Mount Sinai, Hashem instructed him to write down His ordinances. These ordinances are written in the chapter called Judgments or Rules, Exodus chapter 21. Moses wrote down the ordinances on stone and with that he completed the Book of the Covenant which contained the words of Genesis and the first half of Exodus up until the end of chapter 24, including the Ten Commandments.

This book was presented to the Israelites after they heard the Ten Commandments, but before Moses went up on Mount Sinai to get the Tablets.

> Exodus 24:7, "Then he took the Book of the Covenant and read it to the people. They responded, 'We will do everything the LORD has said; we will obey.'"

Then Moses ascended Mount Sinai to accept the Ten Commandments written on the Tablets of the Covenant from God Himself.

> Deuteronomy 9:10, "And the Lord delivered unto me two tables of stone written with the finger of God; and on them was written according to all the words, which the Lord spoke with you in the mount out of the midst of the fire in the day of the assembly."

In the following chapters I will explain each and every commandment so that it can be applied to a modern world. Every commandment has different Biblical verses that teach more about it.

The beauty of this book is that it is not just a book of law. I will teach how Hashem would like the world to be run if he had things going His way.

It would take thousands of people in high places to change the judicial systems of the world, but it is comforting to know how Hashem judges our transgressions. The heavenly judicial system is fair and quite different from our earthly courts.

Chapter 4

"I Am the Lord Your God"

The first of the Ten Commandments is "I am the Lord your God who took you out of Egypt, out of the house of slavery." This doesn't even sound like a commandment. However, it is the first statement that God uttered on Mount Sinai.

This statement says that we must believe that the one God of the universe is the same God that the Holy Bible speaks of. Every man, woman, and child in the whole world is called upon to believe that the God who took the Israelites out of bondage in Egypt, is the only God and He created the universe and all its inhabitants.

In Judges 5:3–5 there is a hint to this first commandment. The Prophetess Deborah here says:

> "Hear this, you kings! Listen, you rulers!
>   I, even I, will sing to the Lord; I will praise the
> Lord, the God of Israel, in song.

> When you, LORD, went out from Seir, when you marched from the land of Edom, the earth shook, the heavens poured, the clouds poured down water. The mountains quaked before the LORD, the One of Sinai, before the LORD, the God of Israel."

The word I is *"Anochi"* in Hebrew. The translation says, "I even I" to denote the strength of this word. It is not your everyday "I," which is *Ani*. Anochi is the first word of the first commandment. It has a more robust meaning than the word *Ani*. It shows importance and pride. The words *you* and *your* in the Ten Commandments are in the singular form, as though God is speaking to just one person.

Deborah says *Anochi* twice in her song. She felt that Hashem cared about her personally. She was responding to the first commandment, sayings that I am for God and God is for me.

The Ten Commandments speak to you personally. Hashem is a personal God; He has time to give you special attention. You should feel important enough that God cares about your small "thank you" or your small prayer, even though you are just one of seven billion people.

The prophetess Deborah also mentions the direction of where Hashem is coming from to give the Torah: "When you, LORD, went out from Seir, when you marched from the land of Edom," The ancient land of Edom was located southeast of Israel, in the territory now occupied by Jordan. Edom was situated from the southern tip of the Dead Sea to the Gulf of Aqaba and extended to the east.

For decades one of the arguments that archeologists have had against the Bible is that they found no evidence to support of any of the stories of Exodus in the Sinai Desert.

Today's Sinai Desert is a barren land. There are no remains of a trek of millions or even thousands of people.

There is a book called *The Gold of Exodus* by Howard Blum. The writer tells the story of two explorers who found, with proof, beyond reasonable doubt, the original site of Mount Sinai in north-west Saudi Arabia.

The Exodus Case by Dr. Lennart Moller gives archeological evidence that the Israelites crossed the Red Sea into Saudi Arabia, where the Ten Commandments were received on Mount Sinai. The book has unbelievable photographs of many archeological findings including Egyptian chariots and fossilized bones of horses and human bones at the bottom of the north-eastern side of the Red Sea.

As you can see in the diagram below, the Jews crossed the Red Sea on the eastern side and entered from there into Saudi Arabia. Remnants of Pharaoh's chariots were also found at the bottom of the Red Sea further north than is depicted in the following diagram. The sea was turbulent during the splitting of the Red Sea so the exact spot where the chariots were found is not a proof of where they crossed. However, the fact that the Egyptian chariots were found, along with skeletons of horses and Egyptian men, which Dr. Moller was able to DNA identify, does prove that the Bible story is true.

God Meets the World

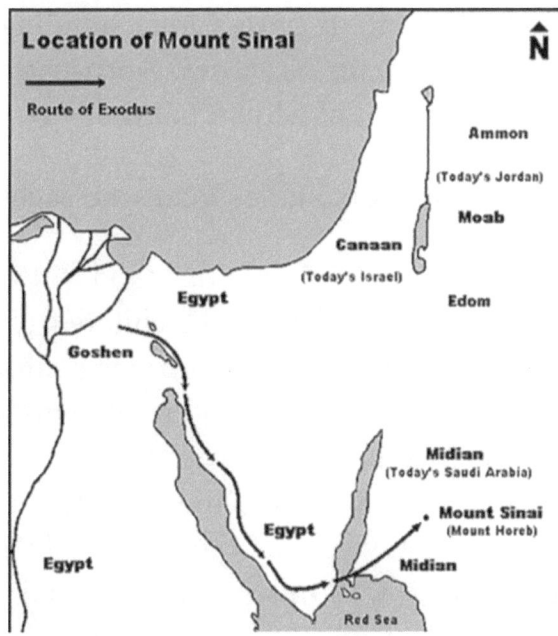

In this diagram you can see where Midian is located. Midian is the home of Jethro, father-in-law of Moses. The Torah says that Jethro came to greet Moses and the Israelites when they came to Mount Sinai.

Before the revelation of God at Mount Sinai, Hashem spoke to Moses at the burning bush, which was also on Mount Sinai.

> Exodus 3:5, "God said to Moses, 'Do not come any closer,' God said. 'Take off your sandals, for the place where you are standing is holy ground.'"

This land was destined to be the site for the giving of the Ten Commandments and the Book of the Covenant. The mountain that was found in Saudi Arabia has many signs that it really was Mount Sinai of the Bible. Some of this information can also be found on line if you look up

Jabal-al-Lawz. The Saudis have a long standing tradition that this in the mountain of Moses. Apparently Deborah knew the exact location of Mount Sinai.

The First Commandment has many messages:

1) To believe in one and only one God.
2) To believe that God took the children of Israel out of Egypt and out of slavery through miracles. This commandment says that God is powerful enough to free a whole nation out of slavery through miracles that defy nature. It is a mitzvah to learn about the Exodus from Egypt every year on the holiday of Passover.
   Exodus 13:8, "On that day tell your son, 'I do this because of what the Lord did for me when I came out of Egypt.'"
3) God is a personal God; you can relate to Him on a one to one level.
4) It's a mitzvah to remember that once we were only slaves. Never have prejudice over those less fortunate than you. God took the Israelites out of Egypt in order to be free. Hashem doesn't want us to be slaves. If we feel like slaves in our jobs or our relationships, we must not allow that situation to continue.
5) It is a mitzvah to remember the Exodus of the Israelites from Egypt and learn about the Jewish holidays of Passover, Sukkoth, and Shavuot. These holidays commemorate the Exodus from slavery to freedom.

Gentiles are to learn about these holidays as part of the whole story of the Exodus from Egypt. Gentiles are not obligated to celebrate these holidays as are Jews.

The Holidays

We had a friend from the Far East who spent a lot of time with us. He saw how many holidays we were celebrating and said, "The Jews are always having a holiday. You never get a chance to work!"

It's true. Jewish holidays are celebrated as major events. Three times a year we have a holiday that lasts a whole week and another two holidays that are two days long and one more for one more day. We also have five fast days. Most of these holidays are actually mentioned in the Torah specifically.

Every holiday has very special activities to do for the whole family to enjoy. Even the Sabbath is a holiday, with two fancy meals and sacramental wine. It is a day of freedom, which includes freedom from the slavery of our jobs and household chores.

In the summer we have a couple of days of mourning on which we fast. When they're all over, after the ninth of Av, in the month of August, most Israelis go on a small vacation. Even people that are poor go on vacation by visiting friends or relatives in another city. Since the whole country is a place of tourism, wherever you end up you'll find something fascinating to do.

The holidays and vacations also give us something to look forward to other than work. Hashem made you in His image. He did not make you a slave. The holidays free us up from slavery. We don't live to work, we live to celebrate! On Shabbat, Passover, Succoth and Shavuot we mention the miracle of the Exodus from Egypt in our prayers of celebration.

No one ever loses money from too many holidays. If you are well rested, you can work better. Of course businesses all love holidays; everyone buys more food and clothing in preparation for the big days ahead. Restaurants, hotels, taxis, and buses all get busy. Somehow there is a very big blessing for everyone.

One and Only One

The first word of the Ten Commandments, "I," is a statement in and of itself. "It is I, Hashem, who is speaking; do not insult me by looking at any other gods." The Egyptians had no trouble believing that the Hebrews had a powerful god. They just didn't believe He was the only one.

When ancient man believed in more than one deity he had the illusion that one god wants one thing and the other god wants something else. He felt that he had the power to choose which god to worship and how. His friend could choose his own god.

This is more or less the basis of modern thinking. Everyone has a right to their own beliefs. This way of thinking has helped many people of different religions survive and thrive in peace and harmony. So what's wrong with it?

The modern world of today has a new ideology, the belief that all religions are created equal. Hashem is not in agreement with this belief, because it brings us back to the ancient sin of idol worship.

Elijah was very concerned that the Israelites were not settled with their faith. They would worship idols for a few months and then look to worship God when they had real hardships.

"How Long Will You Waver between Two Opinions?"

It is not permissible to have two gods even if one of them is the God of Israel. Elijah the prophet reprimanded the people for wavering between two beliefs. Sometimes they worshipped God and sometimes they worshipped the Baal, the god of the false prophets. In the following story Elijah had a plan to convince the Israelites to worship only the God of Abraham.

> 1Kings 18:20-39,
> "So Ahab sent word throughout all Israel and assembled the prophets on Mount Carmel. Elijah went before the people and said, "How long will you waver between two opinions? If the LORD is God, follow him; but if Baal is God, follow him."
> But the people said nothing.
> Then Elijah said to them, "I am the only one of the LORD's prophets left, but Baal has four hundred and fifty prophets. Get two bulls for us. Let Baal's prophets choose one for themselves, and let them cut it into pieces and put it on the wood but not set fire to it. I will prepare the other bull and put it on the wood but not set fire to it. Then you call on the name of your god, and I will call on the name of the LORD. The god who answers by fire—he is God."
> Then all the people said, "What you say is good." Elijah said to the prophets of Baal, "Choose one of the bulls and prepare it first, since there are so many of you. Call on the name of your god, but do not light the fire." So they took the bull given them and prepared it. Then they called on the name of Baal from morning till noon. "Baal, answer us!" they shouted. But there

was no response; no one answered. And they danced around the altar they had made.

At noon Elijah began to taunt them. "Shout louder!" he said. "Surely he is a god! Perhaps he is deep in thought, or busy, or traveling. Maybe he is sleeping and must be awakened." So they shouted louder and slashed themselves with swords and spears, as was their custom, until their blood flowed. Midday passed, and they continued their frantic prophesying until the time for the evening sacrifice. But there was no response, no one answered, no one paid attention.

Then Elijah said to all the people, "Come here to me." They came to him, and he repaired the altar of the LORD, which had been torn down. Elijah took twelve stones, one for each of the tribes descended from Jacob, to whom the word of the LORD had come, saying, "Your name shall be Israel." With the stones he built an altar in the name of the LORD, and he dug a trench around it large enough to hold two seahs of seed. He arranged the wood, cut the bull into pieces and laid it on the wood. Then he said to them, "Fill four large jars with water and pour it on the offering and on the wood."

"Do it again," he said, and they did it again.

"Do it a third time," he ordered, and they did it the third time. The water ran down around the altar and even filled the trench.

At the time of sacrifice, the prophet Elijah stepped forward and prayed: "LORD, the God of Abraham, Isaac and Israel, let it be known today that you are God in Israel and that I am your servant and have done all these things at your command. Answer me, LORD, answer me, so these people will know that you, LORD, are God, and that you are turning their hearts back again."

> Then the fire of the LORD fell and burned up the sacrifice, the wood, the stones and the soil, and also licked up the water in the trench.
>
> When all the people saw this, they fell prostrate and cried, "The LORD—he is the God! The LORD—he is the God!"

The reason I brought you this whole story is for you to realize how silly the idol worshipers were. They truly believed in their gods. The Israelites in the times of Elijah had their service plan. They wanted their god to ignite their sacrifice. They weren't worried about how the god(s) wanted them to behave. They were using God Almighty as an alternative to idols. The worshippers would lay down the rules of the game. Even today in most religions, people write the rules. The whole concept of religion is an attempt to put God into a framework of your religious leader's choice.

In the above story Elijah is upset that the Israelites worshiped other gods whenever they wanted, and returned to the God of Abraham when the idols didn't answer their prayers. Elijah wanted to prove that the God of Abraham is the true God and He is not changeable.

Wavering between two religions is not respectable in Hashem's eyes. It shows lack of values, lack of principles. The original pilgrims came to this country in order to have freedom of religion. In Great Britain and Europe, they were not allowed to have their own beliefs and worship God as they wished. The English monarchy permitted no freedom of religion or freedom of worship. Everything had to be their way.

That is not right. Everyone is different and each has a right to have his own different customs and culture.

However, we all must believe in the one God who created the universe. The Torah, the Pentateuch is a book of God's rules. People did not invent the Torah; it is God given. If humans try to change it in any way, they might come up with a new religion.

We've come a long way since the times of Elijah. We are smarter and more educated but we still believe what we want to believe. The modern idea that everyone can have his own god is based upon the principle that science is the only truth. Everyone may have his own god because religion is just "the opium of the masses," so why not let people do what they want.

Let's say that someone has an argument about their scientific beliefs. Is the American government so accepting of people's different opinions as they are of their different religions?

The answer is no. It's so extreme that if you don't want to vaccinate your children for religious reasons it's fine. However, if you don't want to vaccinate because you think that the vaccines are not safe, that is not tolerated and you may be forced to vaccinate against your better judgement.

Hashem would like everyone to believe in the God of Israel and watch Him perform miracles. The rules are dictated from God to us; we cannot tell God what to do. My father of blessed memory used to say, "You can't engineer God."

The problem is that today even a revelation on Sinai or fire falling from heaven will not change people's minds. The only thing that will help is a change of heart. My mission here is to present you with God's point of view. Through teaching you how to understand His precious book, the Torah, I pray that God's words will enter your heart and soul.

Freedom

Hashem blessed the world with freedom. This includes freedom of speech, freedom of religion, and free choice. He wants us to think and create unimpededly. Freedom of religion is acceptable to Hashem if it is just a matter of how to worship, what prayers to say, and what dress and customs to keep but not in whom to believe in and direct prayers. When we teach religion to our young ones don't emphasize the man made details of worship, emphasize the Ten Commandments.

The Old Testament Bible should be freely available to all, so that all mankind will have free access to learn about the one and only God. The souls of all humankind are yearning to believe in Hashem. By limiting children's access to the Bible they are not given a fair chance to choose their path in life. The Torah is everlasting; it will never change. Malachi the prophet reminded that before the day of salvation you must remember the laws of the Torah.

> Malachi 4:5, "Remember the law of my servant Moses, the decrees and laws I gave him at Horeb for all Israel. "See, I will send the prophet Elijah to you before that great and dreadful day of the LORD comes. He will turn the hearts of the parents to their children, and the hearts of the children to their parents.

Malachi is saying that the children are the key. If you give your children the fundamentals, they will have the insight to strengthen your faith. Every person needs fundamentals. We need ideology to feel human. If we don't get a belief system from our parents, we create one. At Mount Sinai,

God introduced His ideology. It is short, to the point, but from Hashem's point of view, the basis of this ideology is to believe in the correct god—the one and only God who, besides creating the world, also took the Israelites out of Egypt. He is also the only one who vividly spoke to millions of people at the same time, and they all survived to tell the story.

The prophets of the Old Testament envisioned a time when everyone will believe in the God of Israel:

> Zechariah 14:9, "And the LORD shall be king over all the earth: in that day shall there be one LORD, and his name one."

Micah 4:6-7
"In that day," declares the LORD,
"I will gather the lame;
I will assemble the exiles
and those I have brought to grief.
I will make the lame my remnant,
those driven away a strong nation.
The LORD will rule over them in Mount Zion
from that day and forever.

Passover

The holiday of Passover is central in the Jewish calendar because it celebrates the story of the Exodus from Egypt. That grand exodus prepared the Israelites for the big day at Mount Sinai, the giving of the Ten Commandments. This is the holiday designated to teach our children that God took the Israelites out of Egypt.

> Exodus 13:8, "On that day tell your son, 'I do this because of what the LORD did for me when I came out of Egypt.'"

The nation of Israel saw the miracles that Hashem performed in Egypt and the nations of the world heard all about it.

> Exodus 15:14
> The nations will hear and tremble;
> anguish will grip the people of Philistia.

The purpose of the nature defying miracles of Exodus was in order to introduce the world to God, before He comes out in full voice and tells everyone what He wants them to do. That's why adults are also commanded to remember the Exodus from Egypt every day.

> Deuteronomy 15:15
> Remember that you were slaves in Egypt and the LORD your God redeemed you. That is why I give you this command today.

In order to influence children to keep the Ten Commandments, they must understand the source. Many people do not follow in their parents' footsteps because their parents demanded blind faith. Hashem doesn't demand blind faith. He wants us to understand. That's why He wrote the whole Torah, not just a set of commandments.

When rearing children, we should tell them lots of true stories. When they ask, "why?" we should give them the history or science to back up our answer. However, there are some things we have to go on faith, just as in math there are some axioms that we just must believe. The most basic axiom in geometry is: One and only one line can connect between two points. The most basic axiom of the Bible is: One and only one God is connected to you personally.

Which Commandment Is the First One?

Some Christians believe that "I am the Lord your God" is an introduction to all ten, and the first commandment to enumerate is "You shall not have other gods." This is a misunderstanding that stems from the mistranslation of the word *Devarim* in Exodus 34:

> Exodus 34:28
> Moses was there with the LORD forty days and forty nights without eating bread or drinking water. And he wrote on the tablets the words of the covenant—the Ten Commandments.

The Hebrew verse does not say Ten Commandments; it says, Ten Statements. *Devarim* which means statements is traditionally translated as commandments.

The Ten Commandments are not all commandments, but they are all statements. The first statement isn't a clear command, but it is a very powerful proclamation. When referring to the Ten Commandments in Hebrew we say, "*Aseret hadibrot*," literally, the "Ten Statements."

I agree that this first commandment or statement is an introduction. It is the precursor to the whole Torah. The whole Torah depends on the belief in God. Hashem says, "I want you to observe the Torah because you believe in Me and you trust Me. I love you and want to take you under

My wing. My wing is the Ten Commandments, following them will keep you safe from evil's harm."

We are all in agreement that there only Ten Commandments or statements. We also agree that the first statement is an introduction. The only question is how to enumerate them. If the first commandment is not, "I am the Lord your God" but "You shall not have any other gods," then you would have to say that the second commandment would be, "Do not to make yourself an image."

> Exodus 20:3, "You shall have no other gods before me. You shall not make for yourself an image in the form of anything in heaven above or on the earth beneath or in the waters below."

If the commandment to refrain from making images were a commandment on its own, then it would be prohibited to make images of any kind, even stuffed animals! Hashem told me that it's fine to have stuffed animals and little dolls for your children, just as long as you don't worship them or believe they are a vehicle to connect to God, or any other divine being or for witchcraft.

Therefore, the commandment not to make images is connected to the commandment not to have other gods. It's OK to have images that are not gods if you do not give them any type of spiritual sanctity.

Since the Torah specifically says that there are Ten Statements, we have to count the first statement as Commandment number one. The second commandment is all about worshiping other gods. All the other commandments are not divided into two parts so there is no discrepancy as to how they are enumerated.

Chapter 5
Idol Worship

Exodus 20: 3–6 and Deuteronomy 5: 7–10 say: "Do not have any other gods before me. You shall not make for yourself an idol, whether in the form of anything that is in heaven above, or that is on the earth beneath, or that is in the water under the earth. You shall not bow down to them or worship them; for I the Lord your God am a zealous God, punishing children for the iniquity of parents, to the third and the fourth generation of those who reject me, but showing steadfast love to the thousandth generation of those who love me and keep my commandments."

When you get upset, you might go for a drink, a cigarette, or even drugs. If you choose wisely, you may exercise or go to a psychologist or psychiatrist. In ancient times people went temples of idolatry to feel better. The belief was that if you give a sacrifice to the gods, everything would be OK. This calmed the ancient man temporarily.

Monotheism is different. It's not enough to give a sacrifice. God is scrutinizing you. You have to behave. You have to remember that He is watching. Only very strong commitment and trust can calm you down. Believing in God is hard work. It is not magic.

The Israelites worshiped idols in Egypt even before Moses' appearance.

> Joshua 24:14, "Now fear the LORD and serve him with all faithfulness. Throw away the gods your ancestors worshiped beyond the Euphrates River and in Egypt, and serve the LORD."

Just forty days after God announced in a great voice, "Thou shall have no other gods before Me ..." (Exodus 20:3– 5), the Israelites transgressed this commandment at Mount Sinai. In the absence of Moses, they committed the sin of the Golden Calf.

Before Moses returned to Egypt, on a mission to save the Israelites from bondage, the Israelites were accustomed to turning to idols in order to deal with their fears. When Moses didn't return from Mount Sinai, the Israelites slid back into their old custom of idol worship.

In the wilderness after the redemption from Egypt and after being punished for the sin of the golden calf, they sinned again:

> Numbers 25:1, "While Israel was staying in Shittim, the men began to indulge in sexual immorality with Moabite women, who invited them to the sacrifices to their gods. The people ate the sacrificial meal and bowed down before these gods. So Israel yoked themselves to the Baal of Peor. And the LORD's anger burned against them."

Moses foresaw the future downfall of Israel, as they would be influenced by the pagan practices of their neighbors:

> Deuteronomy 31:25, "For now I know that after my death you will become corrupt and you will leave the path that I commanded you to follow. The bad things will happen because you will do evil in the eyes of Hashem, to anger Him with the creations your own hands."

For extended periods of time from even before the death of Joshua and the elders, until the destruction of the Holy Temple, the Israelites had a very hard time believing in God alone. They thought that when they were fearful that it was right to turn to gods for protection.

> Joshua 24:23-26, "'Now then,' said Joshua, 'throw away the foreign gods that are among you and yield your hearts to the LORD, the God of Israel.' And the people said to Joshua, 'We will serve the LORD our God and obey him.' On that day Joshua made a covenant for the people, and there at Shechem he reaffirmed for them decrees and laws. And Joshua recorded these things in the Book of the Law of God. Then he took a large stone and set it up there under the oak near the holy place of the LORD."

I'd just like to make a comment here. The above passage gives evidence that the whole Old Testament Bible is called Torah and is holy to God. The NIV translation says the Book of the Law of God is a translation from the Hebrew, *"Torat Elokim"* meaning "God's Torah" When Joshua wrote things down he wrote it in a new book, in continuation of the first five books of Moses. He knew that his book, the book of Joshua, would not be the last, it would be part of a whole compilation that he called God's Torah and we call the Bible.

In chapter 11, Jeremiah describes how the Jewish people did not keep the covenant made with Hashem at Mount Sinai. Jeremiah lived in the time leading up to and during the destruction of the Holy Temple.

> Jeremiah 11: 6-8
> "The LORD said to me, 'Proclaim all these words in the towns of Judah and in the streets of Jerusalem: Listen to the terms of this covenant and follow them. From the time I brought your ancestors up from Egypt until today, I warned them again and again, saying, "Obey me." But they did not listen or pay attention; instead, they followed the stubbornness of their evil hearts. So I brought on them all the curses of the covenant I had commanded them to follow but that they did not keep.'"

The Bible is filled with different passages describing the sin of idolatry. For modern man, believing that a statue is a god is a hard concept to even contemplate. Therefore, I would like to go back in time a little to explain more about the source of idol worship.

How Did Idol Worship Begin?

There are a few museums in Israel that contain relics from the Holy Temple era. There are idols the size of small dolls twelve inches long, sometimes shorter, sometimes larger, and occasionally with jewelry settings. These are examples of the "foreign gods" that Joshua mentioned.

The curses mentioned in the Bible are first and foremost punishment for worship of idols. The rewards for keeping away from them and loving Hashem are grand: rain, prosperity, sustenance, and long life. These consequences are mentioned many times. One example is in Deuteronomy chapter 11. This chapter is in our daily prayers.

> Deuteronomy 11:13-17
> So if you faithfully obey the commands I am giving you today—to love the LORD your God and to serve him with all your heart and with all your soul—then I will send rain on your land in its season, both autumn and spring rains, so that you may gather in your grain, new wine and olive oil. I will provide grass in the fields for your cattle, and you will eat and be satisfied. Be careful, or you will be enticed to turn away and worship other gods and bow down to them. Then the LORD's anger will burn against you, and he will shut up the heavens so that it will not rain and the ground will yield no produce, and you will soon perish from the good land the LORD is giving you.

Strange Figurines

We saw exhibits of idols in the Israel Museum in Jerusalem and the museum in Hatzor that were found in the ancient land of Canaan. The archeological findings dated around 3500 to 4000 BCE. That's around the time of Moses. They were very strange-looking figures. I asked Hashem, "Why did they make idols that had ugly faces that were disfigured?" Some of them didn't have arms or had horns for noses and other strange appearances. Hashem said that the pagan priests wanted to frighten the people so they made them scary-looking gods.

All of a sudden I understood everything. The pagan priests didn't believe in these gods. Many just promoted the belief in idols for profit and power. The terrifying images of the gods stirred people to fear them. The priests convinced innocent people that the gods needed to be appeased. They had their congregants bring them their jewelry, food, and animals to present to the gods while these priests accumulated riches and became more and more corrupt. Presenting gifts to the gods became a way of worship. The worshipers were brainwashed to dread these make-believe gods. This brainwashing also prevented them from intellectual advancement. The population is subservient to the high priest and they must lose any initiative to change their ways, lest they be punished by the wrath of the gods.

Fear Is the Antidote for Fear

I once had a client who had a fear of traveling. She didn't drive, and she was terrified of buses. She came to me crying because her mother moved out of town. How could she possibly go visit? Medications were not a possibility because this woman had five children, any pill she took made her sleepy—too sleepy to care for her children. I gave her some natural remedies, which she took with her on the bus for local rides. They helped temporarily, but she still didn't have the guts to go out of town.

I thought about it for days, and I came up with a plan. "You are going on a trip out of the country," I commanded her.

"I am?" she asked. "You know my sister is getting married in Belgium, and I came to ask you if I should go to the wedding."

"Yes, yes, this is what you have to do to get better. Do something even more scary than what you are afraid of." I packed her up with more herbal remedies, and she was off. She did it! When she came back, going to visit her mother was a piece of cake!

Why Do We Have to Fear God?

> Deuteronomy 10:12 says, "What am I asking from you? Only to fear me."

Hashem says, "If you think you're afraid of some little idols, then fear Me. Fear what I will do to you because you believe in such nonsense." Fearing Hashem is the cure for all other fears.

Fearing Hashem is the way to prevent idol worship as well as fear of human beings, then and now. For example: If at work you're afraid of your boss, work on yourself to be afraid of God instead. If your boss wants you to do something that Hashem would oppose, then fear God and you will not do what is wrong in His eyes, even at the expense of your job. There are two possible outcomes: You don't lose your job and you get more respect, or you lose your job and you will have more self-respect and respect from Hashem while you're awaiting a much better position. Either way you're ahead.

What Makes Hashem Angry?

There is one commandment when transgressed in the Ten Commandments that makes Hashem angry. This is the sin of idol worship.

> Deuteronomy 6:13–15, "You shall fear only the Lord your God; and you shall worship Him and swear by His name. You shall not follow other gods, any of the gods of the peoples who surround you, for the Lord your God in the midst of you is a zealous God; otherwise the anger of the Lord your God will be kindled against you, and He will wipe you off the face of the earth."

Hashem's relationship to the children of Israel is a core issue in the Torah. Throughout the Holy Temple period, idolatry existed in the land of Israel until it grew to the point that God expelled the children of Israel from the the Land of Israel.

There are a lot of different powers that Hashem created in the world. If you go to a Buddhist temple, you may feel a powerful force there. Many people hear voices of Buddhist gods. Does that mean that the Buddhist idol has any power? No! It's all from Hashem. There is no other source of supernatural power but Hashem. Hashem gives you the choice to believe in Him or not. This is free-will granted to you from Hashem. However, if someone is brainwashed, he loses his free will. The only way he can get it back is for someone else to break the cycle and help him think differently.

Before and after the Torah was given, pagan priests and their hierarchy still had their free choice. Some priests knew that it is nonsense to believe in idols, some actually believed in other gods, but they all influenced, tricked, or forced people into thinking that idols will save them. Even today people may tell each other to look at the picture of a rabbi or saint and they will be saved. If you believe that any power comes from something other than Hashem, the atmosphere changes. You will have an illusion that there is another power other than Hashem. Your belief creates power.

We see this in medicine too. Placebos can heal people miraculously. Hashem doesn't want us to live an illusion. He doesn't want us to have a placebo as a religion. Carl Marx said, "Religion is the opium of the masses." Sometimes it is, but so is atheism. Atheists end up believing in science and medicine as the only truth and accept their opinions even if they are instructed to give up hope.

Another exhibit that we saw in the Israel Museum in Jerusalem was a whole floor of amulets and magical artifacts. The power that the believers gave to these objects turned into bad energy. I felt this negative energy so strongly that I had to leave the hall. When praying to other gods, the worshipers are really praying to Hashem. He's the only one that's listening;

that's why they feel the spirituality and they sometimes get answered. However, Hashem doesn't like this.

My good friend, a school teacher gave a great analogy. Let's say, God forbid, you are suspicious of your husband going to prostitutes. You dress up and flag him down on dark corner late at night. He makes passionate love with you, but you are steaming! *How come he has energy and money for me when he thinks I'm a whore but not for his loyal wife and mother of his children?*

The Bible also compares idol worship to unfaithfulness and prostitution.

> Isaiah 1:21
> "How has the faithful city become a prostitute! She was once full of justice; righteousness used to dwell in her midst but now there are murderers!"

> Ezekiel 6:9
> And they that escape of you shall remember me among the nations whither they shall be carried captives, because I am broken with their whorish heart, which has departed from me, and with their eyes, which go whoring after their idols; and they shall loathe themselves for the evils which they have committed in all their abominations.

Idol worship requires indoctrination as well as a relinquishment of free will and free thinking. If idol worship is a product of brainwashing, why does Hashem get so angry at idol worshippers? Maybe it isn't their fault.

Remember, Hashem has been planning this world for millions of years. He finally created a man who can think independently and have free choice. In pagan religions, unrestricted questioning is prohibited. The more fundamental the religion, the less questions are allowed to be asked.

Judaism prides itself on the ability to listen to all questions. Inquiries are encouraged. However, there are some ultra-Orthodox groups in Judaism and Christianity that do not allow their children to ask questions. Forcing a dogmatic religion is against the Torah, and even though it isn't idol worship, it is blind worship.

After the multitude of miracles that Hashem produced in order to prepare for the Exodus from Egypt the Israelites should have believed that God is going to help them complete their journey. After the ten plagues and the splitting of the Red Sea they still had doubts. The Israelites complained that they didn't have food or water and worst of all they worshipped the Golden Calf.

This is a case of ungratefulness. God got very, very angry and He even wanted to destroy the whole nation. Why did they do it? The answer that I will give you will explain not only why they worshipped the Golden Calf but also why miracles don't help.

When God plagued the Egyptians with the plague of lice the magicians tried to copy the plague but they were not successful.

> Exodus 8:16-19
> Then the LORD said to Moses, "Tell Aaron, 'Stretch out your staff and strike the dust of the ground,' and throughout the land of Egypt the dust will become gnats." They did this, and when Aaron stretched out his hand with the staff and struck the dust of the ground, gnats came on people and animals. All the dust throughout the land of Egypt became gnats. But when the magicians tried to produce gnats by their secret arts, they could not.

Since the gnats were on people and animals everywhere, the magicians said to Pharaoh, "This is the finger of God." But Pharaoh's heart was hard and he would not listen, just as the LORD had said.

The magicians who were intelligent people understood that this miracle is above the ability of a magic trick. It convinced them that it was an act of God. However, Pharaoh believed that even if it was an act of God, maybe there are other gods who can help him. A miracle proves God's strength but it doesn't prove God's absolute oneness.

How does this translate to our generation?

If we know that we were created by God and He has given us food and clothing our whole lives, then why do we suddenly doubt that he will provide? Simply because we aren't thinking that everything is in His hands. When we are thinking that our boss at work can hurt us or the stock market crash will hurt us it's all a result of a lack of awareness. We really believe that there are powers stronger than God Himself.

Constant Awareness

Almost everything we do wrong connects to insufficient awareness on some level. For example, a parent yells at his child because he forgets or is not aware that the child is just an innocent human being. You argue with your spouse because you forgot all the good things she's done for you. A person steals because he lacks the awareness of what the true outcome of his actions will be.

Emotional problems can also be linked to lack of constant awareness of God's presence. Why be depressed or discouraged if Hashem is with me? How can I be angry, if the Creator of the world is in the same room watching me?

When we ignore the blessing that God gave us and believe in the power of others Hashem gets upset. If he wanted to kill you, you can get hit by a car and instantly return to your Creator. If He wants you to live, then He'll give you food to eat and money to pay the rent. The more you are aware of this fact, the more Hashem will look out for you.

Sometimes people can test our patience, especially children. Yelling and abusing children hurts them for life. They are too sensitive to withstand the blows of an adult, especially those of their own parents or guardians.

The truth is that we yell at our kids because we can. There is no visible superior authority hovering over us, and we forget that Hashem is watching. We take advantage of their weakness and inability to manage without us. We feel powerful around our kids. Are we not guilty of sacrificing our children on the altar of pride and power?

Awareness of God's presence would put us in our place. The lack of that awareness is like idol worship. Constant awareness will change our whole demeanor and will give us strength to endure the stumbling blocks that life brings us.

Sacrificing Children

Deuteronomy 18:10, "There shall not be found one who passes his child through fire." Leviticus 20:2, "A man from the children of Israel or from a foreigner who will give his child for a sacrifice to *Molech* shall die."

Molech was an idol that was worshipped by the Israelites. They would prostrate themselves before Molech with a child in their arms. The false prophet would take the child and throw it into the interior cavity of the idol, burning him or her alive. Even nursing babies were sacrificed to this god. This is one of the hidden meanings of the phrase "Do not cook a kid in its mother's milk." (Exodus 23:18)

On the left, is an 18th-century German illustration of the idol called Molech. On the right is the picture of a Babylonian seal depicting child sacrifice. The idol is sitting in a chair and the child was meant to be burned on its lap.

This despicable act of sacrificing children was God's last straw. It made Him angry and he decreed destruction of Jerusalem and of the Holy Temple within.

> Jeremiah 7:31, "They have built the high places of Topheth in the Valley of Ben Hinnom to burn their sons and daughters in the fire, something I did not command, and I didn't even contemplate such a thing."

> In Jeremiah 32:35 he adds: "I didn't even contemplate such a thing to cause the people of Judah to sin."

The Israelites were practicing child sacrifices regularly. Hashem was complaining that not only doesn't He want that, but He never even contemplated it. Worshiping through human sacrifice is not what Hashem wants. He wants us to keep the Torah and the mitzvot that are written in the Torah. If the Torah says that you can't murder, then you can't murder for God either.

In the story of the binding of Isaac, (Genesis 22:1–19) God instructs Abraham to slaughter his own son. The Torah law is that if a prophet tells a nation or even one person man to serve idols, the prophet must be killed. The same goes for murder or rape. Hashem gave the Ten Commandments so we will have red lines. In the case of being told to violate one of the Ten Commandments, we must say no to a prophet and even to God.

Most likely if a man claims to hear God commanding him to violate one of the Ten Commandments, he is hallucinating, lying, or mentally ill. If Hashem told Abraham to kill his son, he should have said emphatically, "No!" If he said yes, then Abraham didn't pass his test.

Hashem does not want us to sacrifice anything for Him. He doesn't need anything. What is more important is that He wants us to have limits. We must have an ideology on which to stand. We must have the ability to say no sometimes. The more strength we have to stand on our values the prouder Hashem is of us.

If a young girl refuses to have an abortion no matter what shame she will have to go through Hashem is proud of her. If a person says the truth in the face of peer pressure, Hashem is proud of that person. He doesn't want us to follow the multitudes. That is what differed Abraham from other people in his time. Abraham was a powerful man with a strong will to go against the whole world and find God. He would have never agreed to sacrifice his son.

Modern Bible researchers assert that the language in this chapter is different, and it comes from a later date, around the end of the Holy Temple period. There was no child sacrifice in the time of Abraham. If he would have heard God say such a thing, it would have been unthinkable. Bible scholars suggest that this story may have been invented during the time of Jeremiah at the time of the Holy Temple in order to stop child sacrifice.

I believe that this chapter was written by false prophets during the Holy Temple period in order to encourage child sacrifice. The words, "You didn't withhold your son, your only one, from me" (Genesis 22:12) are not characteristic of God's merciful attributes. The false prophets wanted the Israelites to be so devoted to their gods that they would be willing to surrender everything they owned, even their own children. That's how the false prophets became so rich and powerful.

Hashem doesn't want us to give up our children for Him. What good does it do for Hashem if someone is killed? If He wants them to die He can kill them in an instant. How is it possible to even contemplate the thought that killing a child is a gift to a god? How is it possible to even contemplate that the death of Jesus is a gift to God?

> Jeremiah 32:35
> And they built the high places of Baal, which are in the valley of the son of Hinnom, to cause their sons and their daughters to pass through the fire unto Molech; which I commanded them not, neither came it into my mind, that they should do this abomination, to cause Judah to sin.

It is the only instance in the entire Bible that God said He never commanded or contemplated commanding a sin. God is saying this passage in a shocking way. The story of the binding of Isaac was a rumor that was spoken of in the times of Jeremiah. When Hashem tells Jeremiah, "neither came into my mind" He means to say, "I would never even think of telling Abraham to kill his own son; this idea is preposterous!" Hashem told Jeremiah that He is angry that the people of Judah even believed this story.

I believe that many people who read this will object to my claim that any part of the Bible is not true. Even if the story was true, the lesson to learn from it is that we should not sacrifice our child to God. In this story the angel stopped Abraham from killing his son.

Hashem is like us. We are created in His image. Would you enjoy people worshipping you by dying for you?

Hashem does not want us to be immersed in worship. He doesn't want us to hurt ourselves in any way. Sacrifice gives the worshipper the illusion that they are giving God something that He needs and in return his prayers will be answered.

Hashem doesn't need anything. He wants our wellbeing. He loves us more when we take care of ourselves and of our children. If we want to give something to God, give to other people, that's what makes Him happy.

> Proverbs 14:31, Whoever oppresses the poor shows contempt for their Maker, but whoever is kind to the needy honors God.

How did the story get into the Bible? The story of the binding of Isaac was found on scroll in one of the biblical libraries just like many other biblical works during the Holy Temple period. It wasn't written on stone like the rest of the Torah. That's why this story begins in Genesis 22, starts with the words, "And it happened after these things," or in free translation, "Once upon a time …"

When the Torah was canonized in the year 200 CE, the rabbis put this story into the book of Genesis believing that it was a true story because it was so well known. Hashem told me that this is the only story that was added to the Five Books of Moses and was not written by Moses. I know that I might get attacked for this statement but I feel sorry for Abraham. He is in heaven watching how everyone is saying that he agreed to kill his only son that was born to him when he was one hundred years old. It's very insulting and it makes Abraham feel falsely accused of something unimaginable!

God doesn't need our sacrifice or our pain. If we suffer it is because He realized that this is the last possible resort that He has, to make us change our ways, improve ourselves and nourish our souls. When we suffer Hashem suffers even more. In order to understand fully the history of the compilation of the Bible as we have it today, please read my book *God's Hidden Treasure*.

Self-Sacrifice

We aren't supposed to love God more than we love our own children. That is another reason why we must love Hashem and fear Him. A parent's love for his or her child is without fear. Love for Hashem is respectful love like love for a parent or a leader and should not be confused with love for a child or a lover.

Hurting someone else for God is absurd. Your child is also Hashem's child. He wants him alive and well, not dead or suffering. Risking your own life to keep your child alive is another story. Many parents would risk their lives to save their child from danger. That's the way it should be. When you run into a roaring sea to save your child, you trust God that if you try with all your strength, He will save you and your son or daughter.

The main purpose of the animal sacrifices in the Holy Temple was to keep the Israelites away from idol worship. They were so deeply immersed in worship through sacrifices that they would be afraid to live without them. Hashem unwillingly allowed the Israelites to give Hashem sacrifices in order to prevent them from sacrificing to other gods.

In reality Hashem doesn't need sacrifices of any kind. As it says in Isaiah 1:11, "Why do I need your sacrifices … I've had enough of your fat sheep."

> Jeremiah 7:22-26 say, "For when I brought your ancestors out of Egypt and spoke to them, I did not just give them commands about burnt offerings and sacrifices, but I gave them this command: Obey me, and I will be your God and you will be my people. Walk in obedience to all I command you, that it may go well with you. But they did not listen or pay attention; instead, they followed the stubborn inclinations of their evil hearts. They went backward and not forward. From the time your ancestors left Egypt until now, day after day, again and again I sent you my servants the prophets. But they did not listen to me or pay attention. They were stiff-necked and did more evil than their ancestors.

From Jeremiah we learn that on the day the Israelites were freed from Egypt, they were told that the purpose of the Exodus from Egypt was not to give sacrifices in the desert, like Moses had originally requested of Pharaoh. Only after the sin of the Golden Calf did God tell the Israelites to build a Tabernacle for ceremonial worship, in order to help restrain them from idol worship.

Nowadays, modern religions don't have sacrifices, but they do have houses of worship. Hashem allows us to have a house of worship because it's better than worshiping other religions, but Hashem doesn't need a house of worship. He doesn't want to be worshipped, He wants to be loved.

Hashem only wants our best, and He doesn't need to be served. He doesn't enjoy people prostrating themselves to Him. He doesn't even want us to cry to Him. All Hashem wants is that we realize that He is there, thank Him, appreciate whatever we have and work on ourselves to do better. He admires us very much if we learn the Bible and implement what we've learned in our daily lives.

The original purpose of the synagogue was to learn Torah. There was only one Torah scroll per city so the people of the town came to the synagogue to learn. Since the Jewish People were exiled they built up new places to learn and pray together for their return to the promised land.

The synagogue is valuable as a place to meet other people and pray together. When we pray together God will answer us, not only for our own merit but in the merits of the entire community.

> Proverbs 14: 28, A large population is a king's glory, but without subjects a prince is ruined.

When you have a serious problem ask for others to pray for you. The more the better. You personally might not have the merit to be saved but if so many good people care about you Hashem will help you just in order not to let them down.

Other actions that we can do to find favor in the eyes of Hashem are to study the Bible, sing and speak to Hashem from the heart and help those in need.

The basic belief that God wants human or nonhuman sacrifices is something that He didn't even think of or contemplate. All He wants is our love and devotion to His rulings. Even though there are death penalties mentioned in the Torah Hashem would much rather that we repent than suffer.

> Ezekiel 13:32 says, "For I do not wish the death of the dead, rather that he returns to Hashem and live."

If we suffer it is usually for the purpose of repentance and change. After we die it is too late to repent. Every morning we should wake up with a prayer, thanking Hashem for giving us life and begging for strength to learn and improve.

Free Will

Free will doesn't begin at birth. Babies start to develop their own tastes and their own will slowly. They get a big boost of free will at two years old, and from then on it grows stronger and stronger as we mature into adulthood. The more we use our brains, the more free will we have and the more we can improve and excel.

Don't destroy children's free choice by being too hard on them. They have to learn how to choose right from wrong. Don't try to program them into doing things your way. Teach them right from wrong. Tell them stories that will help them understand so they have the ability to choose what's right and not be hypnotized by friends who influence them to go the wrong way.

If we program others, or allow ourselves to be programmed, then we are undoing the whole purpose of creation. God wanted to create a being that has its own free will and watch what he will do with it. In my book *Who is God?* I elaborated on the topic of free will, sacrifice and forgiveness. I show evidence that God forgives only those who repent and change their ways.

The whole media is busy hypnotizing people. Just like the pagan priests of ancient times, they are trying to take away our free will. The media attempts to manipulate the public through the use of subliminal messages. Then it was false prophets; now it's false and mesmerizing advertisements.

Idol Worship and Science

The Torah doesn't go against the laws of science, and science doesn't go against the laws of the Torah. During the period of Galileo, the church overruled science. Galileo was imprisoned for promoting the idea that heavenly bodies orbited the sun. The church believed that because Joshua told the sun to stop, the sun must have been circling the earth.

> Joshua 10:12, "On the day the Lord gave the Amorites over to Israel, Joshua said to the Lord in the presence of Israel: "Sun, stand still over Gibeon, and you, moon, over the Valley of Aijalon."

If science proves something beyond the shadow of a doubt, we try to understand the Torah accordingly. Throughout history, Jews were always open to learn about science. Science and nature are both part of learning about Hashem.

What really happened in Joshua's war?

The sun didn't stop; time stopped. Hashem made time stop for the Israelite soldiers. They went into a different dimension while the rest of the world was in slow motion or no motion compared to them. It was a miracle like we see in science fiction movies.

The Theory of Evolution

Some propose that the theory of evolution was just a diabolic plan to get people to stop believing in God. Darwin lost his first daughter and was very angry at God. He wanted desperately to believe that there was no God. After many years of trying to prove his theory, Darwin realized that his observations in nature would justify his proposing theory of evolution only if in the future archeologists discovered the missing links between the different fossils found in archeological excavations.

Many other wealthy men wanted to be free of the church that was very controlling and disturbed the personal freedom of families in England at the time. Darwin was paid well to invent some imaginary theory that had no proof in science and hypnotized the world to believe the impossible. There is a movie called *Darwin* that can be very educational and puts Darwin's theories into another perspective. There is a book called *Darwin's Doubt* by Stephen C. Meyer. He explains how Darwin had his own doubts in his theory but believed that with time, more evidence would be discovered. Today there have been many advances in archeology. Not only didn't modern scientists find the missing links, but archeologists discovered many more remnants of fossils that lack evolutionary development stages.

Approximately 488 million years ago there was an era called the Cambrian period. At this prehistoric time, hundreds of different species appeared suddenly and simultaneously in different parts of the planet with no signs of any intermediary stages.

Darwin knew about the Cambrian explosion and said the future discovery of links before and after this era is the basis on which his whole theory stands. Scientists never discovered any missing links. Some scientists who admit to the lack of missing links, have come to the conclusion that there must be an intelligent creator. This is called the theory of "Intelligent Design." There are also three DVD's called *Intelligent Design* by Illustra Media that give fascinating explanations.

Atheism

Communist Russia tried to persuade their people into believing in a godless world for decades. From a very young age, children were taught to believe in evolution. But it was just hypnotism; it wasn't the truth. The proof of this is that as soon as the communist regime fell, millions of people from the former Soviet Union looked for faith and now believe in God.

Communism as it has been practiced, is another form of controlling the masses. People who have faith have strength. They feel justified in the righteousness of their cause. If the government goes against them, they may feel that the government is unjust. Religious people sense that there is a righteous power, higher than the government, a power worth fighting for and even worth giving up their lives.

In order to acquire increasing power, wealthy Communistic leaders limited their people's access to worldly news and information. They took away their religion, their ideology and their knowledge.

The reason the new generation of Russians are returning to faith is because it isn't natural to be atheistic. The Communist regimes of the world had to be very insistent on instilling non-belief. A Russian friend of mine who lived in Communist Russia told me that when she was in first grade, her teachers in school started to instill negative messages about the faith in God. Every year the new teacher made it her business to put atheism as a top priority. When my friend came to Israel from Russia, it was very hard for her start believing in God. However, her guts told her that she must give her life some spirituality. She started lighting candles on Friday night and was strict not to work or cook on the Sabbath. Slowly she started to feel that there is a God, and her son and his wife became observant Jews.

Atheism is a religion just as any other, and its believers can be even more devout than religious followers. The American educational system separates church from state and forbids communal prayer in school. While the Bible was banned as a source of history or even literature, the "religion" of godless evolution, now disproved by many, was promoted. In America it is also forbidden to teach the theory of Intelligent Design in public schools.

Notwithstanding, in Hashem's opinion, atheism is not a form of idol worship because it lacks an emotional attachment to a god. Scientists with staunch Darwinist beliefs quickly gave up their tenets when they discovered evidence disproving evolution theory.

When compared to atheists, religious people remain loyal to their convictions even after being presented with scientific proofs negating their beliefs. Loyalty to religion is emotional just like the loyalty to Hashem should be.

When people are forced to go against their religion they feel persecuted as if they were being physically hurt. Therefore, we should always respect the convictions of others and try to teach them about Hashem and his Bible without insulting them or being too emotionally forceful.

Teach people to talk to Hashem. The soul of every human being has a need to connect to the One God who created the world. You can talk to Him and trust Him without any special form of worship. If you forget Him and you suddenly remember, He is still there!

One and Only One God

> Psalm 18:32 says, "Who is a god besides Hashem, and who is steadfast like our God?"

Isaiah was a prophet whose main purpose was to spread God's name and bring back people from the belief in other gods.

Isaiah 45:6

In order that it should be known from east to west that I am God there is nothing that exists without me, I am God and there is no other."

Isaiah 44:8

Do not tremble, do not be afraid. Did I not proclaim this and foretell it long ago? You are my witnesses. Is there any God besides me? No, there is no other Rock; I know not one."

Isaiah 45:20-22
"Gather together and come;
assemble, you fugitives from the nations.
Ignorant are those who carry about idols of wood,
who pray to gods that cannot save.
Declare what is to be, present it—
let them take counsel together.
Who foretold this long ago,
who declared it from the distant past?
Was it not I, the LORD?
And there is no God apart from me,
a righteous God and a Savior;
there is none but me.
"Turn to me and be saved,
all you ends of the earth;
for I am God, and there is no other.

Some may say that the Bible was written before Jesus was born and at that time there was no other God but Hashem Himself, but after Jesus was born, things changed. I will answer with another quote that explains that everything that was written in the Torah will never ever change:

Isaiah 59:21,
> As for me, this is my covenant with them," says the LORD. "My Spirit, who is on you, will not depart from you, and my words that I have put in your mouth will always be on your lips, on the lips of your children and on the lips of their descendants—from this time on and forever," says the LORD.

A friend told me a story about a Jewish convert that he met. This woman just got her certificate of conversion and was happy to celebrate. My friend was interested to hear how she fared on her final test. The convert said that she was asked about the prayers of Shabbat and intricate details of the laws. He asked her in a very matter-of-fact manner, "Do you still believe in Jesus?"

"Of course," she said.

"How did you go through conversion school while still believing in Jesus?"

Then came back the innocent answer: "Nobody ever asked."

This convert believed in Jesus since childhood. She couldn't stop believing in him even when she was convinced of the truth in Jewish ideology. The word *Jesus* is so taboo in Jewish circles that no one asks anything about him. Many priests claim that Jesus and God are one. That's how they understand the famous passage, "The Lord is God the Lord is One." (Deuteronomy 6:4)

Isaac Newton, a genius in his time, studied the ancient Christian texts and arrived at the conclusion that it is forbidden to believe in Jesus as a divine being because it says in the Ten Commandments, "Thou shall not have other gods before me." Isaac Newton was a deep thinker and he saw the contradiction.

By the way, if this convert believed in Jesus when she converted, her conversion is not valid. If a person who was born Jewish starts believing in Jesus, or if a convert starts to believe in Jesus after he converted, he is still Jewish but if he wants to return back to Judaism, he must go through a ceremony to return to the faith. Many Marranos from Spain have gone through this procedure when they came to Israel and returned to the faith of their forefathers. (see the glossary for more explanation about Marranos)

Zechariah 14:9 says, "And the day will come God will be King all over that land. He will be one and His name will be one." For years I didn't understand why the prophet had to say that God will have one name. What's so important about a name?

Zechariah was foreseeing our times, when any belief is acceptable. Our generation accepts many different creeds and freedom of religious belief. Most religious people look for a common ground, claiming that they believe in the same God. God really wants us to believe only in Him, the God of Abraham, Isaac and Jacob, without any divisions, interpretations, or other names.

At the site of the burning bush, God revealed His name to Moses. Exodus 3:14-15

> God said to Moses, "I am who I am. This is what you are to say to the Israelites: I am has sent me to you." "Say to the Israelites, Yehoweh the god of your fathers—the God of Abraham, the God of Isaac and the God of Jacob—has sent me to you. This is my name forever; the name you shall call me from generation to generation.'"

The name that Hashem called Himself was *Eheye* which means I will be. That was an introduction to explain His full name, "Yehoweh the God of your fathers…" Yehoweh is a compound word made up of the three words, "I was, I am, and I will be."

Almost every time you read "The Lord" in the English translation of the Bible, the Hebrew says *Yehoweh*. Since there are no vowels in the original Bible we cannot be sure how Hashem's name should be pronounced. Jews were always careful not to say it so there is no known heritage of the exact pronunciation. The Jehovah Witnesses call God Jehovah. That isn't a different name, it is the same name in English, just like Joshua is the same as *Yehoshua* and Abraham is the same as *Avraham*. Many people claim that the pronunciation of God's name should be *Yahweh*. They base this on some archaeological Egyptian writings. It could be that when the Israelites were in Egypt the Egyptians pronounced God's name *Yahweh*.

However, in Hebrew grammar it is not possible that the letter *Hay* after the letter *Yud* would be pronounce *Ya*. *Hay* in the middle of a word is never silent. Since Hebrew is a phonetic language with no exceptions, the only correct pronunciation of the letters in the Torah would be *Yehoweh* or *Yehowah*. Since *Yehowah* would be feminine I wrote *Yehoweh*.

However, in our prayer books the vowels underneath God's name is usually in the feminine form *Yehowah*. In Psalms there are times when the masculine form is written, usually when we mention God's strength and His attribute of justice. In the Bible itself as given to us by Moses there were no vowels. The Torah scrolls in Synagogues are also written without vowels.

In order to avoid saying His name in vain by mistake we never say God's name out loud. When we pray, we say Adonai meaning, "My Lord," but when we speak colloquially we say Hashem, which literally means "the name."

> Zechariah 14:9, "The LORD will be king over the whole earth. On that day there will be one LORD, and his name the only name."

Zechariah didn't mean that we can't call God by other names. When we call God Hashem, The Creator or The Almighty we aren't giving Him a new name, we are giving Him titles. Zechariah wanted to say that the one God, who spoke to Abraham and to Moses, will be the one God of the world. Everyone will know that His name is the name that is written in The Torah, *Yehoweh*. Zechariah prophesized that in the future Hashem would be the one and only God in the world. All will believe in one God that wrote the Torah and told Moses his name. He will be the only God without additions.

Holy War

There are many terrorist groups that scream out the name of God before they throw a bomb or commit suicide, as if God is directing their course of action. The Crusaders of the Dark Ages also claimed to be on a mission from God, killing thousands. This is much worse than just murder; it is murder in God's name.

These terrorist groups are not idolaters; they believe in one God but they do not believe in all of the Ten

Commandments. The second commandment is not only a directive to believe in One God, but to believe in the God that took the Israelites out of Egypt and gave the Ten Commandments. The belief in a God that promotes murder is not a belief in Yehoweh, our God. It is a false god invented by man. Many of these terrorist groups also encourage theft and deception, other transgressions of the Ten Commandments.

Just like you cannot create a god, you also cannot create rules for God. God's way of ruling is written in the Torah. His most important rules are the Ten Commandments. Any law or ideology that opposes any one of the Ten Commandments is man's invention.

The Satan

Another invention of man is the Satan. It was invented in ancient Babylonia for the religion called Zoroastrianism. They believed that there are two powers in the world: the power of good and the power of evil.

Hashem meant that only one supernatural power exists in the world when He said, "Hear O Israel, the Lord is God the Lord is one." (Deuteronomy 6:4) There are no other super powers, good or bad. In Christianity, the Devil or Satan is believed to be a supernatural power that can do things against God's will. That would mean that God is limited and that He has a rival. This belief is contrary to the second commandment.

The Satan in Jewish folklore is a type of angel that reports the evil that people do and has the job of a prosecuting attorney. Every judgement can have a different prosecuting attorney. It's not always the same Satan. The following verses are evidence from the Bible of this kind of Satan.

> Zechariah 3:1-2
> Then he showed me Joshua the high priest standing before the angel of the Lord, and Satan standing at his right side to accuse him. The Lord said to Satan, "The Lord rebuke you, Satan! The Lord, who has chosen Jerusalem, rebuke you! Is not this man a burning stick snatched from the fire?"

> Job 2:3
> Then the Lord said to Satan, "Have you considered my servant Job? There is no one on earth like him; he is blameless and upright, a man who fears God and shuns evil. And he still maintains his integrity, though you incited me against him to ruin him without any reason."

In the above verse Hashem is angry at the Satan or the prosecuting attorney for saying anything bad about Job. Job's children were burned in a fire, so Job is feeling their pain. In his heart, he is a man that is on fire. God is angry at the Satan for attacking Job. Hashem doesn't want to hear anything negative about Job because He has mercy on him.

Hashem doesn't need a Satan or devil to oppose him. Nevertheless and unfortunately, there are people in this world who are devils. A devil is much worse than a common criminal. A devil is a criminal with legal power. He can do evil and get away with it. He can interfere in the stock market, in politics and even in the hospital. He is the one to kick people out of their homes, take away their rights and even take away their children. They are evil men and women who give to the rich and take from the poor. They can lie in court with no repercussions, they can refuse insurance payments to the sick and let them die unnecessarily. I don't think any spiritual devil can compete with the white collared criminals on earth.

People who have been hurt by these devils will surely agree that this is true. Many biblical prophecies that mention the Satan or devil are surely an allegory to these mortal monsters. The clergymen of the past who frightened people with the devil were devils themselves!

The spiritual Satan cannot hurt you, he is just a prosecuting attorney. However, the mortal devils on earth have free choice. They are the source of evil and corruption in the world.

It is a mitzvah to believe that God will punish these evil people. They are not stronger than God. If they were able to hurt others, it was out of their God given free will. We pray to Hashem to save us from evildoers, and at the same time help others to be saved from them, Amen.

Sometimes in the courts of heaven there are angels that convince Hashem to make someone suffer for their own good, or for the good of others. Hashem is very merciful, so it is hard for Him to implement the decree, but He is encouraged by His angels that it must be done. Nothing will happen without God's approval. If you want to call that prosecuting angel the devil or the Satan, that's OK. I wouldn't, because he is not pure evil. He is a messenger who asks Hashem to do bad things for a positive reason. This is the type of Satan that spoke about Job. The ultimate benefit for the person who is suffering is in the future.

The Satan in Job is not above God. He can only do things with His permission.

> Job 1:12, "The Lord said to Satan, "Very well, then, everything he has is in your power, but on the man himself do not lay a finger."

This Satan is looking pessimistically at Job, wanting to test him. He encourages God to test his faith in order to see how righteous Job really is. The only way that Satan even has his day in court is because Job had done something very wrong.

> Job 1:4-5
> His sons used to hold feasts in their homes on their birthdays, and they would invite their three sisters to eat and drink with them. When a period of feasting had run its course, Job would make arrangements for them to be purified. Early in the morning he would sacrifice a burnt offering for each of them, thinking, "Perhaps my children have sinned and cursed God in their hearts." This was Job's regular custom.

Job wasn't at these birthday parties. He did have a feeling that something immoral was occurring. His solution to the problem was to bring a sacrifice, "a fix." God doesn't want this kind of solution. The girls and boys were at this party eating and drinking for days. Why didn't he crash the party? Job was too good, too polite. Sometimes too good is bad in the eyes of Hashem.

What I can say in Job's defense is that he wasn't attached to his money. When troubles struck his home and his livestock he didn't complain. Only when he heard that his children died did he cry, and when he cried he didn't get angry with God.

> Job 1:20-22
> At this, Job got up and tore his robe and shaved his head. Then he fell to the ground in worship and said: "Naked I came from my mother's womb, and naked I will depart. The LORD gave and the LORD has taken away; may the name of the LORD be praised."
> In all this, Job did not sin by charging God with wrongdoing.

We must have faith that there is justice in the world. A devil that can do harm to you even if you don't deserve it, is not just. Hashem is only one and He has total control. Nothing or nobody can hurt you without Hashem's consent. Whatever Hashem does, is a consequence of what man does. Whatever man chooses will bring him closer or further from the protection of the Almighty God.

Job's friend, Bildad, realized that Job was suffering because of the sins of his sons:

> Job 8:3-5
> Does God pervert justice?
> Does the Almighty pervert what is right? When your children sinned against him, he gave them over to the penalty of their sin. But if you will seek God earnestly and plead with the Almighty, if you are pure and upright, even now he will rouse himself on your behalf and restore you to your prosperous state. Your beginnings will seem humble so prosperous will your future be.

If Job's daughters were raped at these parties that was not Hashem's doing. A sacrifice cannot fix that. Job was negligent in checking out what was going on in these parties even though he was suspicious. He was so suspicious that he gave sacrifices in order to absolve his son's sins.

Job was too good. He didn't want to interfere. There are people that are good and strong and there are people that are good but weak. There are people who are bad and strong and there are those who are bad and weak. If you are good and weak, too weak to fight evil, you can end up being bad and weak.

When I was a little girl we used to watch *Mister Rogers* on Television. It was a children's educational show. He sang great songs for children. Here is one example:

Be Brave

> Be brave and then be strong,
> Be brave,
> Do not be wrong if you are right,
> Keep your chin up tight.
> Be brave and then be strong.

This song should be your motto whenever you face the choice between conquering your fears or facing them. One sign that what you are doing is right is that it is not easy. Choosing good from bad takes courage and endurance. Just remember that we must check into the Torah in order to know what is right in God's eyes.

A Copper Serpent

After Aaron died, the children of Israel left Mount Hor, the place where Aaron passed away and started a new route, walking in the hot and dry desert with no end in sight.

They began to complain that they were not happy with the provisions that they were receiving in the desert. Hashem got angry and punished them with fiery serpents that bit them.

> Numbers 21:4-9
>
> They traveled from Mount Hor along the route to the Red Sea, to go around Edom. But the people grew impatient on the way; they spoke against God and against Moses, and said, "Why have you brought us up out of Egypt to die in the wilderness? There is no bread! There is no water! And we detest this miserable food!"
>
> Then the LORD sent venomous snakes among them; they bit the people and many Israelites died. The people came to Moses and said, "We sinned when we spoke against the LORD and against you. Pray that the LORD will take the snakes away from us." So Moses prayed for the people.
>
> The LORD said to Moses, "Make a snake and put it up on a pole; anyone who is bitten can look at it and live." So Moses made a bronze snake and put it up on a pole. Then when anyone was bitten by a snake and looked at the bronze snake, they lived.

In order to heal the people, Moses made a copper serpent and placed it on a pole. If a serpent bit anyone, he would look at the copper serpent and live. Doesn't this appear to be a type of idol worship? If looking at it heals you, doesn't that constitute sorcery?

Indeed, in the times of the Holy Temple, the snake on the pole became an idol:

> 2 Kings 18:1–4 says, "Hezekiah the son of Ahaz king of Judah began to reign ... He broke up the copper snake that Moses had made, for up to that time the Israelites had been burning incense to it."

Hezekiah was a very righteous king, and he did what was right in the eyes of Hashem. He was able to stop idolatry in his days, but years later the nation of Judah resumed idol worship, eventually causing the destruction of the Holy Temple in Jerusalem.

Why did Hashem command Moses to create something that could be made into an idol?

After so many miracles, the children of Israel still complained! So Hashem said to Moses, "Let me test them. Maybe it really is too hard for them to stay in the wilderness for such a long time. Are they really ready to enter the land of the Canaanites and fight to conquer a land that is full of idolatry? I will put them to a test. I will give them one last chance." Hashem allowed the desert serpents to attack, and many of the Israelites died. The people were frightened, but they didn't turn to Hashem for help. Instead they complained even more. Hashem was merciful. He saw the children losing their parents, so He said to Moses, "It's urgent. You have to make them a magical remedy so they will heal. The new generation won't survive without their parents! The Israelites are still so deeply immersed in their beliefs in magic that only a magical cure will help them."

From this story we learn that the Israelites didn't respect Moses or Hashem in the same way that they respected magic. Hashem commanded Moses to create a symbol in the form of a snake on a pole in order to provide a placebo.

Psychologically the Israelites needed a little touch of Egyptian-style medicine to really heal. This proved to Hashem that the Israelites were really not capable of entering the land of Canaan and fighting thousands of idol worshippers.

Medications are not magic; they have actual scientific effects on disease. However, the damage they cause is discounted. When they advertise medications on TV and they enumerate the different side effects, including cancer, I always wonder how people are still willing to take such poison. When I suggest something natural to my patients, if it has even the slightest side effect, they don't want it. Why are people willing to take medicines that have so many risks?

What is the symbol of the American Medical Association? The emblem is one snake around a rod. The origin of this emblem is in Greek mythology, which began about the time of Hezekiah in the Holy Temple about 700–800 BCE. The Greeks took the idea from the Jews, who were worshiping the snake on a rod. The Greeks developed a whole religion of idolatry at the time. The American Medical Association emblem stands for a Greek god of medicine and is called the Rod of Asclepius.

Two snakes on a stick with wings on top of them called the Staff of Hermes is the emblem of the US Army Medical Corps and is used by many other medical organizations and commercial companies.

The American Medical Association, the US Army Medical Corps, and medical organizations use a symbol of a pagan god as their emblem! Be careful not to worship the medical association or doctors in general. Don't be mistaken—the Jewish people do not believe in faith healing as a way of getting healed. People who believe in faith healing don't understand that God created disease as well as medicine. Hashem wants us to use medicine, both conventional and natural, in order that we should be grateful for the miraculous results that His little creations can accomplish.

God gave us medicine, natural and modern, in order to heal ourselves, and we must pray to succeed. If you are not stubborn about the specific way you want get better, you demonstrate your total trust in God. Maybe Hashem wants you to solve your problems in a different way than you originally planned. All possibilities should be left open.

Whether in medicine, in business, or in any domain of life where we may encounter problems, Hashem might want to send us our salvation in ways that we do not expect. Being flexible to any new ideas shows modesty and readiness to accept God's blessings.

Magic

Even today people forget to think of Hashem or turn away from Him and search for magical solutions to their problems. People visit fortune tellers. They may wear an amulet or prayer beads.

I was approached by the mother of a large extended family that had a serious omen from God. The mother told me that six of her grown children were simultaneously having nightmares of death or illness in the mother's house. She asked me what to do. I explained to them that they were receiving a message from Hashem and that they should move to another apartment. The mother and the oldest daughter said it was too hard to move. I told her that what was going to happen was going to be so bad that it would be worth all the trouble to move.

Because my solution was too difficult, they turned to a Kabbalist, an expert in Jewish Kabbalah. Kabbalah is a body of mystical teachings of rabbinical origin. The Kabbalist took one hundred dollars from them and said he would pray and make a "tikun," which is a correction or fixing by some kind of "magical" words he has to say. A week later, the oldest son of twenty-six years was standing and working on the second-story porch of their home. He accidentally fell to his death.

Hashem was giving them clear messages that something very bad was going to happen but they didn't budge. What's even more upsetting, is that after the son died they still stayed in the same apartment.

There are two good ways of solving problems: going with nature, if it means going to a doctor a lawyer or any other earthly way to solve problems, or repenting of your ways and making real changes in your behavior. If you do both then you will really succeed. A magical solution to our problems defeats the whole purpose of having a having a world with its laws of nature. The magic is only temporary, but it sways people away from facing reality.

Just like it's a mitzvah to keep God's commandments, it is also a mitzvah to respect and keep God's laws of nature. Whether it be through conventional or natural medicine, we must protect our God given soul and make every effort to get healthy.

Hashem doesn't want us to not rely on prayer alone. He wants us to try to find a solution to our problems and then do the leg work needed. He especially enjoys our use of his natural world to help ourselves and others. Sometimes the answer to our prayer is finding the right doctor.

Gold and Silver

Psalms 115:4 says, "But their idols are silver and gold, made by human hands." Today, people actually worship the gold and silver no matter the shape. They give too much importance to money. The number one reason that couples divorce is because they fight over money. Parents are cut off from children and children cut off from their parents because of money. Money is the number one reason friendships end. Money is today's biggest idol. Since everyone needs money, how do you know if a person has made money into an idol?

Working hard for your income and being scrupulous over your money doesn't make you an idolater. According to Jewish law, you should donate a minimum of one tenth of your net earnings to charity and not more than twenty percent. Extending money to your own grown children can be counted as part of your charity. As a matter of fact, Hashem doesn't respect those who give charity to large institutions while their own family, or extended family, needs financial assistance.

In ancient times, people sacrificed to their idols. They even sacrificed their own children to gods. If you sacrifice your own children's health or happiness, or if you sacrifice your marriage, your friendship, or family relations because you don't want to share your money, your money is your idol.

The more you trust Hashem, the easier it is for you to share and use your money. Unless there is a medical or situational problem, you don't even think about where your next breath of air is coming from. As long as you have a healthy heart, you don't worry that your heart will stop beating before you wake up in the morning.

When you have enough money for your daily needs and you trust Hashem that you will have enough also for tomorrow, you can also breathe easily, knowing that Hashem can give you all the money you need, even in a heartbeat.

All You Need Is Love

The second commandment specifically says that Hashem will reward those who love him.

Exodus 20:4-6,

> "You shall not make for yourself an image in the form of anything in heaven above or on the earth beneath or in the waters below. You shall not bow down to them or worship them; for I, the LORD your God, am a jealous God, punishing the children for the sin of the parents to the third and fourth generation of those who hate me, but showing love to a thousand generations of those who love me and keep my commandments."

Deuteronomy also gives great reward to those who love Hashem. Deuteronomy 11:13–15,

> "So if you faithfully obey the commands I am giving you today, to love the Lord your God and to serve him with all your heart and with all your soul, then I will send rain on your land in its season, both autumn and spring rains, so that you may gather in your grain, new wine and olive oil. I will provide grass in the fields for your cattle, and you will eat and be satisfied."

The main thing God wants is our love. How do we show our love? When we keep the laws of the Bible with enthusiasm, tell Hashem that we love and trust Him, and thank Him for everything we have, Hashem will definitely feel that you love Him.

Monotheism

Abraham believed in a one and only God, in spite of the cultural and social pressures and customs of his day. The greatness of Abraham is that he was brought up believing in idols and he changed. He figured out on his own, that an idol couldn't be a creator.

Maimonides, a Torah scholar and philosopher from the 12th century, writes in *The Guide to the Perplexed,* that Abraham was known in the history of the gentiles as well as the Jews to be a man who rebelled against the faith of his people and believed in only one God. In a sense he was a man who changed his ways. He did what he thought was right and not what society dictated. Abraham was way ahead of his time.

One of the reasons that the Torah takes away blessings from those who worship idols is because these people do not want to think on their own, they don't want to change. When you do things just because that's what everyone else does, you can get in trouble. Kids learn how to smoke from their friends and do things that they would never dream of doing alone. In order to get Hashem's blessings, you must be a free thinker. You cannot follow the beliefs of others blindly. When you think for yourself you will come to the conclusion that there really is one Creator because that is what is instilled in your soul. If you don't think for yourself, you are just like a sheep following the herd.

The Next Generation

It took the Israelites many generations to be totally free of idol worship. Israeli archeologists found thousands of artifacts of idol worship from the Holy Temple period. In 586 BCE the Holy Temple was destroyed and the Jews were exiled to Babylonia. There are no idols found in the archeological digs in Israel that date after this period. Even though the Jews were very bad at the end of the Holy Temple as they were killing each other in civil war, they still didn't worship idols.

Before the destruction of the Holy Temple there were various factions that rose. The two main groups were the *Tzdokim* or Sadducees and the *Perushim* or Pharisees. The Sadducees believed that the most important thing was the worship of God through sacrifice in the Holy Temple . The Pharisees scrutinized the Bible word by word and made interpretations. The Pharisees are the precursors of today's Orthodox Judaism. Another sect was the Essenes, who ran away to the Dead Sea and secluded themselves from society. The Essenes copied and preserved the most ancient Torah and Biblical scrolls that have survived until today. The scrolls were discovered in caves close to the community they established. These are the famous Dead Sea Scrolls. The original scrolls are almost identical to the Torah that all Jews of today have in their synagogues.

Zealots formed another group that would rather die than submit to the Roman conquerors. The people of Masada were zealots. There were also Torah scrolls discovered in Masada that were identical to the ones at the Dead Sea. The last Jewish sect was the Christian sect.

All these groups of Jews believed in the Bible. They all believed in God as the one and only God. Only a few centuries later did Christianity formally give divinity to Jesus and call him God.

In the year 325 AD the Council of Nicaea under the Emperor Constantinople voted that Jesus is to be worshipped as a divine power. The vote to decide whether Jesus was divine or just a great man was of a political nature, with the Roman hierarchy favoring the faction promoting divinity because it would help them politically. Constantinople forced the council to vote and decide under pressure. They decided that declaring Jesus a god would be a good tactic to scare and control the masses. A three-hundred-year civil war ensued between the two Christian sides, those who believed in Jesus to be divine and those who believe Jesus to be a mortal teacher.

God's Children

The Torah teaches us that we are all children of Hashem. Deuteronomy 14:1 says, "You are sons to Hashem your God." We also call Hashem our Father. We are all created equal, just like it says in the Declaration of Independence. Jesus was the son of God just as we all are sons and daughters of Hashem.

Hashem wants us to believe in Him, the one and only one God—not because He is too proud or egocentric to have a partner. The other way around; He doesn't want any intermediaries. He loves you and wants you to pray to Him. He has known you since you were an embryo in your mother's womb. He doesn't need any go-betweens in order to connect with you. God is not too busy to hear prayers from those who love Him.

The Torah advocates a personal relationship with God. This is what He wants most. Hashem wants so much to be our friend that He is willing to create millions of people just so a few will be close to Him.

To understand more please read my book *Who is God?* In the chapter entitled "Who is the Messiah?" I explain that there will be a time of redemption in the future when the whole world will believe in the one God. As it says in Zechariah 14:9, "And the Lord shall be king over all the earth: in that day shall there be one Lord, and his name one." Amen.

Chapter 6

Do Not Take God's Name in Vain

> Exodus 20:6 says, "Thou shall not take God's name in vain. God will not clear those who take His name in vain."

The most basic understanding of this commandment is not to swear falsely in Hashem's name. Are you allowed to swear falsely if you don't say God's name? Of course not. There is also a commandment against lying in court, "Do not bear false witness," so why have two similar commandments?

The Ten Commandments must be basic to the foundation of our faith. There are so many laws that seem much more basic than this one, that are in the Torah but are not in the Ten Commandments. There must be a more all-encompassing meaning to this commandment.

The explanation lies in the translation. The Hebrew word *Tisa*, which is translated as "take or swear," does not mean take or swear at all. Tisa comes from the root *Nasa*, meaning to carry or lift. An example is found in the phrase "The Levites carried the Holy Ark" (Deuteronomy 31:9).

How does one carry God's name?

There was a famous actor in Israel who was interested in becoming religious. During a television interview he said, "I've got to be very sure that this is the right way to go because a lot of people will follow me if I do change my way of life." He had the right idea. When you present yourself as a religious Jew, you better behave. You are carrying God's name. That doesn't mean that if you are not religious then you can do what you want. However, if you do act against the Torah, then it's between you and God and possibly any offended party.

If you are dressed as a religious Jew, you are representing God. Of course if a rabbi, minister or priest commits any known crime, it is hypocrisy, a profanity of God's name, and a public sacrilege. This kind of two-facedness could also lead the public to scorn religious leaders and God.

Chaplains, parents, or teachers who claim to teach God's word, must be careful because they are carrying Hashem's name. Hashem judges religious leaders much more strictly than common folk. Of course everyone can make mistakes in the content of their speech, but the tone of voice and the attitude can be even more destructive. Worst of all, there have been people in our history who have lied and spread falsehoods to very innocent people, who trusted them innately. The naïve masses believed that their clergymen are emissaries to relate God's will to them.

Unless God is telling you what to say, when you speak before an assembly, you must remind the listeners that you are voicing your opinion or the opinion of someone else. If you give the congregation some kind of leeway to decide whether they agree with you or not, they will actually listen with more interest than if you force the issue. This is also a good rule for any teacher or psychologist that is conveying a philosophical doctrine; how much more so if the educator is claiming to speak in the name of God.

Even if you are not a chaplain, just an Orthodox Jew, it is possible that what you do and how you act will give Hashem a good or bad name. People in the giving professions like a doctor, a nurse or a psychologist must also be careful with their attitudes because they are doing God's work.

God's Representatives

This commandment has a specific directive. It is addressed to all those who represent God. You may think that you are a simple person, but you may be someone people look up to for guidance and faith. For example, as teacher or a parent you are expected to be an example for children to emulate. They imitate you much more than they obey you.

The Ten Commandments have an amazing quality. Each commandment has an aspect of all ten. In the following paragraphs, I will go through each of the Ten Commandments and how they apply to someone who is special in the eyes of Hashem, a person who is carrying God's name.

These commandments will be further explored in later chapters. For now, let's see how the Ten Commandments pertain to the righteous: leaders, parents, teachers, doctors and social workers, even adolescents who are admired by their peers. These are the Ten Commandments for any man, women or child that wants to be the best that they can be. This is God's way to make a simple person become a holy person.

1) "I am the Lord your God."

You should love Hashem with all your heart and all your soul. If you don't feel it, just start thanking Him for every little thing. Say, "Thank You" and "I love You." If you start to appreciate the things God gave you, you will begin to feel love for Him in your heart. Even when things go wrong, trust Hashem that everything is from Him. If you trust that everything will turn out for the best, then it really does.

2) "You shall not have any other gods."

Don't make yourself into a god. Rabbis, priests, leaders, teachers, and parents must understand the importance of being approachable. There are many influential people who keep a distance from the members of their congregation, their patients, their students, or their clients. If you are approachable, no one will make you into an idol. Some professionals like to keep their knowledge to themselves. That makes them feel important and superior. Teach what you know to others. Your knowledge and talents are gifts from Hashem; share them. When you give to others, Hashem will give you more.

Idol worship is a way of ignoring Hashem. The complete opposite of idol worship is a constant awareness of God. Never stop thinking of Hashem, and never stop talking about the divine providence and miracles in your life. It is a big mitzvah to tell stories of Hashem's work at every opportunity.

False Prophets

Falsely representing oneself as a prophet is definitely a very serious transgression. False prophecy is compared to idol worship. Many false prophets in history caused people to worship idols and even convinced the Israelites to sacrifice their own children.

False prophets were common in the times of the Holy Temple. They claimed that God or gods told them things. There is a specific prohibition against false prophets in the Torah:

> Deuteronomy 18:20-22, "But a prophet who presumes to speak in my name anything I have not commanded, or a prophet who speaks in the name of other gods, is to be put to death. You may say to yourselves, "How can we know when a message has not been spoken by the LORD?" If what a prophet proclaims in the name of the LORD does not take place or come true, that is a message the LORD has not spoken. That prophet has spoken presumptuously, so do not be alarmed."

The worst kind of false prophecy is a prophecy of the future. Just to be safe, don't tell people the future at all. Since telling the future is common practice among doctors and lawyers, it is a mitzvah not to believe them. They are essentially acting as false prophets. If the doctor tells you that you need surgery, you should take it seriously but, if for example, a doctor tells you that you are going to die in a few months, don't believe it. Keep faith that Hashem will help.

Sometimes I like to watch game shows on TV. On one show the contestant has to guess numbers and take risks. Relatives of the contestant are called in to cheer up the contestant but sometimes they insist and use psychological force to convince their relative take a risk against all reasonable probability. What gets me very upset is that the relatives are not prophets but they are pushing their opinion as if they are.

This happens with many different people who are so sure about their opinion that they leave no room to even listen to anyone else. Lawyers, judges, teachers and doctors must be careful not to insist that their opinion is the only opinion. If they allow for a second opinion or even suggest it, the person can have free choice. God doesn't force us to do thing why should mortals?

3) "Do not take God's name in vain."

Deuteronomy 14:1 says, "You are children of the Lord your God." Act accordingly. Your speech and demeanor should be that of a prince of princess. No foul language, no foul play. If someone insults you, react as if they said nothing. As a son or daughter of God, what can a human being do to hurt you? The above quote comes from Deuteronomy14:1, "You are children of the Lord your God. Do not cut yourselves or shave your forehead bald for the sake of the dead." Princes don't cut themselves or take out blood. This includes tattoos. There is actually a special prohibition against tattoos in Leviticus 19:28,

> "You shall not make any cuts in your body for the dead nor make any tattoo marks on yourselves."

Our body is just a temporary loan. While in this body, we have an obligation to take care of it. We can't mutilate it, and we cannot do anything that would damage it, including eating unhealthy foods.

A righteous person in the eyes of God is someone who cares about his or her health. No smoking, no drugs, only tiny amounts of sugar or alcohol, and no tattoos! That is why so many healers are blessed with clairvoyance. By caring about their health and the health of others, they find favor in God's eyes.

Many people want to feel righteous by praying at length from a prayer book. If you pray by saying words from a book as if the recitation were an incantation, you may very well be taking God's name in vain. Hashem would much rather that you talk to Him from your heart or even sing and dance to Him as you would to a beloved father. This would not be in vain because Hashem will really come down and listen. On the other hand, if you start praying by just mumbling words from a prayer book, why should Hashem bother paying attention? If He's not listening, aren't all your words in vain?

There is an exception to this rule. If you say words from the Bible even without understanding the meaning, you are performing the mitzvah of reciting the words of Torah. As it says in Deuteronomy 6:7, "You should teach your children these words again and again and speak about them ..."

I've had experience with myself and with many others that reciting those words in Deuteronomy before going to sleep help immensely against nightmares and negative thoughts. Any recitation of the Torah should help, especially from Deuteronomy.

Deuteronomy 6:4–9 and Deuteronomy 13:11–21 are examples of good verses to recite. It is not saying Hashem's name in vain because a recitation of words of any parts of the Bible is never in vain. These verses are part of the Jewish prayer book and in our daily prayers.

Psalms is a book of prayer. Open the Book of Psalms when you are feeling bad and you will find the chapter that was meant for you. Psalms has a quality of instilling the feeling of the prayer in your heart so it is never in vain.

4) "Remember the Sabbath to keep it holy."

The Sabbath is not only a day to rest your body, it is also a day to rest your mind. If you don't think about any of your worries on the seventh day of the week, you will have energy for the whole week, and you will succeed much more in all your earthly endeavors.

One of the reasons that Hashem gave us the Sabbath is so we won't be slaves. However, in this day and age, taking off one day a week might not be enough to call yourself "free." Many men and woman feel like slaves even if they work five days a week. In order not to be a slave, you must do more than just work, sleep, and eat. When your life has meaning, you are not a slave. You feel fulfilled.

I advised an elderly woman, who was feeling depressed, to go to a class on the Bible. She found a weekly class. She enjoyed it so much that her depression left her. She felt she had something to look forward to all week long, and that made all the difference.

Something else special to do in order not to feel like a slave is to pray. I don't mean praying while you work. I mean setting aside time in the day to meditate with your

Father in heaven. Even fifteen minutes can break the cycle of the mundane.

If you have workers, you must be understanding of their needs, even when it isn't Shabbat. For example, a cashier deserves to have a chair to sit on while working. If your worker has a child who is sick, don't deny her the right to stay home. One of the most important parts of keeping Shabbat is not to enslave others. Make sure that your workers and family members do not work seven days a week, and when they do work, remember that they are not your slaves.

If you are suffering in your job, or your job is causing you physical illness, do not be afraid to quit. Hashem will bless you with a better job. Our life experience has taught us that you have to get rid of the bad to let in the good. How are you going to get a better job if you are still stuck in a bad place? Trusting Hashem takes righteousness, but we must believe that God will provide. Staying in a job that makes you into a slave is against His will and it may ruin your life.

5) "Honor you father and mother."

Hashem commanded us to respect our parents just for bringing us into the world. This means He wants us to be thankful that we are alive. Life is a blessing. Without it, none of the wonders of life have any meaning. We should be so happy to be alive that we are in awe and appreciation of our parents. If you want to be close to God, the One who gives life, don't complain that life isn't good enough.

Righteous people are very careful to take good care of their parents when they age. It's important to forgive your parents for any wrong doing, especially after they passed on. Holding a grudge can seriously hurt your parents in the next world and even cause a block in your eternal relationship. Hashem forgives us when we forgive others. If you have a good heart you will believe that whatever happened to you in your childhood was predestined. It is better to release any blame you have against your parents and forgive them.

This doesn't mean that you have to forgive them for the unforgivable. You are not obligated to forgive actions like sexual molestation and serious physical abuse, but aside from serious transgressions to the Ten Commandments try to be understanding. Your parents should be first on the list of people to forgive. Read more about this in the chapter entitled, *"Honor your Father and Mother."*

6) "Do not murder."

Love people, and pray for them. If you help others and take care of them, you are fulfilling the commandment not to kill to its fullest in a positive way. Of course when you save someone's life in any way, you can join the ranks of being a righteous person. Our sages say that if you embarrass someone in public or tease him or her to the point of hurting him or her emotionally, it is likened to killing. There are many young people today who are mentally ill because family or friends hurt them emotionally, so much that they cannot lead normal lives.

I have heard an upset parent say to his child, "I'll kill you." It is an unrealistic threat, and it makes Hashem cringe when He hears it. Threatening is a bad way to educate. It also calls for a rift between you and your child.

Nevertheless, if you must reprimand, it must be without anger. Otherwise, the child just feels hurt and distant. The emotional or physical pain is all he or she will remember, the point of the reprimand gets totally lost.

A righteous person praises his or her friends and family. Encouraging words and constructive ideas are essential with children, and the most important of all is clear explanations. Children have a very strong will to live, be healthy, grow and be smart. If you explain gently why something is dangerous or bad for them, they will listen and learn. Forcefulness never changes people's hearts. They may change their actions, but when you're not around, they will do what they want. Remember, your children are not your merchandise. They are with you for a while until they're on their own. Your job is to prepare them for the big world.

We mentioned earlier that Hashem looks up to those who take care of their health. If you give your family healthy food, you are giving them life. If you give them unhealthy food, you are killing them.

In my experience as a healer, I see that people who are careful about what they eat are righteous people. They are willing to avoid foods they love in order to be healthy. Even more righteous are parents who are strict about what their children eat. Food is the fuel of life or the fuel of death. We can give life to our family by giving them healthy food and a healthy atmosphere.

7) "Do not commit adultery."

Clothing is your banner. You are what you wear. A righteous man or woman should dress very modestly. Dressing provocatively reflects a lack of respect for the mitzvah of not committing adultery. Even your speech should not be too friendly or provocative with the opposite sex. For example, if you are friendlier with a co-worker than with your own spouse, it is not looked upon with respect, even if the co-worker acts nicely. If he or she knows that you are married, he won't like it, and if he does like it, it's even worse.

8) "Do not steal."

Honesty is rare. Pure honesty means admitting the truth even to yourself. One of the big success stories of the world is AA, Alcoholics Anonymous. Their methods include the first step to successfully changing your life. This is admitting you have a problem. To be honest enough to see yourself is to be humble. Being humble is the first step to being close to God.

Honesty with money is even a harder quality to find. You should say something if the cashier made a mistake. Sometimes people lie in order to get a discount. Insisting on a discount against the owner's will could be considered dishonest. It is definitely not the way of the righteous.

> Deuteronomy 23:19
> No Israelite man or woman is to become a shrine prostitute. You must not bring the earnings of a female prostitute or of a male prostitute into the house of the LORD your God to pay any vow, because the LORD your God detests them both.

The Torah forbids us to use the money that a harlot earned in order to bring a sacrifice. This shows that the money itself is tainted. From here we learn that we should be careful not to buy stolen goods. We should never desire wealth that derived from dishonesty or any other transgression.

In other words, there is no blessing in stolen goods, stolen property or even in a stolen inheritance.

9) "Do not bear false witness"

Every night when we go to sleep, we are judged for what we did that day. We sometimes may be called to be a witness in a heavenly court for judgment of a family member or a friend. People who have had near-death experiences were sometimes able to see people who are still alive witnessing on their behalf.

If you judge people favorably in your heart, then you will find a way to forgive them. There is a beautiful book called *Courtrooms of the Mind* by Chanoch Teller. The author tells stories that teach you how people should be given the benefit of the doubt because the truth is not always obvious. Gossiping is another form of bearing false witness. People talk and do not give others the benefit of the doubt. Gossipers judge others with little or no evidence and with their words they can cause serious damage.

As a healer, I see how people can be angry or thoughtless just because of nutritional deficiencies or medical weakness. I also see how they've been hurt by others. I always judge people favorably by telling myself that they have mental, emotional and physical weaknesses because of physical or emotional health issues.

Having mercy on people is an attribute of a righteous person. If you see the good in people, you are not bearing false witness. You are seeking the optimistic truth and

Hashem will love you for your giving others the benefit of the doubt. Then, Hashem will connect you with others who will judge you favorably as well.

10) "Do not covet."

Not only should you not be jealous, but you should not make others envious of you. Your friend shouldn't feel covetous of what you have. A true friend feels lucky that she has a friend like you.

How do you make this happen? If you feel your friend is interested in what you have, you should give him or her a present. Lend her a book or a CD. Make her feel fortunate to have you as a friend.

The last commandment, "Do not covet," is also a mitzvah to trust Hashem that what you have is what is best for you. The ancient Jewish book called *Ethics of the Fathers says*, "Who is rich? The one who is happy with his lot."

You should also not covet people whose lives are simpler than yours. Not everyone is here on the same mission. While your neighbor is jealous of your success, you may be envious that she can stay home and take care of her children. Each of you must look at your own mission in life. Hashem has different missions for each and every person. This doesn't mean that you shouldn't change your lot. Change is the best way to solve problems. Do so because it's best for you and not because you compare yourself to others.

Conclusion

The third commandment, "Do not carry God's name in vain," speaks to the believers, the thinkers, and the leaders. Before God tells the world the rest of His commandments, the leaders are addressed. Whether you swear in God's name or just speak in God's name, as I do, you must be careful to say the truth or you'll even be in more trouble if you put God's name to shame, because of your actions.

CHAPTER 7

The Sabbath

Shabbat, which is Sabbath in Hebrew, is very important to Hashem. It is already mentioned in the first chapter of the Bible.

> Genesis 2:2–3, "And on the seventh day God ended his work which he had made; and He rested on the seventh day from all his work which He had made. And God blessed the seventh day, and sanctified it, because that in it He had rested from all his work which God created and made."

Shabbat has a special holiness that Hashem created on the seventh day. I can feel this holiness soon after I light the Shabbat candles on Friday night. Even before Hashem gave the Ten Commandments, Hashem told the children of Israel that Shabbat is holy:

> Exodus 17:22–30, "And he said to them, "This is what Hashem has spoken; Tomorrow is a rest day, a holy Sabbath for Hashem. Bake what you wish to bake and cook what you wish to cook; and whatever is left over, put away for yourselves to be kept until

the morning." And they laid it up till the morning, as Moses had commanded; and it did not stink, neither was there any worm in it. And Moses said: "Eat it today; for today is a Sabbath for Hashem, today you shall not find it in the field. Six days you shall gather it; but the seventh day is a Sabbath, on it there will be none." And it came to pass, that some of the people went out on the seventh day to gather, and they found none. And Hashem said to Moses, "How long will you refuse to keep my commandments and my teachings? See, that Hashem has given you the Sabbath, therefore He gives you on the sixth day bread for two days; let every man return to his place, let no man go out of his place on the seventh day." And the people rested on the seventh day."

Before the giving of the Ten Commandments and the Torah, Hashem instructed the children of Israel to prepare their food on Friday and rest on Shabbat! The manna, which is the food that fell from the sky when the Israelites lived in the wilderness, didn't fall on the Sabbath. Hashem sent fresh manna daily and it would become rotten if left overnight.

The manna was very versatile and could be cooked in different ways. The Israelites prepared their Sabbath meals on Friday, and the prepared manna didn't rot on Saturday, even though they had no refrigeration. On weekdays each family got enough manna for only one day. Any manna that was leftover would become rotten. Miraculously, two portions fell from the sky every Friday and kept fresh until Sunday morning. Even today, religious Jews do not cook on Shabbat; we prepare everything in advance.

Friday is to be the day for preparation. Shabbat begins on Friday at sunset and ends at nightfall Saturday night. In

Israel today, stores and businesses are closed on Saturday and there is no public transportation. Some restaurants and pubs are open Friday night, but they aren't kosher. The Israeli rabbinate will not give a kosher certificate to any restaurant that is open on Shabbat. Most public offices, companies and universities are also closed on Friday as well, so that people can have time to prepare for Shabbat. The weekend starts on Friday. Sunday is a regular business day.

Jerusalem is especially quiet on Shabbat. People take walks with their families. In some neighborhoods the streets are totally blocked to traffic. Hashem feels good on Shabbat. For the first time in two thousand years there is a Sabbath atmosphere in the Holy Land. When we take walks on Saturday afternoon, we see families having fun on their day off and wearing their best clothing in honor of the Sabbath. The following is a poem I wrote about my personal feelings for Shabbat.

I Just Love Shabbos

Every Friday afternoon,
Before the sun goes down,
It's quiet in Jerusalem,
Seems like no one's in the town.
Everyone is home,
No one is alone,
They're preparing for the best day of the week.

As the sun is setting,
There is magic in the air,
The smell of Shabbos food,

Prepared with loving care.
Everything is clear,
There's a change in atmosphere.
As I light the candles,
Shabbos will appear.

I just love Shabbos; it is in my soul.
I just love Shabbos,
It's my day to unfold.
It's time to get back my strength.
To sing and pray at length.
To remember why we're here, to love Hashem and fear.

I just love Shabbos, it's my day to be free.
There's just one Shabbos for society.
Every chore has got to stop
You can't work, and you can't shop.
With all worries you'll be through.
Hashem gave this gift to you.

****

The Israelites had to collect the manna and prepare it on Friday for both Friday and Shabbat. They were prohibited from gathering on Shabbat. Gathering was their daily work to obtain food, so it was prohibited.

Aside from not going to work on Shabbat, we also refrain from doing daily chores like cooking, cleaning, and shopping. Housework is a never-ending job. We not only avoid doing housework on Shabbat we avoid thinking about it. We free our minds to enjoy life worry-free and have a weekly vacation for our body and soul!

Two Sets of Ten Commandments

The Ten Commandments are mentioned in the Bible twice. They first appear in the book of Exodus when God announced them in full voice on Mount Sinai. In Deuteronomy chapter 4, Moses teaches the Ten Commandments to the new generation before entering the land of Israel and he repeated the Ten Commandments to the new generation. The only differences between these two sets of commandments is in the fourth commandment. Here they are for comparison:

> Exodus 20:8-11, "Remember the Sabbath day by keeping it holy. Six days you shall labor and do all your work, but the seventh day is a Sabbath to the LORD your God. On it you shall not do any work, neither you, nor your son or daughter, nor your male or female servant, nor your animals, nor any foreigner residing in your towns. For in six days the LORD made the heavens and the earth, the sea, and all that is in them, but he rested on the seventh day. Therefore, the LORD blessed the Sabbath day and made it holy."

Deuteronomy 5:12-14

> Observe the Sabbath day by keeping it holy, as the LORD your God has commanded you. Six days you shall labor and do all your work, but the seventh day is a Sabbath to the LORD your God. On it you shall not do any work, neither you, nor your son or daughter, nor your male or female servant, nor your ox, your donkey or any of your animals, nor any foreigner residing in your towns, so that your male and female servants may rest, as you do. Remember that you were slaves in Egypt and that the LORD your God brought you out of there with a mighty hand and

an outstretched arm. Therefore, the LORD your God has commanded you to observe the Sabbath day.

In Exodus 20:8 the Bible gives the commandment, "Remember the Sabbath and keep it holy." This means that the Sabbath must be kept on Saturday. You can't switch it to another day. Deuteronomy 5:12 says, "Observe the Sabbath to keep it holy." This verse is referring to avoiding the actions that are prohibited on the Sabbath. The first Ten Commandments were uttered by God. He was speaking to a generation of slaves. They had to remember not to work on Sabbath because as slaves they were accustomed to working without stop. The second time the Ten Commandments were said, Moses was speaking to the generation that would be entering the Holy Land. To this generation it would be important to protect the holiness of Shabbat from outside influence of the other nations.

> The reason for keeping Shabbos in Exodus 20:11 is: "For in six days God created the heaven and the earth, and on the seventh day he rested."

In Deuteronomy 5:15 the purpose for the Sabbath changes:

> "And you shall remember that you were a slave in Egypt and Hashem your God took you out with an outstretched arm, therefore He commanded you to keep the Sabbath."

The first time the Ten Commandments were said, they were said for the whole world. Remember the Sabbath because God created the world. That's a message for Jews and non-Jews alike. The second time it is Moses telling the Israelites about the Sabbath, and he tells the Israelites to watch over the Shabbat and keep it holy because they were slaves in Egypt. This seems like it is more specifically for the children of Israel. Nevertheless, today we know how much slavery there was in the world and there still is.

A slave works for his minimal needs for food and shelter. Many people who have jobs only make enough for that modicum. Workers are sometimes even in a worse predicament than a slave because they are worried about paying bills and debts, two worries that a slave does not have. Therefore, I would conclude that the reason given for observing Shabbat in Deuteronomy is also applicable to the whole world. Keep Shabbat in order not to become a slave.

On Shabbat we feel like royalty. For one day a week, we free ourselves from work and worry. People that work seven days a week are slaves even if they make a good living, because they do nothing but work.

Many people use their Saturday to clean the house or do yard work. Hashem knows that we need total rest once a week and that means one day without taking care of our responsibilities. The reason that Hashem wrote the Torah is to guide us with His supreme genius. On our own, humans would not have the intelligence to make the best laws. Only the one who created the world knows that a human being needs an entire day free of work in order to be physically and emotionally healthy.

Moses was a prophet, and sometimes he could see the distant future. He knew how important Shabbat was. Moses thought to himself, *"What if people start having doubts as to the truth about the story of creation?"* Just in case they would doubt the account of genesis, he didn't want to risk Shabbat. So as a back-up plan to the first set of

Ten Commandments, Moses said, "Listen, guys, God took your parents out of Egypt so you won't be slaves. Don't undo His work by making yourselves slaves and working seven days a week. In the future you may have doubts about the story of creation. While waiting for the scientists of the world to figure out how, when, and why the world was created, just keep Shabbat anyway. Do it in memory of the Exodus from Egypt."

Sabbath for Gentiles

The Ten Commandments are for all humankind, not only the children of Israel. Non-Jews are also obliged to make Sabbath a day of rest. Certainly many non-Jews have had their share of slavery. Hashem doesn't want us to be slaves even out of our own choice. Therefore, even if you are not Jewish, Hashem would like you to rest on Saturday. This day has special energy. Shabbat has the energy of the seventh chakra or the spiritual realm of our soul, so it is also a day for spiritual pleasure.

Shabbat was given to the world right after the first man was created. It was a gift for all mankind. It says in the Fourth Commandment that the reason for the existence of Shabbat is because God created the world in six days and He rested on the seventh day. Hashem created the energy of Shabbat for the whole world. He is waiting for the day when everyone makes the Sabbath their day of rest.

In the following verse, a eunuch was a non-Jewish servant of the king who was castrated in order to be able to guard the women in the palace. A eunuch in this verse has a double meaning. A eunuch is a symbol is of anyone who doesn't have children or even if he does, he is not proud of them. It also means a non-Jew who worked closely with the Jews.

> Isaiah 56:3-8, "Neither let a man from another nation, that has joined himself to Hashem, speak; saying, "Hashem will completely separate me from his people;" neither let the eunuch say, "Behold, I am a dry tree." For thus Hashem said to the eunuchs that keep my Sabbaths, and choose the things that I desire, and hold fast to my covenant—I will give them in my house walls, a place and a name better than sons and of daughters—I will give them an everlasting name, that will not be cut off. And the sons of a man from another nation that join themselves Hashem to serve Him, and to love the name of Hashem, to be His servants, all that keep the Sabbath from desecrating it, and take hold of My covenant—I will bring them to my holy mountain, and make them joyful in My house of prayer—their burnt offerings and their sacrifices shall be accepted on My altar; for my house shall be called a house of prayer for all peoples. The Lord God who gathers the dispersed of Israel said, I will gather more than are already gathered to Israel."

Thus, from Isaiah we learn that the way for a non-Jew to be close to Hashem is by keeping Shabbat. The foreigner referred to in the scripture, is the non-Jew. Furthermore, the eunuch, a man who is castrated, should not feel that he is worthless like a dry tree. This includes every barren man or woman. Isaiah says that keeping the Sabbath will give you a name better than being a parent of sons and daughters, and your name will never be cut off.

Why? How can anything be instead of children?

Even if we have children, who is to ensure that they will follow our heritage?

As important it is to have children, it is even more important to Hashem that we keep Shabbat. A Jew is cut off from the Jewish nation for not keeping Shabbat. They aren't considered as being among the children of Abraham. Any person who keeps Shabbat whether he is of the Israelite nation or not, can enjoy the feeling of Hashem's holiness and share it with others. He can invite his friends to feel that Shabbat spirit and he can teach his friends to do the same. This "eunuch" can have spiritual children that will be with him forever.

When you were a baby, your mother loved you and wished greatness for you. She wasn't thinking of the grandchildren. We are Hashem's babies. We can be His pride and joy. Hashem says, "If you keep Shabbat I will be so pleased with you that I will be satisfied."

If you do have children, keeping the Sabbath can be a way to ensure that your children will be loyal to your family. The Sabbath is a day for family time with no distractions from the TV or telephones. It's a time for extended family to convene and sleep in the same house because we do not drive a car or bus on Shabbat. Aunts, uncles, in-laws, cousins and friends have time to develop solid relationships. When we were growing up, I went to a different classmate's home for a Shabbat approximately once a month. In the afternoon all the girls in the class got together to talk, sing and dance. Since the girls were used to having guests for Shabbat, they extended their invitations to weekday visits too.

Hashem wrote about Shabbat in the very beginning of the Bible.

> Genesis 2: 1-2
>
> Thus the heavens and the earth were completed in all their vast array.
>
> By the seventh day God had finished the work he had been doing; so on the seventh day he rested from all his work. Then God blessed the seventh day and made it holy, because on it he rested from all the work of creating that he had done.

He created the energy of the Sabbath before He wrote the Torah. Shabbat is dear to Him, as is every man or woman from all walks of life who want to observe it. When we observe Shabbat, it shows complete trust in God. It is a celebration of life without worldly worries. This is God's pleasure, just as it is a mother's pleasure to see her children happy and without worry.

Of all the Ten Commandments this is the one that separates us from the secular world. This is a fascinating concept. We discussed earlier that God commanded us to love him, an emotional commandment. Here Hashem is commanding us to be spiritual, not all the time, just one day a week. We are commanded to have a day of holiness not only for ourselves, but for the whole community. Observing Shabbat will enable us to have time to feel God's presence and to learn to love Him. In order to achieve this spirit of holiness you must have a complete cessation of all work, with no exceptions.

Melacha

In my song about Shabbat I wrote, "Every chore has got to stop, you can't work and you can't shop." Melacha, which is usually translated as work, is prohibited on Shabbat (Exodus 20:10, 23:12, 31:14–15, 34:21, 35:2, Leviticus 23:3, Deuteronomy 5:13–14).

Exodus 34:21 says, "Six days thou shall work, but on the seventh day thou shall rest; you shall rest from plowing and harvesting." In modern Hebrew we use the word *melacha* for the skilled work of a craftsman as in arts and crafts; for example, a shoemaker, a painter or a carpenter. *Melacha* in the Torah also means craftsmanship as well as hard work, like building houses or planting in the field. The rabbis of the second century CE in Israel expanded the meaning of work to thirty-nine different actions as follows.

1. Sowing
2. Plowing
3. Reaping
4. Binding sheaves
5. Threshing
6. Winnowing
7. Selecting
8. Grinding
9. Sifting
10. Kneading
11. Baking
12. Shearing wool
13. Washing wool
14. Beating wool

15. Dyeing wool
16. Spinning
17. Weaving
18. Making two loops
19. Weaving two threads
20. Separating two threads
21. Tying
22. Untying
23. Sewing stitches
24. Tearing
25. Trapping
26. Slaughtering
27. Flaying
28. Tanning
29. Scraping hide
30. Marking hides
31. Cutting hide to shape
32. Writing two or more letters
33. Erasing two or more letters
34. Building
35. Demolishing
36. Extinguishing a fire
37. Kindling a fire
38. Putting the finishing touch on an object
39. Transporting an object between a private domain and the public domain

This list was developed in the period of Rabbi Judah the Prince about 200 CE. It defined what constituted work. Religious Jews today abstain from these thirty-nine activities on Shabbat. Because this list is rabbinical, it is not mandatory that a non-Jew abstains from all of them.

However, the above actions are all hard work. If you are not Jewish but you wish to observe Shabbat, use your discretion as to what not to do on Shabbat. The most important thing to avoid is your job, or anything that you do that you also do on your job, like working on a computer or fixing the electric wiring or the car. On Shabbat you should be so busy spending time with your family that you don't want to perform any work or household duties. If you do not have a family, use this time to study Bible, pray and rest and spend time with friends. Hashem knows that we need twenty-five hours to recuperate from our work week. If we only rest for half a day our souls will not be sufficiently energized. Not only that, if you do one thing that is work on Shabbat, the whole Shabbat will not be the same. Even one action that is forbidden affects that feeling of complete peace and relaxation which we all need.

Nevertheless, a little bit of Shabbat is better than no Shabbat. Therefore, if you are forced into a situation that you cannot change, give your body and soul a rest from the remainder of the Sabbath day.

Shabbat and Fire

> Exodus 35:3 says, "You shall not burn a fire in your dwelling on the day of Shabbat."

Why is there a specific mention of a prohibition not to set a fire at home on Shabbat? One of the famous arguments that secular Jews have against religious Jews is that in the past it was hard work to light a fire. Today it is easy with the strike of a match so why is it forbidden?

Hashem saw that in the future it wouldn't take work in the sense of physical effort to create fire. Even in the past it was not so hard to transfer one flame to the next. Neighbors shared flames with one another in case of need. The prohibition of igniting or transferring fire is not necessarily forbidden because it's difficult work. It's a separate prohibition.

Light is the first of God's handiworks in the creation story of Genesis (Genesis 1:3). Shabbat is a day of remembrance, the day that God rested from the work of creating the world. Therefore, there is special importance to abstaining from lighting fire or creating light.

Nevertheless, the main reason Hashem wrote prohibiting us from lighting a fire on Shabbat is because fire is dangerous. Having a fire in a fireplace is worrisome as it can ignite and spread. If there is a pot on the fire, there is a fear that the food may burn and a fire may ensue.

A Rest for Hashem

When something dangerous happens, we beg Hashem for help, and even for miraculous intervention. When Hashem makes a miracle, He doesn't allow nature to continue automatically. He has to intervene. You can pray for miracles, but not on Shabbat. We must try to avoid the need for miracles on Shabbat. That's why the Torah says not to make fires on Shabbat. Cars and buses are run by fire; therefore, it is forbidden to ride in a car or bus on the Sabbath. A vehicle that is not run by fire is also forbidden because it is still dangerous.

Choose Life

> Deuteronomy 30:19
> "I call heaven and earth today to bear witness against you: I have placed life and death before you, blessing and curse; and you shall choose life, so that you will live, you and your offspring."

The Torah was given in order to help us have a better life. If a situation occurs that endangers your health, always choose life, even if it is not in accordance with Torah law.

If someone is sick on Shabbat, we must do whatever we can to help, even if it violates Shabbat. If one is in any life-threatening danger, or even danger to a body part, like a broken leg, God Forbid, you drive on Shabbat to the hospital or clinic. You undergo an operation or whatever is needed, even when it violates Shabbat. All rabbis agree with this.

This law makes us different from other faiths that do not break the rules of the religion for any reason at all. Jewish people get along with doctors and hospitals very well because we don't put up any religious arguments if our health is at stake.

> Exodus 31:17
> "Shabbat is an everlasting sign between Me and the children of Israel because in six days Hashem created the heaven and the earth and on the seventh day He rested and refreshed His soul."

Hashem's strength is infinite. Why are any miracles that He makes considered work? Why would He need to be refreshed?

Of course it takes no effort for God to make miracles. However, He doesn't want to change nature. A miracle within nature is fine, but a change of nature like the splitting of the Red Sea is something that Hashem would like to avoid. He wants people to understand His natural world and find natural solutions to everyday problems.

In my book *Who is God?* I explained that Hashem created many worlds before this one. When He was not happy with what He created, He destroyed it. Scientists have found many fossils but there are not enough links or stages to prove a slow progressive evolution. Many scientists that have discovered this to be true, believe in the theory called Intelligent Design.

Hashem was refreshed on the first Shabbat because He saw that, after millions of years of creating and destroying worlds, He finally created a world that He thought was good. This feeling of accomplishment is what caused Hashem to be refreshed. When we do things that are dangerous Hashem is watching us and may change nature in order to avoid a disaster. On Shabbat Hashem would like us to let Him enjoy the world He created without any dramatic interventions.

Time

When Hashem created this world He started with land, water and the Spirit of God.

> Genesis 1:2, "Now the earth was formless and empty, darkness was over the surface of the deep, and the Spirit of God was hovering over the waters."

God is everywhere. How can He be hovering over the waters?

If scripture says that there was a Spirit of God that means that Hashem already created His Spirit. His Spirit was hovering over the waters which means that it was moving. Maimonides of blessed memory said, "There is no movement without time." In order for something to go from place to place there must be a before and after. If there was movement of God's Spirit, that means that He had already created time. As a matter of fact, by the movement of Hashem's Spirit, He is constantly creating time.

God is everywhere but there are places where we feel God's presence more prominently. When we feel a spiritual feeling in the atmosphere, we are feeling God's Spirit.

It doesn't take Hashem millions of years to figure out that a world is not to His liking. Those worlds were not only different physically than this one, they were on a different timeline. Hashem is above time, so for Hashem it could have been hundreds of years for each world, just like it took hundreds of years for Him to decide to destroy the people of Noah's generation. This is a difficult concept to comprehend. Think of the following allegory:

Let's say you are watching a film and it's going too slow. You fast forward, stop to watch and then fast forward again. You finish the whole film in half an hour. It still is a two-hour film but for you it only took half an hour to watch it. You also got the idea of the story and really enjoyed the conclusion. We are only mortal so we can't watch every detail of the film and enjoy it in fast forward mode, but Hashem can.

In the beginning of creation, Genesis 1:2 says, "there was a spirit of God hovering over the waters." That spirit of God is time. When the spirit goes faster, time goes faster. The timeline changed when Hashem created Shabbat.

Every nation on earth recognizes the seven-day week. It is instilled in nature. The last day, the Sabbath, was sanctified. It was sanctified on the seventh day of creation. In this world, Hashem was not planning to speed watch. He wants to see everything. Hashem gave us a timeline that was much slower than in the worlds before this one.

Did the dinosaurs exist for millions of years? Maybe, but that's compared to our current perception of time. For them it felt like a short time. Did archeologists find thousands of layers of dinosaur fossils at different stages of evolution? Not at all. Hashem created worlds of many different animals to see what powers He had. He saw that those realms were pointless and destroyed them at will. Hashem continued making other worlds afterwards but they also were not to His liking.

Imagine how good Hashem felt when He finally created this world, the world of a speaking man. When He finished His prize creation, He felt a big sigh of relief. This feeling of happiness celebrating the creation of our beautiful world is a reason to observe Shabbat.

Sometimes Hashem gets upset with us. Shabbat reminds Him that we are His prize creation, so He should have patience with us. This is the time to just be God's friend and thank Him for what we have and pray.

Creation

> Exodus 31:16–17
> The children of Israel shall keep the Sabbath, to make the Sabbath an eternal covenant for their generations. It is a sign forever between Me and the children of Israel that in six days Hashem made heaven and earth, and on the seventh day He rested and was refreshed.

Shabbat is a sign forever! That is quite a dramatic statement!

Why does Hashem need a sign?

When we tell time we can make order in our day. The clock is the sign that it is time to change activities. The calendar is a sign that it is time to plan a holiday or seasonal activities. Shabbat is a sign that there is a seven-day cycle in this world. Hashem created the seven-day cycle as well as the seven chakras of our soul as we learn in the Ayurveda philosophy.

When we observe the Sabbath our body doesn't stop functioning and Hashem doesn't stop taking care of His world. We just stop working and doing our daily chores as a sign that we join God in the celebration of the birth of a world that has a seven-day cycle. We emulate Hashem on Shabbat by not making even the slightest change in nature. We honor Hashem's final successful creation of the world by suspending our own work and refreshing ourselves. We give ourselves a total rest on Shabbat and celebrate with good food and good family time.

In Genesis 1:2 it says that before the six days of creation, the world was a mess and a spirit of God hovered above the water in darkness. On the first day Hashem added light and separated it from the darkness. He shined light on the total chaos and started making order.

On the Sabbath, we do not create light from a match, a light switch, a flashlight or from a television. We don't turn on electrical devices one day a week. On the first day of creation, Hashem created light and separated light and darkness (Genesis 1:3–4). He set up a system so that the world would have light and darkness in it every day and night automatically. He doesn't have to create light and darkness every day.

We can use an automatic timer, just like Hashem has His automatic timer running the lights of heaven. The atmosphere in the home is totally transformed when you don't use electricity. If it were every day, it would be a burden. However, if you are in a totally modern home with all the conveniences and suddenly you stop, it brings a feeling of utopia. As you watch the Shabbat candles you will feel a long-lasting sense of peacefulness in the air.

This is a song about Shabbat that my husband wrote to the tune of a famous Beatles song:

A Little Help from Hashem

What would you do if you knew I'm a Jew?
Would you stand up and walk out on me?
Lend me your ears, and I'll teach you Torah,
And you'll open your eyes and you'll see.

Oh, I get by with a little help from Hashem.
Mm, I get high with a little help from Hashem.
Mm, I'm gonna try with a little love from Hashem.
With a little love from Hashem…

What do I do when the heat hits a peak?
Are you sorry that Israel's so hot?
How do I feel by the end of the week?
Are you nuts because you keep Shabbat?
No, I get by with a little help from Hashem.
Mm, I get high with a little help from Hashem.
Mm, I'm gonna try with a little love from Hashem.

Do you need any learning?
I need some Torah to learn.
Could it be any learning?
I want some Torah to learn.

Would you believe in insight at first sight?
Yes, I'm certain that it happens all the time.
When it's Shabbat, do you turn on the light?

No I can't, it's Shabbat, it's divine.
No, I get by with a little help from Hashem.
Mm, I get high with a little help from Hashem.
Mm, I'm gonna try with a little love from Hashem.
With a little love from Hashem …

****

Refreshment

> Exodus 23:12 says, "Six days shall you do your activities, and on the seventh day you shall desist, so that your ox and donkey may rest and your maidservant's son and the sojourner may be refreshed."

Refreshment means recuperation. We recuperate and recharge through eating, resting, spending quality time with our family, and having relaxed loving moments with our spouse.

Friday

Friday is a celebration of the creation of man. It is a day that is remarkably productive. If you watch a Jewish homemaker prepare for Shabbat, she will seem to you like a superwoman, preparing two full-course meals, cleaning the house and showering and dressing all of her children before sundown.

In modern time we have refrigeration so we can divide the work into two and start on Thursday. The Jewish day starts at sundown, so the magical Friday spirit is also present on Thursday night.

> Isaiah 58:13-14, "If you keep your feet from breaking the Sabbath and from doing as you please on my holy day, if you call the Sabbath a delight and the LORD's holy day honorable, and if you honor it by not going your own way and not doing as you please or speaking idle words, then you will find your joy in the LORD, and I will cause you to ride in triumph on the heights

of the land and to feast on the inheritance of your father Jacob. For the mouth of the LORD has spoken."

I would suggest a more accurate Hebrew translation as follows:

"If you return home in honor of the Sabbath, your festival, in order to prepare your needs on My holy day, you will call the Sabbath a delight, to sanctify Hashem who is to be honored. And you honor it from doing and making your things, from looking for and finding your desires and talking about things. Then you will delight in Hashem, and He will give you to a ride on high places, and feed you from the inheritance of your father Jacob. For the mouth of the LORD has spoken."

In Isaiah 58:13 the Hebrew word *tashiv* is mentioned in nineteen places in the Bible, including this verse. In the other eighteen places, *tashiv* is translated as meaning to return. For example, in Genesis 21:6,

"Make sure that you do not take my son back there," Abraham said."

Only in Isaiah 58:13 *"tashiv"* is traditionally translated to mean restrain or keep away, even in Jewish Bibles. The whole meaning changes when you change the meaning of one word. Where do you return to? Return from work to your home!

The next word that is mistakenly translated is *"raglecha."* This means your foot not your feet, as it is spelled in singular. I cannot accept a theory that the prophet made grammar mistakes. Even if a prophet or scribe did make a spelling or grammar mistake, it would have been corrected by the scribes who copied and recopied the Bible until it was canonized in the year 200CE.

Therefore, what makes more sense is that the prophet intended to use this word for its other meaning; *your festival*.

In Numbers 22:28 this word *"raglecha"* means *times*:

> "Then the LORD opened the donkey's mouth, and it said to Balaam, "What have I done to you to make you beat me these three times?"

In Hebrew our holidays are called *"shalosh regalim."* These are the three special times of the year of holidays: Succoth, Passover and Shavuot. The prophet is saying that you must make every Shabbat a festival, a special time. In honor of this festival you must come home early from your work on Friday and not do anything or discuss anything aside from the preparation for Shabbat. If you do this, you will be respected and blessed.

In my corrected translation I wrote, "In order to prepare your needs on my holy day." According to my translation it seems like Friday, the day before Shabbat, is a holy day. How can Friday be a holy day?

The word *kodesh* is translated as holy but what it really means is set aside. The root of this word is also used as a verb. If you would like to donate money you can set it aside for a specific charity and you would use the root of this same word to say so. In the following verse, the word *kadesh,* stemming from the same root, is used and translated to mean *consecrate*.

> Exodus 13:2, "Consecrate to me every firstborn male. The first offspring of every womb among the Israelites belongs to me, whether human or animal."

Friday is a day that is consecrated or set aside for a holy purpose - the preparation of Shabbat. The power of Shabbat gives you extra strength on Friday to prepare for Shabbat. If you work in town, at sea or in the field, you must return home by Friday before noon. You need enough time to prepare your needs and desires for Shabbat. Cooking and cleaning takes time. Hashem gives extra energy on that day to prepare for Shabbat which begins on Friday evening eighteen minutes before sunset.

Even though this translation is not written in any Jewish Bibles, the conclusions from this message, are definitely part of Jewish culture. I believe that the tradition of preparing festive meals on Friday for Shabbat was set by Isaiah.

Some families have a custom of tasting the Shabbat food on Friday. Some Sephardic Jews have a special meal on Friday. This is a great custom. If on the day you need the most strength you don't eat, you will get nervous, angry, and hypoglycemic. Sit down to a proper lunch on Friday—not too heavy so it won't weigh you down, but healthy so you will be calm and have vigor to get ready for Shabbat.

When you do everything you can, to arrange for the Sabbath on Friday, then the Sabbath surely is a delight.

The reward for preparing for Shabbat is that you will enjoy Shabbat and feel the pleasure of Hashem's presence. Anyone who keeps Shabbat can testify that they can feel the holiness of the day.

The "ride on high places" is a spiritual ride. The "food of Jacobs's heritage" is the taste of the Shabbat food, which has its own special flavor that cannot be compared to even the most expensive restaurant. The verse in Isaiah ends, "For the mouth of the Lord has spoken." This is just another way of saying, "I promise."

"Idle Words"

According to my translation Friday is the day not to speak idle words because you should be busy cooking and cleaning and showering. This is a major change in the implementation of the advice of the prophet. Isaiah is giving us an order to "get to work, there is no time to goof around on Friday."

On Shabbat we can speak idle words of love and play, but we cannot talk about work or worries. Religious Jewish people do not turn on a radio or television on Shabbat even with a timer, because it brings in an atmosphere of everyday living.

Shabbat should be a day to talk. Talk about Torah, about faith, about the delicious food, and even about nature. Playing games is very important; if not then, when? It's a day to give attention to your children and family.

Singing is part of the spirit of the day, peaceful singing with no instruments or loudspeakers. Playing an instrument is a skilled profession and is forbidden on the Sabbath.

When we sing together without the distraction of amplifiers and accompaniment it's a lot of fun. My sister and I used to rehearse with our neighbor, and give my parents a choir performance on Friday night.

On Shabbat the family assembles around the table to enjoy delicious food that everyone helped to prepare. The house is clean, and everyone is showered and dressed in their best clothing. We sing Sabbath hymns together, before and after the meal. It is also a time to tell narratives. The children have a chance to tell their own stories or sing songs that they learned in school, while everyone listens. Every child gets a chance to be on center stage.

In Orthodox Jewish communities in Israel the streets are silent as no cars are running and all the stores are closed. At home no telephones ring, and there is no television or Internet for twenty-five hours. In all the Jewish hospitals in Israel there are special Shabbat meals and prayers for the patients and their families. They are organized by a non-profit organization that prepares meals for visitors of the sick, not only for Shabbat but all week long.

The Sabbath begins eighteen minutes before sunset and ends the next day after twilight. Religious Jews keep Shabbat in this way and are very strict to clear their minds of worry for twenty-five hours. They enjoy a vacation every week for a full day.

Shabbat Protects against Idol Worship

Ezekiel 20:13
> But the House of Israel rebelled against Me in the wilderness. They did not follow My decrees and they spurned My laws, through which, if a man fulfills them, he will live through them; and they desecrated My Sabbaths exceedingly.

When Moses was on Mount Sinai, Hashem told him about the commandment to keep Shabbat right before he went down with the two tablets:

> Exodus 31:16-18
> The Israelites are to observe the Sabbath, celebrating it for the generations to come as a lasting covenant. It will be a sign between me and the Israelites forever, for in six days the LORD made the heavens and the earth, and on the seventh day he rested and was refreshed." When the LORD finished speaking to Moses on Mount Sinai, he gave him the two tablets of the covenant law, the tablets of stone inscribed by the finger of God.

Hashem saw that the Israelites were sinning, but He didn't tell Moses. Instead, He completed His discourse by reminding him again about Shabbat, as if to say, "If the Israelites keep Shabbat, they will not worship other gods."

By keeping Shabbat, you avoid becoming a slave. When someone stops all labor on Shabbat, he has to trust that Hashem will take care of him. Even if you don't work on Shabbat in your regular job, you still have to abstain from cleaning, cooking, laundry, and other household chores. You must stop for a whole day and fall into Hashem's lap, just like it says in Psalm 131:2, "Like a weaned child on his mother's lap, that's how my soul is with you."

Every Shabbat is a day to practice having faith and complete trust in Hashem. Pagan religions emphasize obligations to your gods and not your gods' promises to you. It's actually harder to trust Hashem than it is to worship Him. If you get used to letting go of your worries once a week you have a chance to realize that it is God that helps you and no one else. On Shabbat we tune out of our problems. Good company and good food set the tone and the table, for the day of rest.

Shabbat is also a day especially dedicated to Torah study. During the week, we are always in a rush. Now we have once a week to enjoy Torah learning without pressure. Even though learning is a daily mitzvah, the Shabbat learning is of a different quality, we enjoy discussions and interactions with our family and friends.

Shabbat is not purely spiritual. In order to keep Shabbat, you have to prepare in advance. You also have to watch the clock. The candles are to be lit eighteen minutes before sundown. The time is written on every Jewish calendar and online. It changes every week.

We prepare fancy meals for Shabbat, another indulgence in worldly pleasures. We also try to nap and make time for romance with our spouse. Sabbath brings us down to earth in order to connect with each other and have time for spiritual and physical pleasure. This combination is special to Judaism. We don't believe in disconnecting from this world. We believe in connecting to the world and God at the same time. Pagan religions cannot do that. Why?

The minute you encourage being practical, you also encourage being realistic. If you are realistic, you can ask questions. How can you possibly believe that an idol or a man is a god? How can you believe that God who created the world has needs? Any belief in other than the one and only God, comes from suggestions of other people. You would not contemplate that an idol is a god if no one suggested it. However, if you think all by yourself just like Abraham, you can find the one and only God without any outside influence. Many American Indian tribes found God or the "Great Spirit," even though they had no connection to the Western world.

Therefore, we work hard to prepare for a day to stop and rest, a time that you can enjoy discussions about the Bible and ideology. Shabbat is a day to give yourself and your children a chance to ask questions. A free, relaxed atmosphere with plenty of healthy, delicious food and good, healthy play will help create a mind-set for true spirituality. True spirituality does not ignore our world; it finds God in our world.

The Karaites

The Karaites were a Jewish sect that originated in the seventh century CE. They believed in the written Torah but they were against the rabbis and all the commentaries on the Torah. The problem with this way of thinking is because the Torah is so versatile and all-encompassing that it is always in need of commentary. Hashem wrote the Torah in a way that it could be interpreted differently by diverse people, because He wanted to make the Torah eternal and applicable in all times. He likes us to learn and make explanations on the words of the Torah, that's what keeps the Torah alive and applicable to everyone. However, we are prohibited to add or subtract any Torah laws. Any commentaries or insights on the Torah can never contradict the Ten Commandments.

Deuteronomy 4:2, "Do not add to what I command you and do not subtract from it, but keep the commands of the Lord your God that I give you."

Shabbos Candles

Exodus 35:3 says "You shall not burn fire in your house on the Sabbath day."

The Karaites interpreted this verse to mean that all fires are prohibited in the home on Shabbat. They don't light candles Friday night before dark so there would be no fire left burning on Shabbat. Before the invention of electricity they would eat in the dark Friday night.

The idea that there is a prohibition to have a fire in the home that was lit before Shabbat doesn't make sense. That would mean that there is a prohibition for lighting a fire on Friday to prepare for Shabbat. That is not possible because Friday is the day to cook in preparation for Shabbat. Secondly, the exact translation of the verse in the Torah is, "Don't upkeep fire in all your dwellings." This means, "do not keep the fire alive." In other words, do not to add fuel to a fire or transfer it to another source of fuel.

The Karaites, who lived in the Middle Ages, didn't understand the Hebrew properly. Today we can understand Hebrew text better than ever before, thanks to the work of Eliezer Ben Yehuda. He was a great Zionist from Russia who lived in the Holy Land about 150 years ago. He labored to revive the Hebrew language and decided that we would use grammar as it was used in the Bible. He also invented many new words that are needed for modern life. In his merit, Hebrew is a very living language today, and Torah learning is so much easier and more comprehensible than ever before.

The mitzvah of lighting candles before Shabbat produced one of the classic arguments that the Karaites had against the rabbis. The prohibition against lighting a fire is actually lighting it on Shabbat or adding fuel to the flame. When you watch the lit Shabbat candles, you are enjoying the fruit of your labor just like you enjoy the food that you cooked on Friday.

When a Jewish woman lights the candles, she feels the spirituality enter her home. That is why I wrote in my poem, "When I light the candles Shabbos will appear".

In the age before electricity, keeping the fireplace lit was a full-time job. Women and children collected wood to keep the fire alive. Because it was so hard to start a fire from scratch, there was an extra log in the back of the fireplace called the backlog. Just in case the wood was consumed the backlog served as protection against losing the fire altogether because of a lack of fuel. The term "backlog" originates from this use of reserve wood to maintain a fire in the hearth.

For Jewish people, there would be no way to keep the fire ignited for the twenty-five hours of Shabbat without adding wood to the fire. The backlog lasted till late morning. After morning prayers, it was customary to eat a bean soup that was kept warm throughout the night. The afternoon meal was a festive meal eaten cold, including smoked, salted, or pickled fish, raw fruit and vegetables, bread, and cake.

Since it is prohibited to supply wood to a fire on Shabbat, the custom arose to cover it with a piece of metal to indicate that you cannot add firewood. When I was growing up, we had a casing made of copper utilized to cover the stove, and all the knobs were concealed to illustrate that Shabbat is not a day to raise or lower the flames. Today we use an electric hot plate, which is better and safer.

Let's go back in time again. What happened in a Jewish home after the fire went out? When Shabbat ended, how did they bear the trouble of igniting a new fire with no matches? After a day of rest, such a bother could readily diminish the recollection of the joy of Shabbat.

Originally, Shabbos candles had to be large enough to last the whole day, twenty-five hours. That's what differentiated them from the regular four- to seven-hour candles that were used daily. When Shabbat was over, the custom was to take fire from the existing Shabbos candles and light a torch or a braided candle to resemble a torch, and start a new fire in the fireplace.

Following the completion of Shabbat, the ceremony of Havdalah with its prayers is sung to separate the holy Sabbath from the rest of the week. In this prayer we make a blessing on a glass of wine, we smell a scent of herbs or spices, and a light a multi-wick candle. Wine is used as a sacramental drink. The blessing over the smell is a sign that we can begin cooking again.

The highlight of Havdalah is the beautiful braided candle lit in the dark room. We thank Hashem for creating the light of fire. Succeeding to kindle a new fire gave reason to thank Hashem enthusiastically for the element necessary for heat, cooking, and industrious work to sustain us during the demands of the work-week. Nowadays we don't have a fireplace to throw in our torch, but we have a special Havdalah candle, that we extinguish in a bit of the leftover wine. Then we sing special songs together, inviting the new and blessed week.

Death Penalty

> Exodus 35:2, "Six days shall work be done, but on the seventh day there shall be to you a holy day, a Sabbath of rest to Hashem; whoever works on it shall be put to death."

> Exodus 31:13–15, "Observe the Sabbath, because it is holy to you. Anyone who desecrates it is to be put to death; those who do any work on that day must be cut off from their people. For six days, work is to be done, but the seventh day is a day of Sabbath rest, holy to the LORD. Whoever does any work on the Sabbath day is to be put to death."

Why is this mitzvah so serious that it deserves a death penalty? For the nonobservant, this is the most shocking of all statements in the Torah. The death penalty is given to murderers, adulterers, and even to kidnappers, but why is there a death penalty for violating Shabbat?

First of all, the death penalty is mentioned alongside another penalty: "that soul shall be cut off from among its people." Hashem took the Israelites out of Egypt by miracle in order that they could be free. If they want to be continue being slaves to their job or their money after all the miracles that Hashem made in Egypt and in the Red Sea, He would be very upset to say the least. Violating Shabbat would be a statement that you don't want to be part of the Jewish people. If that's the case, then Hashem doesn't consider you Jewish.

Aside from the example in Numbers, the death sentence was never applied. This is because the death penalty is only applicable to someone who is knowledgeable of the laws of Shabbat and warned by two witnesses. If the Shabbat violator is warned, he may repent and can be forgiven. If someone doesn't know or understand what Shabbat is, he is innocent.

In New York city between 1850 through the 1910s, adults and even children were forced to work six days a week under inhumane conditions. The workers were sewing in clothing factories that were nicknamed sweatshops. Many Jews surrendered to working on Shabbat because otherwise they wouldn't have employment and would have no food to eat. Many died from the inhumane treatment. Who gets the death penalty here?

The company owners, not the workers. The new immigrants were going to die of starvation if they didn't work on Shabbat, and they were treated like slaves. The owners, who happen to have been mostly assimilated German Jews, had no right to force their workers to work on Shabbat. Hashem says that there is a death penalty for a Jew who forces others to work on Shabbat against their will.

Nowadays, we cannot practice corporal punishment because we don't have a Sanhedrin or Jewish court of law. The Supreme Jewish Court or Sanhedrin consisted of a body of seventy-one judges, and each city had its own Sanhedrin of twenty-three judges. Jewish law required that the Shabbat violator had to be warned and observed profaning the Shabbat in public by at least two witnesses (Deuteronomy 17:6, 19:15). Since there is no Sanhedrin (Jewish Supreme court) today we have to trust Hashem to do justice. The death penalty in the Torah was intended for Jewish people who force others, whether they are Jews, non-Jews or even animals to work on Shabbat. Just as is stated in the fourth commandment.

> Exodus 20:10
> But the seventh day is a sabbath to the Lord your God. On it you shall not do any work, neither you, nor your son or daughter, nor your male or female servant, nor your animals, nor any foreigner residing in your towns.

Many rabbis claim that a non Jew is forbidden to keep the Sabbath. They base it on the writings of Maimonides that says that an idolater is forbidden to keep the Sabbath. This is because he is not observing Shabbat for Hashem but in honor of his god. If a non-Jew wants to observe the Sabbath as an act of respect to the God of Israel, he is certainly welcome.

Wikipedia has a very nice article called, "Capital and Corporal Punishment in Judaism," that explains the difficult terms that were needed to actually execute someone in a Jewish court of law. In the year 70 CE, the Sanhedrin, stopped all capital punishment. Until this day, except for one exception of a Nazi war criminal, there is no capital punishment in Jewish courts, or in Israel.

Kareit

Death is not the only punishment for the desecration of Shabbat. There is another punishment, Kareit, which in English means "cut off from your people."

> Exodus 31:14
> Observe the Sabbath, because it is holy to you. Anyone who desecrates it is to be put to death; those who do any work on that day must be cut off from their people.

If you chose to work on Shabbat, then your work is not really the work of a slave because you are doing it out of choice. However, if you are Jewish then you are not joining your brothers in their observance, so therefore you are "cut off from your nation."

Lots of Jews would take offense to the statement that you are not Jewish if you don't keep Shabbat. However, you cannot be considered part of the people of Israel who Hashem chose to be a light unto the nations. As I explained in the chapter entitled, *"The Book of the Covenant,"* we are called the "Chosen People" with the condition that we keep the Ten Commandments. By observing Shabbat, we are making a statement: "We accept God's Commandments in entirety whether they are accepted by the general population or not. Just as I observe Shabbat because it is God's law, I don't steal, kill or commit adultery because they are God's laws, not just because they make sense."

With the proper learning and repentance a secular Jew can return to his nation. A non-Jew must go through a year of studies and immerse in a ritual bath, in order to convert to Judaism. Nevertheless, Hashem invites all the nations of the world to be part of the covenant of the Ten Commandments and enjoy the Sabbath even if they are not Jewish.

A Day of Rest

> Exodus 23:12, "In order that your ox and donkey should rest and the child of your handmaid and the stranger that lives among you."

One of the purposes of Shabbat is to let others rest. Hundreds of men, women, and children died throughout history because of their harsh labor conditions. Hashem prohibits any type of forced labor, and He had to make a red line. The red line is Friday at sundown. From that time on, until Saturday night, nobody can work—not your children, not even your animals. Just let your family and animals rest and take a break before unrelenting work breaks them.

Can we deny nature? No matter what you do, if you work seven days a week, you will not be as healthy as if you worked six days. There is and always will be a natural consequence for violating Shabbat. Today we know that overworking can lead to heart and other health problems. The death penalty may not be immediate, just as Adam didn't get his death penalty as soon as he ate from the forbidden fruit. If you work seven days a week, even if you don't force others to work you are still in trouble because you are hurting your body, and literally killing yourself. If you are not Jewish, as long as you have a complete rest once a week and you don't abuse your workers or employ them seven days a week then you don't have to worry about a death penalty.

Why do we have to rest on Saturday; why not choose any other day? On the seventh day of creation God created the Sabbath. No other worlds had Sabbath. In our world, the seventh day is a day that has been segregated for resting.

It's also a day for song and prayer. Even if you do work on this day, there will be no blessing in your labor. If you rest any other day, you won't really be as restored as you would be if you rested on Shabbat. However, if you did not have a whole day of respite on Shabbat for any reason, even a legitimate one, it is better to rest any other day in order not to damage your health.

I realized this when one Sabbath we had a flood in the house. A pipe busted, and the water just kept coming. We had to gather the water immediately before the neighbors in the apartment below would get flooded also. It was dangerous because the water could seep into their ceilings and cause an electrical fire. We were finally able to shut off the water, but we still had a very hard day. The next day, Sunday, we were zonked. We decided not to take clients or even phone calls. We had to repose.

Likewise, if you were deserted on an island and had no idea what day it is, you could choose any day to make Shabbat once in seven days. Even though Isaiah says that a non-Jew is welcome to observe Shabbat, a gentile doesn't get punished for desecrating the Sabbath. Nevertheless, everyone gets punished for working seven days a week—the punishment of ill health and lack of quality of life.

Some people must work on the Sabbath because they work in a hospital or a home for the elderly or handicapped. Of course they can work on Saturday if there are mandatory shifts but they should rest another day instead. Soldiers in the line of duty are totally exempt from any days of rest, especially in the middle of war. Nevertheless, soldiers in Israel have shifts that allow them to come home for the Sabbath as often as possible. The soldiers that have to stay on guard celebrate festive meals and prayers in the barracks, if the situation permits.

Even if you are not a descendant of the Israelites, who were redeemed from slavery in ancient Egypt, you do not want to be a slave. In order to really be free you must take one day off every week with no distractions, not even shopping malls and advertisements.

Some people say that they are working very hard and when they get older they will relax. This is a bad tactic. First of all, who promises you that you will get older? Second of all, it is very difficult to acquire new habits when you are a senior. If you aren't used to having quality time even one day a week, you won't start when you're sixty-five years old. Many people say that they will vacation and spend money when they get old, but the majority doesn't. Most people past retirement age are set in their ways.

Hashem wants you to live now. If He wanted you let up and enjoy life only when you've aged, He could have skipped all the years and created you as a seventy-year-old. Our bodies are created in a way that we need time off, not only when a big vacation comes up but one day of rest every week for the mind, body, and soul.

I have a Russian friend in Israel. She came into the Promised Land from Communist Russia, where there was no religion at all—a spiritual desert. She told me that she loves Shabbat so much that even after twenty years she enjoys every Shabbat as if it were her first. She can't believe how she could have lived without it. In her words, "To have one day with no media, no phone, not even the tension of house cleaning, doesn't exist in Russia. Now we have this wonderful day of peace and quiet every week! It's amazing!"

Sunday

Why was Sunday dedicated as the day of worship in the Christian faith?

Early Christians continued to pray and rest on the seventh day. They also observed Sunday, the day of the week on which Jesus had risen from the dead and on which the Holy Spirit had come to the apostles, according to their tradition.

The early Christians were Sabbath observing Jews. Since it is forbidden to use money on the Sabbath all the donations were collected on the Sunday services.

It was probably hard to get people to come to services twice a week so eventually *The Church Council of Laodicea* circa 364 CE, ordered that future religious observances were to be conducted on Sunday. The Seventh Day Baptist Church in the 17th century reverted to the practice of the primitive Christian church and adopted Saturday for religious services. The Seventh-day Adventist Church followed suit.

Even when the religious observance was changed to Sunday, no one claimed that Sunday was the seventh day. Nevertheless, there were many Christians who observe Sunday as a Sabbath. In Early America a colonist could be arrested for going into their workplace or lighting a fire on Sunday.

There is nothing wrong with praying on Sunday as well as on Saturday. Jews go to synagogue every day. However, the Sabbath services in synagogue are longer, there are added prayers for the Sabbath and we read a portion of the Torah.

During the Shabbat services, a hand written Torah scroll made from parchment is removed from the holy ark in the front of the synagogue that faces towards Jerusalem. We stand up in honor of the Torah and sing songs in its praise. The cantor carries an open scroll all around the synagogue, to show the congregants, and they have an opportunity to touch the holy words and send a kiss.

The Jewish Bible is divided into portions. Every week we read one portion of the Torah on Shabbat so that we complete the Five Books of Moses in one year. Aside from the congregational reading we also study the Torah portion from a printed text at home and have Torah discussions with the family. The children learn about the Shabbat portion in kindergarten and in school, they discuss what they learned at the Shabbat table for all to listen. Shabbat is a day to add Torah into our lives.

Sunday does not have the holiness of Saturday. The practice of observing Sunday is not keeping with the spirit of the Bible that the Christians study and cherish. If we love Hashem, we should feel a strong longing to observe Sabbath on Saturday, the seventh day that was created to nourish our body and soul.

Conclusion

The day of Sabbath is a rest day for the whole world. It is a day to stop and think on our own, to get away from our daily chores and for introspection. It is a day of special foods and fancy clothes. The death penalty for desecration Shabbat is aimed toward those who force labor on others on the Sabbath. This also includes a prohibition to persecute anyone who observes the Sabbath or forces them to break the holiness of this day. Even if a court doesn't give the death penalty, Hashem has His ways of punishing evil people.

In the chapter on the second commandment, we wrote that idol worship was always the result of brain washing. Shabbat protects us from being brainwashed. We have no television, no telephones, and no internet for twenty-five hours. Quality time with family and friends is what we need in order to think, trade thoughts, take leisurely strolls, and feel alive!

Chapter 8

Honor Your Father and Mother

The Ten Commandments are the pillars of our Torah and the first directives from God to the world. They have to be commandments that everyone can keep. Of all the Ten Commandments, the fifth, "Honor your father and mother," is the hardest one to observe.

For many people, respecting parents is very difficult or may even be impossible. Others simply don't have parents. The Ten Commandments are meant for everyone. How can people who have no parents fulfill this commandment?

When you teach someone to respect his or her parents, you are also fulfilling the fifth commandment. The act of respecting parents in front of their children is another way of fulfilling this commandment. Never reprimand or criticize a parent in front of his or her child. Children are so easily influenced that everything you say in front of them may be imbedded in their souls, almost like hypnosis. If you don't have children or parents, you can still fulfill this mitzvah by praising and honoring your friends in front of their children, thereby encouraging them to respect their parents.

Lengthen Your Days

> Exodus 20:12 says, "Respect your father and mother so that your days shall be lengthened." Who is going to lengthen your days?

The traditional interpretation is that Hashem will lengthen your days as a reward for respecting your parents. According to the accurate Hebrew grammar, this verse says, "Respect your father and mother in order that they will lengthen your days." If you respect your parents, they will in turn give you love, understanding, caring counsel, financial support, and more. Your days are lengthened as a natural outcome of your parents' support, which is a result of your good relationship with them.

What if your parents are very bad, God forbid, and they just shorten your days? What if they attempt to turn you against God? What if they injure you financially, emotionally, physically, and even sexually? What if you honor them and they do not provide good counsel, understanding, love and support?

Surely you are not supposed to go to your parents to receive additional doses of neglect or abuse. You don't have to forgive them for doing unforgivable things. If our parents do something that will shorten our days, we must keep away, for our own health. How do we know where to draw that line?

I had a patient who was raped by her father many times during her childhood. Many psychologists convinced her to forgive him. Even though my husband and I counseled her to cut off from her father, she obeyed her other therapists, visited her father and spoke to him on regular basis. This young woman consequently developed cancer in her twenties and died in her thirties after years of suffering. Cancer is an autoimmune disease, a disease that is caused by emotional trauma. This woman was given counsel by professionals to forgive her father and even keep in contact with him. She felt that if she didn't forgive him, then she must be at fault—so much so, that her own immune system turned against her.

These professionals caused an iatrogenic auto immune illness. She developed spinal cancer and died an early death. She was misdirected by therapists who were following the classic ideology that everything is forgivable. This is a misdirection from those who were never personally challenged to overcome such abuse. My husband, who is a clinical psychologist, attempted to boost her heart by encouraging her to not cover over her long-suffering, justified anger and even hate, with forgiveness. He wanted to instill her with a stronger backbone to stand up to those who beg to forgive the unforgivable. She had to leave Israel and unfortunately returned to influential professional malpractice. Ironically, she died of cancer of the spine.

Hashem gave us our emotional constitutions. His laws are also for our psychological well-being. Healthy anger serves to defend a person from attack. There is no mitzvah to forgive a capital offense in the sinner's lifetime, even if the sinner is your spouse or parent.

> Psalm 131:21, "Do I not hate those who hate you Lord, and abhor those who are in rebellion against you?"

Hashem is our mother and father and He doesn't tolerate abuse, especially to the point of physical death or even emotional death which can be a fate worse than death. A mother feels the need to protect her children and can even perform super-human feats of strength to save a child such as lifting a car so a little one may escape. A mother can overcome her love of an abusive husband when she protects her child. Often a mother can amass the strength to ward off an abuser when she does so in service of her child. Maybe we should start calling Hashem our mother instead of our father? He created that feminine strength, it's part of God's image within the female soul.

Hashem wrote the Torah in order give us boundaries. Even though today we cannot implement capital punishment, the mere fact that the Torah gives a death penalty for a specific transgression, means that it is an unforgivable act. If the sinner truly repents he will be forgiven after he dies, even if he dies a natural death.

The sin that the rapist father committed was a transgression of the commandment not to commit incest and it has a death penalty. If a rapist father repents and has a real change of heart Hashem will forgive him after death. He must repent and ask forgiveness from everyone that he hurt, otherwise even death doesn't atone for such a grave sin. He may even be blessed with a long life but he doesn't have the right to demand contact with his daughter. His daughter may also forgive him after he dies, but while he is still alive, she doesn't have to go visit him and give him respect.

In the book *Love Medicine and Miracles* by Bernie Siegel, the author writes about the work he did with cancer patients and was even able to cure many of them just by delving into their true emotions.

There are many other examples of parental abuse that can shorten your life. If your parents offer drugs, cigarettes, or even unhealthy food, you shouldn't listen to them. If your parents talk badly against your spouse, this can shorten your days by ruining your marriage. If, God forbid, your parents try to turn your children against you, pick up your children and run for your life. Children are very fragile, if the bond they have with their parents is weakened, it can interfere with normal healthy development.

Respect doesn't necessarily mean to obey. Even if your parents discourage you, or your children, from fulfilling your dreams, you are not obligated to obey them. If your parents command you to do something against Torah law, you are obligated not to obey them. How do we know this?

> Leviticus 19:3 says, "A man should fear his mother and father, and my Sabbaths you shall observe, I am the Lord."

From the above verse we learn that keeping the Sabbath takes precedence over your parents' ruling. When my mother was only twelve years old she decided to observe Shabbat even though her parents were not religious. Her parents purposely went shopping on Saturday with her sisters in order to try to get her to desecrate the Sabbath. She didn't go with them; she never gave in. My mother kept Shabbat against her parents' wishes and wore her sisters' hand-me-downs until her mother finally surrendered. My grandmother began to respect my own mother's convictions when she was seventeen. She even drove her to classes in a Jewish seminary out of town, three times a week.

Respecting Our Children

Hashem, the God of the universe, has put into His utmost important commandments to give respect to someone other than Himself. This alone shows the humble nature of the Almighty. He commands us to respect our parents not for Himself, but for us. Hashem knows that the best thing for us is to respect our parents. In turn, we as parents have to model that respect in our home.

Although we are much more experienced and intelligent than our children when they are young, we are only human. We should not give ourselves too much importance. Many parents yell at their children because they have a feeling of superiority over them.

The difference between our intelligence and Hashem's intelligence is infinite compared to the difference between our intelligence and our children's. We are called upon to remain humble before God in our relationships with our children. We should bond with our children to help them meet life's challenges with Hashem's help. When we regard our children as our little friends, we can help them overcome life's tests without dominating over them. This way, we maximize their growth and promote the greatest degree of mutual respect and independence.

Good parents who help their young ones, should be respected and praised. When you grow up and have your own children if your parents are supportive of your devotion for your children, they already deserve your respect.

Parents who teach you to believe in God and trust Him, should be admired and honored. If you are honest and you keep your word, you teach your child to trust you, and that child will in turn learn to trust God.

Many people insist that children must have rules and structure so they will be disciplined. Children who learn to behave because of a strict environment, will either grow up disciplined but with fears, or grow up rebellious. If they are reared with encouragement, friendship and love they will establish rules and structure for themselves.

Home should not be a place of fear or punishment. A child should feel so much love and joy from her parents that she admires and respects them without any disciplinary measures.

As children mature, set an example by respecting your spouse. The children will imitate your attitude, especially after they leave your nest. Children mirror what's happening at home. If the parents lovingly respect each other, the children will respect them. If children view their parents hard work, they will work hard at their schoolwork. The influences of your discourses have no effect at all in comparison with the influence of your actions.

Nevertheless, it is important to have lengthy discussions with your children about your knowledge and your beliefs. Teach them to fear Hashem and not you. Teach them to be respectful of you because Hashem says so in the Ten Commandments. If they don't understand, their souls will. If you teach them loyalty to the Torah they will respect you. Just the tone of your voice as you speak about the Creator of the universe will give them a feeling that you are a wise parent, worthy of their respect. I conclude that the best way to teach your children to respect you, is to respect them, the Torah and Hashem.

Born Free

From the moment we are born, we begin to protest. Babies scream for what they need with no regard to their caretakers. When they grow up, they continue to have demands. Hashem made us naturally demanding because if they were really thinking clearly, they would worship their parents. As babies we depend on them for everything. Hashem wants us to feel from birth that our parents are not God. That is why we are born with an egotistical will to fight for our rights. Don't fight your child's inclination, calm them down and help them understand that you are there to help them.

When our children are about three years old, we can begin to instill them with faith in God. When children realize that God alone is our Master, they can begin to lose that egotistical streak and be very respectful of their parents without worshiping them.

People of all ages who have faith in God are blessed with a goodness and innocence. If your child is impudent, try to find ways to teach him about God rather than punish him.

I have a friend who is an elementary school English teacher in Israel. Every time her students fight, she calls them over and explains that Hashem is watching them and He would like them to love each other. She spends a lot of time teaching about faith instead of their English studies. Other educators might think that she is wasting time, but the results are in her favor. Last year her class won an award of the highest grades in the country on an Israeli national achievement test, in English. The respect the children had for their wonderful teacher and for each other helped them to be studious, mature and smart.

The following Song can be sung to the melody of *Every Breath You Take*. It is a song addressed to your children in order to teach them that God is always watching. This song is also praise to Hashem for having children to love and cherish.

God is Watching You

Every breath you take,
Every move you make,
Every bond you create,
Every step you take,
God is watching you.

Every single day,
Every word you say,
Every game you play,
Every time you pray,
God is watching you.

Can't you see what's more
Hashem knows what's in store.
He is always awake, for every step you take.

Every move you make,
Every record you break,
Every time you ache,
Every breath you take,
God is watching you.

Since you're born we've felt that we've been graced.
Asleep or awake, we love to see your face.
We look around and it's you, no one can replace.
We feel so warm, and we long for your embrace.
We keep thanking Hashem, Hashem, please...

Hashem can give a test,
Because He knows what's best.
Hashem is always awake, for every step you take.

Every move you make,
Every record you break,
Every time you ache.
Every breath you take,
God is watching you.

Every move you make,
Every step you take,
God is watching you...

Every breath you take,
Every move you make,
Every bond you create,
Every step you take,
God is watching you.

Every single day,
Every word you say,
Every game you play,
Every time you pray,
God is watching you.

Every move you make,
Every record you break,

Every time you ache,
Every breath you take,
God is watching you.

Every single day,
Every word you say,
Every game you play,
Every time you pray,
God is watching you.

Every breath you take,
Every move you make,
Every bond you create,
Every step you take,
God is watching you.

****

A Peaceful Atmosphere at Home

Just as Hashem despises promiscuity, He loves a peaceful and loving home. When children grow up in a home of innocence and loyalty, they learn how to make a proper home for their own families. Establishing patience is the first step to making a beautiful atmosphere in the home. As Hashem is very patient with us, we are called upon to be patient with our spouse and our children. Yelling at children is not in keeping with the mitzvah to emulate Hashem. We ourselves are the children of Hashem. He does not rush to reprimand or punish us for every little error. He can wait for many years until we finally learn to change our ways for the better. In Deuteronomy 30:16, when the Torah says to go in Hashem's ways, the NIV translates it as "to walk in obedience to him." The KJV is more accurate.

> Deuteronomy 30:16 KJV, "In that I command thee this day to love the LORD thy God, to walk in his ways, and to keep his commandments and his statutes and his judgments, that thou mayest live and multiply: and the LORD thy God shall bless thee in the land whither thou goest to possess it."

In the above translation it is more clearly articulated that we are commanded to copy Hashem. We are adjured not only to observe His laws, but to go in His ways; to be like Him. If we set a good example to our children, we are emulating Hashem so they will follow us.

Education through Example

> Deuteronomy 6:7 says, "And you shall teach these words to your children repeatedly and talk about them."

If our children do something against the Torah, then they need to be taught and reprimanded. Hashem doesn't want us yelling at a child for making his room a mess. Even if the child does something against the Torah, like lying or stealing, you still have to be patient to explain what's right and what's wrong. God forbid, never use scare tactics to get children to be good. It is always counterproductive.

As bad as it is to yell at your children, it is incomparably worse to yell at your spouse. If you yell at your spouse, you teach your child to disrespect his parents. Even if you are angry at each other in your heart, the tension can be felt by the children. When children see that their parents get along, it causes them to admire Mom and Dad and to look forward to having family of their own.

If you are divorced, you are still obligated to respect the parent of your child and teach your children to respect their mother and father. The only time that it would be permissible to say anything bad about a parent is, if it was dangerous for the child to be alone with him. At that point all your children must be warned.

Respect Your Parents and Observe the Sabbath

"A man must fear his mother and father and keep my Sabbaths" (Leviticus 19:3). Sabbaths in plural, includes all the holidays on which we are prohibited to do work. The traditional commentary for this verse is, that if your parents command you to violate Shabbat, then you should not listen to them. Another explanation of this passage is that, as a result of fearing your father and mother, you will be able to keep a lot of Sabbaths. If you have the experience of obeying and respecting authority, so it won't be hard for you to keep Shabbat, or any other mitzvah that demands obedience without full understanding.

Shabbat is a family holiday and the children are invited to participate in the preparations. Likewise, children learn to model their parents' religious or nonreligious behavior. Children who grow up with parents who smoke in front of them are much more likely to smoke when they become adults compared to children of nonsmokers. Like any religious teaching, parental modeling holds the strongest influence.

My Father, My Teacher

If children become God fearing later in life due to the influence of another parental model, should that parental model be honored as much as the biological parents?

Our sages say, "Your father gives you this world; your teacher gives you the world to come." We have many teachers in life. We should listen to wise people and learn from them our whole life. Even if we are not in touch with them, we should honor them by following in their footsteps. However, you don't owe them the respect that you owe your parents. When your parents are old or sick, you are obligated to take care of them to the best of your abilities. You have a responsibility toward them, just as they had a responsibility toward you when you were growing up. If you are adopted, you must respect your adoptive parents even more than your true biological parents. Their efforts, including financial, emotional, physical, and mental efforts to rear you, demand your utmost esteem.

Interestingly enough you also have to respect your biological parents if you were adopted and you have the opportunity to find them. Just the fact that your parents were partners with Hashem, in your creation, is a reason to respect them. Of course, you also should respect a parent who was absent during your childhood, unless respecting him or her will cause disrespect to your attending parent, biological or adoptive.

Learning History

> Deuteronomy 32:7 says, "Remember the days of old, study the years of every generation. Ask your father and he will tell you, your wise men and they will say."

We must honor our parents in order to learn our heritage from them. We have to pass on our life stories from generation to generation.

The mitzvah to honor our parents also includes honoring our grandparents, great grandparents and ancestors throughout the generations. We must respect the founding fathers and mothers of monotheism even if we aren't biologically related to them. Hashem wants us to acknowledge, respect, and appreciate our parents and teachers for their leadership.

As parents we have the responsibility to teach our heritage to our children. We learn from the above verse Deuteronomy 32:7 that it is a mitzvah to learn history. Learning history helps children develop a personal ideology.

When I was a young girl, our school emphasized history and Jewish culture. The teachers were very humble and treated us as friends. I remember asking my math teacher a question that she couldn't answer. I asked, "When is there a situation in life where we would use a negative number multiplied by a negative number?" She came back the next day telling us how she discussed this with the other teachers, and we all shared our thoughts on it. This provided significantly more important learning than concentrating on more math exercises. The atmosphere in our seventh and eighth grade classes was that of acquiring knowledge and expanding our ideas. Almost all my classmates turned out to be teachers or leaders in their communities.

The new generation across the whole world has become exposed to booming multimedia. Millions of visual minutiae come screaming to their faces, but for the children there is no background picture. As a parent, you are called upon to place the world into perspective. Tell them lots of true stories and expose them to historical novels, world history and the history of the different religions of the world. By teaching world history, you are teaching children to be tolerant of other people for their beliefs, their customs and even their external features. My mother used to say, "School is just a high level babysitting service, real education is in the home." She learned this from Mark Twain who said, "I have never let my school interfere with my education."

Honesty Is the Best Policy

The way the schools teach history is sometimes very boring and lacks the dramatic affect needed to make an impression on young minds. Through books, DVD's and the internet, children can learn a lot about the world of the past. Some parents are not even honest with children about their own past. Being honest with children will help them much more than any damage that might occur because of the child's exposure to life's problems and shortcomings.

I met a young woman who was so overprotected by her parents that she was not told that she was born with a medical problem that required lifelong treatment with medication. Her mother would give her medicine every morning and say that it was a vitamin. The child's life was perfect. She had no knowledge of any problems in her family; everything was a secret. Finally, in high school she was not accepted for a main part in the school play that she really wanted. Disaster followed the stress of rejection. She was sixteen years old and suffered panic attacks so terrible that she actually experienced a stroke. The whole right side of her body became paralyzed. This is an exaggerated example, but it is a true story.

Peace in the Home

Children become upset and even traumatized by small things that their parents get upset about, and they can also be traumatized by big things like moving to a new neighborhood or even suffering through their parents' divorce. Very young children may even acquire neurochemical brain imbalances from exposure to hearing screeching in the house. On the other hand, children seem to learn and grow, even in the face of really strong life challenges or changes of circumstances when they have their parents' support in a peaceful home environment.

What is it that makes us get more emotionally expressive about small things then big ones? Why do we yell about our gloves that are missing and we have patience for a tooth extraction?

At the dentist we are on guard. We are trained to behave in public but somehow at home we feel relaxed and let loose. We should let loose at home in order to laugh, not to yell. Try to make jokes at home instead of being serious all the time. The laughter will conquer all. If when we feel free at home we yell, our children will have no respect for us. They see how we act in public but our manners are all false, because the minute the doors close our behavior changes.

Yelling at children doesn't teach them anything, except how to yell. The point that you are trying to get across becomes oblivious as it gets drowned out in the shocking sound waves.

Positive Reinforcement

As parents we are called upon to focus more on what our children do correctly, than where they can improve. When parents concentrate on what their children do right, rather than what they do wrong, good perspective is projected. Children subsequently feel good about themselves and develop self-confidence.

Their natural instincts will blossom, and they will find their own faith and love of God from within. Speak to your children at bedtime. Tell them to ask God for something for the next day. Ask them to pray, for themselves, their friends and their family. Teach them how important the prayers of children are, as it says in Psalm 8:3, 'From the mouths of babies and nursing children you put down the foundation of strength.'"

Before the children are old enough to understand who Hashem is, it is important for them to realize they can trust you, the parents. From the time they are born, tell them how Mommy and Daddy are going to take care of them. Always be mature and self-confident when they cry or complain, so that they learn to rely on you. Children who can count on their parents can easily learn to have faith in Hashem. Do not tell children about your financial issues or other problems before they are old enough to help you. When children hear that you don't have money, they can develop unnecessary fears. Children should feel that they can be free to have fun and play because Mommy and Daddy will take care of them and solve all their problems.

Hashem has great pleasure watching children who really have faith in Him. He enjoys when they sing songs to Hashem.

When you teach your children to sing to Hashem, you also instill the words of the song in their hearts and in their souls.

A child must be encouraged to ask questions. Even if you don't know the answers, try to help her find the answer to her inquiry. Don't ever make light of a question about life. Everything should be open, from Darwinism to Freud, to whatever speculations the child or adolescent has or makes him wonder. The trouble is that nowadays with time-consuming work, school, and activities, some parents don't spend enough time with their children to even know what questions they have. Conversing or playing with your child may be even more important than taking them on a special trip or attending an after-school recreational activity with them.

In a book called *Off the Derech* (*Derech* means path) by Faranak Margolese, the author reviews her interviews with hundreds of Jewish youth who left Judaism and God. She concluded that if these children were allowed to ask questions and discuss possible answers freely, they would never have left their faith. In my books I want to reach those people who are looking for answers and give them new ideas and a new perspective.

CHAPTER 9

Do Not Murder

Genesis 27 begins with the story of Jacob and Esau coming to their father Isaac to be blessed before his death.

> Genesis 27:42, "When Rebekah was told what her older son Esau had said, she sent for her younger son Jacob and said to him, "Your brother Esau is planning to avenge himself by killing you. Now then, my son, do what I say: Flee at once to my brother Laban in Harran. Stay with him for a while until your brother's fury subsides. When your brother is no longer angry with you and forgets what you did to him, I'll send word for you to come back from there. Why should I lose both of you in one day?"

What is the meaning of mourning for both on the same day? Obviously, Jacob would be mourned should Esau actually murder him. Why mourn for Esau? He would still be alive.

Esau did not care for the first-born status. He traded it for lentil soup. He hardly lost out on the material benefits from his inheritance compared to his brother's inheritance. However, when he discovered that he was destined to serve his brother and his kin would be Jacob's slaves, he was enraged.

Hashem told Rebecca that Esau was planning to murder his brother so he would never have to serve him (Genesis 27:41). Rebecca feared he would succeed. Should he murder Jacob, on the same day she would disinherit Esau as a son. From that day onward, Esau would be as good as dead to Rebecca, and she would mourn for the loss of both her murdered son and her murdering son.

Rebecca sent Jacob to her brother because she knew he had wonderful daughters who believed in God. With this act Rebecca determined from whom the Jewish people should arise. It took many generations until the Jewish people decided to follow the maternal line. In my book *God's Hidden Treasure*, I wrote a chapter entitled "The Woman's Role" where I reveal a big secret about the women of Israel that was never told before.

We learn from the story of Jacob and Esau that a murderer has a spiritual death sentence even if he isn't convicted in a court of law. With the mere thought of murder, Esau already forfeited his rights to inherit the blessing of the inheritance of the Land of Israel from Abraham his grandfather.

> Psalm 115:17-18
> "It is not the dead who praise the LORD,
> those who go down to the place of silence;
> it is we who extol the LORD,
> both now and forevermore.

In my book *Who is God?* in the chapter entitled "Life after Life," I describe how our relatives who were righteous souls and have passed on, praise Hashem in heaven. Dead people do praise Hashem.

The dead in Psalms are the living dead. A sinner is compared to a dead person. The sinners do not praise Hashem. We can also learn from this verse that if you do praise God, you are not a sinner. Praising Hashem will lift you from the abyss. Therefore, if you want to repent and change your ways, start by praising God for everything He gave you, and for the beautiful world that we live in.

Another example where dead means a bad person is in Ezekiel.

> Ezekiel 13:32 says, "For I do not wish the death of the dead, rather that he returns to Hashem and live."

If a sinner is called a dead person then if you influence someone to sin, it is like killing them. Therefore, the prohibition of the commandment, "Do not murder" includes influencing others to do bad things.

On the other hand, influencing wayward wrongdoers to return to Hashem is like giving them life and will surely atone for the sin of persuasion to do evil. So, if in your youth you persuaded your buddies to steal or do drugs, God forbid, you can fix that by influencing them or other people to go in the path of God.

Accidental Manslaughter

The Torah gives a death penalty for premeditated murder. Contrary to modern law, the Biblical law is that the death penalty cannot be given because of circumstantial evidence. There must be two eyewitnesses. The witnesses have to be sure that the murder was purposeful. Accidental killings are not punished. If someone killed another human being inadvertently they would need protection because a relative of the deceased might not be so forgiving.

> Numbers 35:22–25, "But if without enmity someone suddenly pushes another or throws something at them unintentionally or, without seeing them, drops a stone heavy enough to kill them, and they die, then since that other person was not an enemy and no harm was intended, the assembly must judge between the accused and the avenger of blood according to these regulations. The assembly must protect the one accused of murder from the avenger of blood and send the accused back to the city of refuge to which they fled."

The above verses are referring to the time when there would be six cities of refuge in the Land of Israel. These were walled cities, and they were to be the homes of the Levites and Cohanim (priests). The Levites and priests did not own land. Their job was to teach the Torah. They would reside in cities where they could learn Torah and get a worldly education too. They prepared their kin to serve in the Holy Temple and trained them to become educators all over the land. The other purpose for the cities of refuge was to protect someone who killed by accident.

> Deuteronomy 19:5, "If a man may go into the forest with his friend to cut wood, and as he swings his ax to fell a tree, the head of the ax may fly off and hit his neighbor and kill him. That man may flee to one of these cities and he shall live."

Accidental manslaughter cannot go unnoticed because the relatives of the deceased will be mightily angry. In the cities of refuge, the killer will be safe. The gates are guarded, and the guards do not allow anyone to pass unless they have special permission.

Being thoughtless and irresponsible to the point of causing death is very serious. The killer must learn how to behave from the Levites and priests. He must stay in the city of refuge and he may bring his family with him.

Nowadays people get long jail sentences for manslaughter, and shorter terms for involuntary manslaughter or accidental killing. In the Bible, the person responsible for accidental death is not incarcerated at all. The Torah offers an alternative, a way to prevent mishaps and help people who are still capable of improving. The killer has to live in a city of refuge with the Levites and the priests, the ones who teach and learn the Torah. This way the offender could learn to improve and be cautious in everything he does. This system is much better than jail and less painful because the perpetrator's family would be readily allowed to come with him to live in the city of refuge. As a matter of fact, it was advisable, because the avenger might choose to hurt the killer's family too. This system would work like today's witness protection program.

According to the Bible, intentional murder is punishable by death. However, the only way to prosecute a person for murder is with two eyewitnesses that are heavily cross-examined. If they tell different stories their testimony is not accepted. If they have identical stories in the same exact language, their testimony is thrown out, because that might mean that it is a planned set-up. They are in big trouble if they conspired against the accused. The law is that they get prosecuted for the felony of the accused as if they did it themselves.

If there is not enough evidence to prosecute a suspect, the alleged murderer can go to the city of refuge to be protected from the avengers. The Torah does not condone revenge. However, if a man did avenge the killing of his wife or child, he would not be arraigned because he could claim temporary insanity. Therefore, the Torah prepares six cities of refuge to flee to safety from those who may legally take revenge.

An Accidental Injury

> Exodus 21:22, "If people are fighting and hit a pregnant woman and she gives birth prematurely but there is no serious injury, the offender must be fined whatever the woman's husband demands and the court allows. But if there is serious injury, you are to take life for life, eye for eye, tooth for tooth, hand for hand, foot for foot, burn for burn, wound for wound, bruise for bruise."

In the above scenario a pregnant woman gets in-between two people fighting and gets hurt or her unborn baby gets hurt. The translation says "You are to take a life for a life..." However, the Hebrew says *venatata*, which means: and you should give. There's a big difference between giving and taking. To give means to give money, monetary compensation for the injury. One of the compensations stated is *a tooth for a tooth*. An unborn child doesn't have teeth which means that the woman or the father lost a tooth. The Torah doesn't demand you to punch out someone's tooth. That would be revenge; another prohibition from the Torah.

In this scenario the pregnant woman who was hurt may have lost her unborn child. However, it is not without fault; therefore, the law demands monetary compensation. There is no need to run to the city of refuge. The father and mother will be consoled by payment. If the fighters accidently kill the mother, they must run to a city of refuge for safety.

Choose Life Reexamined

The prohibition against murder includes the positive commandment to choose life. In Deuteronomy 30:19 it says, "I have given before you, life and goodness, death and evil, and you shall choose life." Don't bring death to yourself and your family by choosing evil. Deuteronomy teaches us that choosing wickedness causes death because of all the consequences that will come to you as a result of bad choices. Hashem created the world and also made all the rules of nature. If you go against the rules of nature, such as by smoking, drinking, eating unhealthy food, taking drugs, not sleeping, and so forth, you are choosing death.

> Deuteronomy 30:19–20, "This day I call the heavens and the earth as witnesses against you that I have set before you, life and death, blessings and curses. Now choose life, so that you and your children may live and that you may love the LORD your God, listen to his voice, and hold fast to him."

The above verse in the Torah is telling us that death is bad; contrary to some religions that sanctify death. The Torah does not allow us to kill ourselves or even cause damage to ourselves or others and thereby shorten life. God gave us our bodies and our health, and He wants us take care of them.

> Deuteronomy 14:1, "You are children to the Lord your God; do not scratch yourself and do not put a bald spot between your eyes for the dead."

This phrase is referring to an old custom of mourners to take out blood by scratching themselves with a knife. Even today, there are rituals in other religions that have the mourners injure their bodies by wounding themselves.

God calls upon us to do what's right by choosing what the Torah teaches us to do and by choosing what naturally prolongs and improves our lives. This is one reason why many people who are emissaries of Hashem are given the power to become healers.

Because the Torah says to choose life we are not obligated to die for any mitzvah. However, there are three mitzvoth that our sages say we must die for: "Do not murder," "Do not commit adultery or incest" and "Do not worship other gods."

However, it is not possible that we have to die rather than to kill because that would make it forbidden to fight in self-defense or in war. On the other hand, adultery and incest are sins that damage your soul. Therefore, it would be better to die than to consent to having sex with a family member or a married woman.

If a married woman is threatened with rape, God forbid, she certainly must fight to protect herself but, if she can't, she is not held accountable and her husband must forgive her. However, if for example if a married woman wants to become a prostitute because she has no food to eat she should rather starve than sin.

There was a true story of an orthodox Jewish woman who was raped and got pregnant. She decided to keep the pregnancy and gave birth to a set of black twins. She raised them as good Jewish children and her husband raised them as if they were his own. According to Jewish law a child is Jewish if the mother is Jewish, so this woman definitely did the right thing.

Religious Persecution

Idol worship is not something that you must die for if it is done outwardly and there is no change of heart. The Marranos of Spain were outwardly worshipping in the church but keeping their own faith in their homes. In this case they should have worked hard to escape to other countries while they hide their identity. Christopher Columbus was a Jewish man who did just that. Researchers found proof that he was Jewish because they found Hebrew initials in the right-hand corner of his letters. These initials stand for, "With God's help." Every orthodox Jew puts these letters on every page that they write. A set of phylacteries (see glossary) was also found in his cabin. The reason that he asked the queen for three ships was in order to take as many Jews as possible out of Spain.

The Jews of Spain were given a chance to leave Spain in order to stay Jewish. Many of them did. My father's family comes from Jews who escaped from Spain and fled to Turkey where they built up a flourishing Jewish community.

If a person were threatened with his life, or put to the stake in order to be killed for believing in only one God,

Hashem will respect their choice. They can either die for the cause, agree to convert and in secret keep the faith, or agree to convert and in secret help others to escape this persecution as many did in the Holocaust.

The belief in Hitler as the Fuhrer was also idol worship. Therefore, if people were outwardly willing to agree to comply with him but secretly saved Jews, as did Oskar Shindler, they are righteous people. Holocaust Memorial Museum in Jerusalem currently recognizes 24,811 saviors. These heroes performed the mitzvot, "Do not murder" and "Do not worship other gods," to the fullest.

Modern-Day Killers

Modern industry tempts and attempts to kill us all the time. The market is flooded with dangerous drugs, cancerous foods, and endless ways to hurt you, just so the rich and ambitious can make more and more money.

Every time you decide to choose the right food, the right exercise, the right good deed, you are choosing life. You are choosing not to support murder and not to be brainwashed into nutritional suicide, however quickly or slowly.

Leviticus 19:15 says, "Don't stand over your brother's blood." The medical and food corporations that are creating poisonous food and drugs are standing over us and watching their brothers bleed. Many doctors are also victims to the processed foods and unnecessary drugs that they ingest and give their own families. In my book *Choose Life* I wrote details of what food is good for you and how to stay healthy through diet, herbs and food supplements.

Help Your Friends

"Don't stand over your brother's blood" also means that you can't watch your friends suffer and not do anything about it. Even though you are not actively hurting them, it doesn't absolve you from withholding information that might help them immensely.

For example, when you hear of somebody's legal problem and you know of a great lawyer who is a real expert in that field, you must tell them. Don't say to yourself, "Maybe they don't have the money to afford him." Give them the information, and they will have the free choice to use it or not. If you see someone with flu and you have a great herbal remedy to help him or her, give him or her the information. If you don't, you'll never know what his or her reaction might have been. If they don't want the information, you still get the mitzvah or merit for trying to help.

Suicide

Suicide is murder. You don't own your body and you don't have permission to hurt yourself. People who even consider suicide think that if they die they won't have any more problems. The truth is that you can't really kill yourself. You'll still be around. You will have the same feelings that you had when you were alive, only you will have to face heavenly courts on the conviction of murder! Now you're really in trouble. You'll wish that you had the problems you had when you were on earth.

This commandment, "Do not murder," is the sixth of the Ten Commandments. It follows the commandment to honor your parents. The worst thing that a child, youth or adult, can do to his parents is to commit suicide. It is an act of extreme disrespect for all the work that his parents did to bring him up. The one who suicides bears total disregard for all the suffering his loved ones will have to endure with their loss. Sometimes the suicide is planned in order to instill anguish in the parents. The killer may have entertained thoughts of making his parents, friends, or spouse feel guilty. He feels miserable and blames others for his misery. He faults them for inadequately rearing him. He thereby makes this ultimate statement by taking his own life, thereby attesting to their failure to make him happy. He truly believes his parents will react with guilt. This gives him pleasure and even strength to take his own life and to kill whatever joy his parents could have for the rest of their lives. Even after your parents passed away the least you owe them is to try to stay alive. How do you think your parents would feel if they saw you take your own life as they watch the suicide from heaven and don't have the ability to stop you?

Consequently, besides transgressing the commandment not to kill, someone who plans and commits suicide violates the fifth commandment, "Honor Your Father and Mother."

If someone is threatening to suicide, immediate action should be taken to give him or her the help he or she needs. The will to die is against nature and is usually caused by mental disease. Please take threats of suicide seriously, even if the person who is threatening says that he or she isn't serious. In the past a person who suicided was buried outside the gates of the cemetery because of the disgrace that this was for his relatives. Today Jewish law considers suicide a tragedy caused by mental illness and the victim of the disease has a respectful funeral.

This is a poem of encouragement to anyone who is feeling low:

Choose Life, Take the Task

Sometimes you feel that your soul is sinking
All you feel on your face is a frown
When your plans have failed you stop thinking.
Why is everything upside-down?

Every day we go to work and what's the point?
The get up the next morning to go to the same old joint?

Choose Life,
Take the task.
There isn't a question you shouldn't ask.
Sing a song that comes from the heart,
It's a trip to heaven.
From Hashem don't be apart.

It's difficult to find yourself from the depths of despair.
It's an unjust world,
Only Hashem really cares.

Return to Hashem even if it takes a fight.
You are an image of God
And must love Him with all your might.

From the depths of darkness,
Look to the stars.
Just like Abraham,
And you'll go far.

Wake up in the morning,
With a prayer in your heart.
Sing aloud,
And your soul,
Will have a good start.

****

Abortion

Now for the big question—Is abortion considered murder in the eyes of Hashem?

In the Discussion in Chapter One, under the heading Ten Commandments for Noah on page 10, there is a direct quote from the Bible, a commandment given to Noah after the flood. Genesis 9:6 states: "Whoever sheds human blood, by humans shall their blood be shed; for in the image of God has God made mankind." The literal translation is; "The one who spills blood of a human inside a human, his blood will be spilled."

While this shows that abortion is against the Torah, it doesn't mean that a court will order the spilling of a perpetrator's blood. It's a natural consequence, meaning abortion has repercussions, as I will explain.

The English translation of the NIV Exodus 21:22-25 read "If people are fighting and hit a pregnant woman and she gives birth prematurely but there is no serious injury, the offender must be fined whatever the woman's husband demands and the court allows. But if there is serious injury, you are to take life for life, eye for eye, tooth for tooth, hand for hand, foot for foot, burn for burn, wound for wound, bruise for bruise." However, the Hebrew word ason, translated as serious injury in the NIV, is properly translated in English as tragedy. A tragedy would be when the mother loses her child.

The answer to the question, "Is abortion murder?" demands consideration that the Hebrew term lo tirtzach, literally "Don't murder, "as written in The Ten Commandments in Exodus 20:13, is not used in Genesis 9:6, when discussing a man shedding human blood inside a man or in Exodus 21:23 where it says "If there is a tragedy" when referring to the death of an unborn baby. An abortion is not permissible by God's Law, and it is a tragedy to at least the mother. Many women suffer from PASS, Post Abortion Stress Syndrome. Women might suffer their whole lives because of one abortion. Giving up a baby to adoption may cause severe prolonged post-partum depression, but God will understand and forgive.

Another damage caused by an abortion is to the parents' soul. A child was assigned to be born to them and the parents interfered with the plan, changing the whole course of their future or fate. Aborting a child comes from a severe lack of faith. The parents feel that whatever God planned for them is not acceptable. Before a child is born, its soul has the right to choose his or her parents. However, if instead of accepting that choice the parents say, "No, you are not welcome," this soul who is part of your spiritual family may meet you in heaven and may not be very happy or forgiving.

Those who abort for financial reasons don't realize that God who gives them food and shelter will also care for a baby.

We all live from God's gifts even though we may live in the illusion that we are supporting ourselves. There are many organizations world-wide to help poor women financially who decide to keep their babies.

To summarize, the Torah doesn't consider abortion as murder in the traditional sense of the word, lo tirtzach. There are no clear Torah callings for the perpetrator of an accidental, or even a purposeful abortion, to be put to death. An unintentional feticide, by definition, is considered a disaster. All the more so, an intentional abortion is an even greater disaster.

If you did have an intentional abortion, the best is to have a baby yourself. If you cannot try again, pray to Hashem that your child's soul will be born to someone else close to you.

When it Comes to Babies Trust No One

A daughter of a friend of mine was expecting, and from the seventh month the doctors were telling the mother that the baby had a deadly disease and would die either in the womb or right after birth. They had stacks of medical records all about this baby's grave situation.

In the beginning of the ninth month, the child was not doing well, and the doctors were saying to let the baby die in the womb and wait for a stillbirth. I told the mother to demand an immediate Caesarian section. I said, "You can't wait for a child to die. Whether he will die later is up to God." The parents did the operation, and the baby was small but fine. All the diagnoses proved wrong. The child is now three years old. She is a happy and healthy little girl.

Another mother I knew had German measles early in her second month of pregnancy. She was totally calm throughout the pregnancy because she had faith that whatever child God would give her would be fine. She delivered a perfectly healthy baby boy.

Another example was a woman who became pregnant when she was forty years old. The ultrasound showed some discrepancies between the gestational age and weight. The doctors were suspicious that the fetus was not developing properly and suggested the baby might have Down's syndrome. The mother was so emotionally compromised and distraught that the rabbi finally permitted her to do the amniocentesis test, a test that Jewish people usually do not do. There were no genetic issues discovered. However, the anxiety that the mother endured in addition to the dangerous testing, caused the mother to have early contractions which resulted in a premature birth in the seventh month. Today the child is healthy with some learning problems that are a result of the prematurity. If she would have been calm and just trusted Hashem, the child would have been perfectly healthy.

As I wrote previously, since telling the future is common practice among doctors, it is a mitzvah not to believe them. Medical predictions of health and illness or life and death are best taken with a grain of salt, especially when it comes to birth defects.

Pregnant Girls

Many young, unmarried Israeli Jewish girls who fall into the hands of the wrong guys, choose not to abort. They would rather give the child up for adoption. If the pregnant girl's parents are willing to help, they will almost always choose to keep the baby. These are girls who were brought up religious and gave up keeping Torah, usually for rebellious reasons. No matter how secular they are, they usually have a red line: they will not murder their unborn child.

What is it that makes a teenager choose the life of her fetus above her own, even if she will have to endure a lot of embarrassment and inconvenience?

In Jewish religious education, the first stories taught are about the lives of the forefathers and foremothers. Sarah, Rebecca and Rachel all had trouble conceiving. At home and in school, the stories are told and retold. The characters of the women in the Bible become part of the primordial psyche of every religious Jewish girl. No matter what happens later in life, whether they stay religious or not, when they discover at any age that they are about to become mothers, they are delighted and excited! Subconsciously they know how precious that baby is because of the stories they were taught at such a young and tender age.

From this example we can learn how important history is for our children's education and their emotional development. Stories sink deep, much deeper than chastisement or reprimand. If there were more emphasis on Bible history and culture through stories and songs and less emphasis on prohibitions and obligations, children would become much more happily attached to their heritage. They would then make much healthier, life-promoting, and enduring choices throughout their lives. This is true for Jews and non-Jews alike.

A Mitzvah to Learn History

Deuteronomy 32:5-7
"They are corrupt and not his children; to their shame they are a warped and crooked generation. Is this the way you repay the LORD, you foolish and unwise people? Is he not your Father, your Creator, who made you and formed you? Remember the days of old; consider the generations long past. Ask your father and he will tell you, your elders, and they will explain to you."

Moses mentions this phrase before he dies. It is right after he prophesies how bad the children of Israel were going to be. Moses gave a solution for having turned to an evil path. Remember the days of old, and then you will have a generation that continues your heritage.

When an unmarried woman becomes pregnant, she starts to feel guilty for her behavior and for everything that she did wrong to get her into the mess that she's in. The most basic instinct for a mother is to protect her offspring. The Jewish mother has an even stronger instinct than most because of the frightening history the Jews have of pogroms and murders that were all part of her education.

If a young woman is already feeling guilty, the last anchor that she has to hold on to, is that ideology that is shared by

Jews and non-Jews, the preservation of an innocent life. She wants to feel that she has something to live for.

Lots of Children

Orthodox Jewish woman have many children. A recent statistic was done in Israel. The general average birth rate was 3.11 children per family. In ultra-Orthodox Jewish families, whether rich or poor, the average number of children is 7.8. In modern Orthodox Jewish families it is 5.6. These numbers are statistical averages. It includes families who have no children and those who are just starting to have their first child. I have many friends who have more than ten children and they are all well-dressed well-mannered, respectful and loving. Even those who leave the ultra-orthodox way of life, continue to respect their parents forever.

Israeli Orthodox mothers and fathers don't feel that their children are a burden or an expense. They actually go to the doctor even after they've had six children in order to get help to successfully conceive the seventh. These parents have faith that Hashem will provide for their children and that every child brings a blessing with him or her. They also help their offspring financially even after they are married and have their own children. The contact between parents and children lasts a lifetime.

The nonbeliever thinks it is selfish to bring another child into the world that he may or may not be able to afford to support. The religious believe that they are bringing down a soul that is waiting to be born. They have faith that

Hashem will provide the finances for the needs of the child and are proud to give a good education, instilling values on which he or she can flourish and be part of the community.

Rabbis allow contraceptives but only in order to space the children, not to stop having children entirely. The Orthodox Jewish women don't complain. I asked a friend who has eight children how she manages. She says that she loves her children and enjoys caring for them. This is what she said: "If you have less children it's harder. In a large family, there is more discipline. The older children help and the children always have someone with whom to play. The Sabbath table is a pleasure, with each child telling stories he or she learned from school." The children in these families actually get more positive attention because the mother isn't wiped out from yelling at them. She doesn't feel free to scream, because the other children are watching and she doesn't have to scream because the children have older siblings who take over the police work. The Mama is the judge. If that doesn't work, it goes to the Papa!

Of course, these mothers can't work very many hours outside of the home. However, when their offspring are older and are more independent, these mothers develop to be super-talented as office managers, teachers, therapists, cooks, and anything else mothering has taught them.

In old age the children take turns caring for their parents. They may chip in to get full time help if necessary. The option of an old age home is only a very last resort, but if there is no choice, the elderly parents continue to see one of their children or grandchildren almost every day.

It is a very big mitzvah to visit the elderly even if they are not your relatives. When you visit them you give them life. If you make a regular schedule to visit, you are giving them something to live for and anticipate.

Do not murder is not only a commandment not to kill, it is also a commandment to give life to those who are alive and to save lives.

War

The Torah values life, but it also teaches us to kill our enemies. The lives of our families and the lives our people are to be protected, even at the cost of the lives of others.

> Deuteronomy 29:16 says, "From the nations of the cities that I gave you for an inheritance, do not allow any soul to live."

If someone tries to kill you, you have to attack first. If a nation plans to go to war with you, you have to start. When you go to war to protect your country, you are actually fulfilling the commandment not to murder, by defending your brothers.

Leviticus 19:18 says, "You shall love your friend as yourself." The word for friend in this text is *"raya"* in Hebrew. Raya can also mean comrade or fellow soldier on the battlefield. Many movies portray how close and how loyal some soldiers are to each other in a time of war. War is a time when you must sacrifice everything for your fellow soldier and your people. Many have commented that a soldier's primary and major motivation to fight is to preserve the lives of their comrades, over and above love of country.

Let's pray for a time that there will be no war as it says in Isaiah 2:4, "No nation will raise a sword against another nation and they will not learn the trade of war anymore."

King David

King David had a lot of trouble deciding whom to kill and with whom to have mercy.

> 1 Samuel 24:6 says, "God forbid that I should raise a hand over my master who is anointed by God …"

This is a phrase taken from the story of David and King Saul, Israel's first anointed monarch. King Saul personally pursued against David, chasing him with his army in order to kill him. David had the opportunity to slay Saul while he was sleeping, but instead he cut the corner of his coat to prove that he could have killed him but didn't. Later on in 2 Samuel 19 when David's son Absalom dies trying to kill his father, David mourns him. King David's first general, Joab, gets very cross with David and gives him the following speech:

> 2 Samuel 19:6–8
>
> And it was told to Joab, "Behold, the king weeps and mourns for Absalom." And the victory that day turned into mourning for all the people as the people heard that day how the king grieved for his son. And the people snuck that day into the city, ashamed as if they were fleeing in battle. But the king covered his face and cried with a loud voice, "Oh my son Absalom, Oh Absalom, my son, my son!" And Joab

came into the house and said to the king, "You have shamed this day the faces of all your servants, which this day have saved your life, and the lives of your sons and daughters, as well as the lives of your wives and your concubines. Thus you love your enemies and you hate your friends for you have declared this day a day of mourning. You have no regard for princes or servants; for I understand that on this day, if Absalom had lived, and all we had died instead on this day, then it would have well pleased you. Now therefore arise, go forth, and speak to comfort your servants; for I swear by the Lord, if you don't go forth, no one else will remain with you tonight and it will also be worse for you than all the evil that has come upon you since your youth until now." Then the king arose, and sat in the gate. And the people were told, "Behold, the king sits at the gate." Then all the people returned to the king for every Israelite had fled to his tent.

David had trouble his whole life saving his enemies and killing his friends. As a matter of fact, before he died, he ordered his son Solomon to kill Joab his first general, blaming him for the death of Abner, a general from the enemy's side, (1 Kings who took the life of Joab's brother, Asahel (2 Samuel 2). Joab was impudent, but he was correct in his assumptions.

He observed how David sometimes forgave and even loved his enemies whether they were family or not, and hated his friends and loyal subjects in the case of war with Absalom.

Sometimes we also have to judge our priorities. We should protect our spouse and children with our lives and not let others interfere with the peace in our home. See who your enemies are and cut off relationships with them lest they cause more damage.

The state of Israel arose after almost two thousand years of slaughter and persecution, in the merit of simple Jews who were willing to fight, kill, and be killed for their people and their country. We don't love to kill and we don't live to kill, but sometimes we have to kill to live.

By fighting your enemy, you are protecting your country and family from being killed. Therefore, not only is fighting in the army not a transgression of the sixth Commandment "Do not murder," but your soldiers are actually fulfilling the mitzvah not to murder by protecting their country and the people in it from enemies who would slaughter every man, woman and child if given the chance.

Chapter 10

Do Not Commit Adultery or Incest

Let's start this chapter with a joke: Once upon a time, a man wondered if sex was work or play. He was not sure if having sex on the Sabbath was a sin. He sought out a priest and asked him his opinion. After reviewing his Bible, the priest finally announced that he was certain that sex was work and therefore not permitted on the Sabbath.

The man thought, *"What could a priest know about sex?"*

So he went to a minister, who after all was a married man and experienced in this matter.

The minister reviewed his Bible extensively and subsequently replied the same as the priest. The minister ruled that sex was work and forbidden on the Sabbath.

Still unsatisfied, the man sought out the highest authority he could imagine. He thought that a rabbi must have studied many volumes of books of wisdom and Torah knowledge. So he asked the rabbi. He expected he would also have to wait a while to receive an answer. To his surprise, the rabbi responded immediately, " Sex is definitely to be considered as play and permitted on the Sabbath."

The man was astonished. *"How could the rabbi answer so promptly and definitely without taking time to pour over the Bible and the Talmud?"* He asked the rabbi, "How could you be so sure, when others studied the question so much more extensively and disagreed?" The rabbi answered softly, " If sex were work, my wife would have the maid do it!"

****

Even though Orthodox Jews are very modest and strict with their unmarried offspring, once they are engaged to marry, their adult children are introduced to a culture that has a very positive, and good-humored outlook towards marital sex.

The Torah has a lot of different names for sex. The very first word used for sex is "to know." The exact translation of Genesis 4:1 is, "Adam knew Eve his wife and she became pregnant and bore Cain …"

The second name that is used is for sex is "playing." Genesis 26:8 says, "Isaac is playing with his wife Rebecca."

The English translation of this commandment is not really accurate. Adultery in English is defined as one spouse cheating on the other. *"Lo Tinaf "* in the Hebrew means, "Do not have any prohibited relationship," the worst of all being incest. Some of the laws of prohibited relationships are mentioned in detail in Leviticus 18:6: "Every man should not get close to his blood relative to reveal nudity." Revealing nudity is another term used for sex, usually forbidden sex. The most common terms used in the Bible for sex is "to know" and to "lay down with."

In addition to the incestual and forbidden sexual bondings that are included in the Seventh Commandment, "Lo Tinaf,"

Do Not Commit Adultery, comes the proscription not to allow your child to become a prostitute. A prostitute in Torah terms means any promiscuous activity, one-night stands, continual changing and exchanging partners, even if the swapping of bodily fluids or partners are not for money.

Are Men and Women Created Equal?

The Torah does not forgive any sexual transgressions. There is a death penalty for incest whether the sinner is male or female. As far as infidelity is concerned, any man, single or married, who has sex together with a married woman is considered an adulterer. A married woman who, with mutual consent, has sex with any male, other than her husband, is an adulteress. If a married woman is raped, of course she is not considered an adulteress as this would be an exception to this rule. The Torah is more forgiving to a man who cheats on his wife with a single woman. If she was innocent and did not know that he was married, he may have to give her a monetary compensation. In fact, polygamy is not forbidden by Torah law as long as the first wife agrees.

The prophets compare the children of Israel worshiping idols to an adulterous married woman.

> Jeremiah 3:20, But like a woman unfaithful to her husband, so you, Israel, have been unfaithful to me," declares the Lord.

Sometimes the wayward Israelites are compared to a prostitute.

> Jeremiah 3:1, "If a man divorces his wife and she leaves him and marries another man, should he return to her again? Would not the land be completely defiled? But you have lived as a prostitute with many lovers—would you now return to me?" declares the Lord.

We never see any comparison between the children of Israel with a cheating husband. This is not because the Torah is prejudiced against women; on the contrary, the Torah considers women to be on a higher level than men and therefore less forgivable.

> Isaiah 4:3-5
> Those who are left in Zion, who remain in Jerusalem, will be called holy, all who are recorded among the living in Jerusalem. The Lord will wash away the filth of the women of Zion; he will cleanse the bloodstains from Jerusalem by a spirit of judgment and a spirit of fire. Then the LORD will create over all of Mount Zion and over those who assemble there a cloud of smoke by day and a glow of flaming fire by night; over everything the glory will be a canopy.

Isaiah is describing a future redemption where the women will be cleansed before the men. After the women are cleansed the city of Jerusalem will be cleansed. It is much easier for women to feel God's presence and holiness. If they even think of sinning by breaking their marital loyalty, their soul screams out. If they sin anyway, it is much more grievous than if a man sins.

This prophecy was already fulfilled. When Ezra retuned to Israel to build the Holy Temple, he commanded the Israeli inhabitants to leave their idol worshipping heathen wives and take Jewish wives to build new families. You can learn more about that in my new book, *God's Hidden Treasure*.

Be Holy

Leviticus 19:1 reads: "Be holy for I am holy." This is a general and everlasting statement that means, "Don't play tricks on God." You know in your heart what a respectable holy person should be doing. This is the opening statement of a chapter all about forbidden relationships. From this passage we should understand that a man shouldn't cheat on his wife or on anybody, whether sexually, financially, or otherwise. A man who cheats on his wife is breaking his marriage contract; that is his covenant between man, woman and God. If a married woman sleeps with a man other than her husband, the man cannot forgive her and take her back unless the woman was raped or forced to have sex against her will.

The Torah cannot give a death penalty to someone who has sex with a person he is allowed to marry. Marrying more than one wife was a normal, accepted practice at the time when the Torah was given and for centuries afterwards.

Historically, even up until the past century, divorce was a fate worse than death for women. There were no jobs for women. If the ancient man wanted to divorce his wife because she didn't bear children or because she was emotionally ill, he would just take another wife and continue to support her.

If a man cheated on his wife, what good would it do the woman if her husband got the death penalty? Who would support her? God wants her husband to be strong and healthy so he can support her for the rest of his life, even if he divorces her.

Before every Jewish couple gets married, the groom is asked how much money he wants to put on the marriage contract or *Ketuba,* in case of divorce. Usually it is a large sum of money, and it is announced at the site of the wedding ceremony. If a court finds a man guilty of infidelity, he must pay his wife the full amount of money that is written on their *Ketuba,* in addition to all their mutually owned property and full support. In other words, an unfaithful man would have to forfeit his house and support his ex-wife and children, even if she remarries.

OK, so I understand why the man doesn't get the death penalty, but why should an adulterous woman be put to death?

First of all, death penalty was never instituted in Jewish courts without the required two eyewitnesses and a warning. A guilty plea is not acceptable. However, the Torah does institute a special procedure for a woman who is suspected of infidelity.

In Numbers chapter 5:11-31, there is a law pertaining to a married woman who was seen going into a room alone with another man after her husband already warned her not to have anything to do with that person.

The woman is to be brought to the high priest in a public ceremony. She must swear that she did not sleep with the man in question. If at this point she wants to confess she can. If she swears to her innocence, her hair is uncovered and untied, and she must drink bitter water from a clay cup that had Torah verses, written inside of it. If she is guilty, her whole insides explode but if she is innocent, then she is blessed to have a child.

The Torah makes this whole embarrassing procedure in order to cure the husband's jealousy. He himself might be hesitant to bring his wife up for charges if she had to go through a public ordeal like that.

In a society where men were very jealous, it was important to have a sure fire way to stop jealousy from ruining a marriage. A threat of a death penalty was another important factor. When a woman knew that she is under threat of a death penalty she would probably be very cautious to avoid flirtatious men.

In actuality, the death penalty for promiscuity meant that this is an unforgivable sin. The woman must be divorced and can only be forgiven after she dies. In a small town, a woman who was divorced because of such a suspicion, might also be excommunicated, but there is no historical accounting, that we know of, about an actual execution for the crime of infidelity in a Jewish court of law.

Seduction

If an unmarried man seduces a virgin, the punishment is either monetary payment or he is obligated to marry her and never divorce her for the rest of his life. Seducing a woman who is engaged or married is another story. It's a death penalty for the man and woman.

In this day and age, there is no death penalty for adultery. After the destruction of the Holy Temple, Hashem changed his attitude toward the death penalty.

> Ezekiel 33:11, "Say to them, 'As surely as I live, declares the Sovereign LORD, I take no pleasure in the death of the wicked, but rather that they turn from their ways and live. Turn! Turn from your evil ways! Why will you die, people of Israel?'"

Hashem saw that even after thousands of people died for their sins during the horrific wars leading to the destruction of the Holy Temple, the people didn't change. The only ones who changed were those who had a change of heart. That is true today as well. Threats and punishment don't help so much, only learning and understanding can bring about a change of heart.

However, even to this day, if a woman cheats on her husband or fiancé, she is forbidden to return to her man. She is also forbidden to marry the man with whom she cheated. The Israeli rabbinate will not allow a couple to marry if they cheated together while either one of them was married. If two divorcees wish to marry and one of them was divorced because of infidelity, the rabbis may demand the couple to take an oath that they did not sleep with each other when they were married to their former spouses, before allowing the couple to get married.

Sexual Intercourse out of Wedlock

The Torah does not specifically explain the laws of marriage and did not include a prohibition against premarital sex in the Ten Commandments. However, Hashem feels very strongly against premarital sex. Sex has a very powerful energy to bond two people. It is very painful to have an intimate relationship and then separate, Hashem cannot condone a relationship with no commitment.

If that is the case, why is there not a clear prohibition in the Ten Commandments or in the Torah against premarital sex? Here are a few reasons:

1) It is up to man to create laws of marriage and divorce. Ancient men had no wedding; they just took a wife for themselves and brought her into their cave. That's the way Adam and Eve did it and that was acceptable.
2) As mentioned previously, there is prohibition on prostitution. You are forbidden to let your child become a prostitute or a gigolo. Throughout history, and even in parts of the world today, parents have forced and nowadays do coerce their children to make money for the family through harlotry. Child brides historically and even today made and make the big bucks for the parents.

   The restriction against whoring includes all sexual activity that is not faithful to one partner. Sexual relations with multiple partners are not allowed. Such would be considered prostitution and a direct violation of the Seventh Commandment, forbidding said activity in Deuteronomy 23:18.

   Deuteronomy 23:18
   "No Israelite man or woman is to become a shrine prostitute. You must not bring the earnings of a female prostitute or of a male prostitute into the house of the LORD your God to pay any vow, because the LORD your God detests them both."

3) If a couple already has a relationship and wish to marry, they might be soul mates. Hashem doesn't want to punish the couple because that might discourage them from getting married. If premarital sex was prohibited in the Ten Commandments, you would have to break up with the partner with whom you sinned.
4) There is a law in the Torah for a man who has sex with a virgin who is single without her consent:

> Deuteronomy 22:28-29, "If a man happens to meet a virgin who is not pledged to be married and rapes her and they are discovered, he shall pay her father fifty shekels of silver. He must marry the young woman, for he has violated her. Because he made her suffer he can never divorce her as long as he lives.

The NIV translation above says that the man raped the woman. This is an incorrect translation of the word *shachav* which means lay. Secondly, the scripture says that the couple were discovered. It suggests that they are both together in action and in mind. The man must marry the woman or he must pay her father fifty shekels of silver.

Why would there be such a big mistake in the NIV? That's because at the end of the paragraph the scripture says because the man made her suffer he cannot divorce her for the rest of his life.

This word suffer, *enah,* is used in the story of Dinah denoting rape. There is no question that Dinah was raped. However, in this case the suffering will be corrected by having the man pledge never to divorce her. It is obviously not a rape, the Torah would not recommend that the rapist marry his victim. The suffering here is the shame that she feels because she is not a virgin anymore.

This woman might have agreed to have sex because she was seduced. Then she wanted to marry her beloved but he may not have wanted to marry her. This happens a lot in modern society, men don't want to commit. This causes women tremendous suffering so that the remedy "he may never divorce her the rest of his life," surely fits. The man has the choice to marry her or to make a payment to her father, which would serve as the girl's future dowry.

If the father sees that this man will not be a good husband for his daughter, he has the veto power to prevent the couple from marrying, take the money in order to give his daughter a bigger dowry and marry someone else.

Transgressions that have a monetary punishment are not mentioned in the Ten Commandments. The Ten Commandments are like the Constitution, only the basics. Details are written in the Torah.

It is possible that the virgin just said that the man seduced her against her will, in order to save face. That's OK—the father doesn't have to know exactly what happened. He just has to consent to the marriage and not disown her, like some cultures used to in ancient times. This teaches us that the Bible does not want you to disown children because they had premarital sex.

5) The laws of the Ten Commandments are very strict, and they apply to the whole world. They are commandments that are necessary to have a properly functioning society. The lack of a marriage contract between two adults is not detrimental to society if the couple stays loyal to each other. Some places in

the world may not even have had a written language in which to write a contract.

The sin of not being married is not against society; it is against your intimate partner. Each partner in an intimate relationship deserves to feel secure and have a sense of belonging to a family. When you marry publically, especially when you have a nice big wedding, aside from the legal bond, a spiritual bond is created, even if the wedding is not ceremoniously religious. Without a binding marriage contract to the present partner, given in front of two witnesses, the relationship can never reach full mutual trust in which each spouse can feel relaxed belongingness.

Premarital sex is not specifically forbidden in the Ten Commandments. Nevertheless, promiscuous sex breeds jealously, a violation of the Tenth Commandment, "Do not Covet."

Any corruption of courts of justice violates the Ninth Commandment, "Do Not Bear False Witness." Remarkably, bribes of sex for acquittal from legal charges are well enough known. This is perverse and considered sexual debasement of both judge and/or other court member(s) and defendant. The heavenly punishment for perjury is a lot worse than earthy verdicts, as bad as they can be, in terms of fines and even prison terms.

Non-consensual sex, date rape and forced rape at the threat of bodily harm to the point of death at the point of a knife or gun, are all forms of theft much worse than stealing money or goods. All these violent crimes are not crimes of passion. They are all crimes of power known simply as kidnapping. Abduction for the purpose of sex or money is the most severe violent violation of the Seventh Commandment, "Do Not Steal."

Countless murders are committed by rapists in addition to jealous partners. Wanton killing violates the prohibition of the Sixth Commandment, "Do Not Murder".

Now let us consider a modern-day phenomenon that occurs throughout the world. Currently, American middle schools through twelfth grade curriculums teach sex education classes. Some schools begin their sex education classes as early as the fourth grade. These classes teach youth and teenagers the subjects of equality and freedom of choice in the United States. Sex education teachers supposedly implant their students with a sense to responsibly engage in sexual relations before the age of consent to marry. Of course, the eager students are warned that the teen male partner, no matter the age of teen or adult partner of heterosexual or homosexual intercourse, uses a condom to prevent from disease and possible unwanted teen pregnancy. Female teens may double down on any contraceptive they wish, with or without parental consent. All possible birth control options are available at pharmacies and especially at Planned Parenthood Clinics. Even if the prevention method or device fails and pregnancy ensues, the young female teens may choose to receive abortions at some state Planned Parenthood Clinics, without either cost or their parents' knowledge and approval, as the girls exercise their so-called rights.

Countless lives of teenagers have been damaged psychologically, mentally, physically, and spiritually from being exposed to sex education by teachers under the public schools' authority in the name of freedom, racial and gender choice equality. Assault, one on one rape, group rape and murder have become too commonplace in the school systems as a result of teaching free sex, however responsible the students are taught to be.

Teens under the age of eighteen are prohibited to purchase alcohol and tobacco. However, with the blessing of public schools, teens at any age can go into any store to purchase condoms and use them to their hearts content in order to have sex with either gender. Consent to marry is required if they wish to marry before eighteen years of age, but it is not required to have parental consent to attend sex education classes which permit and encourage sexual activity to teenagers, well under age eighteen.

When youngsters have sex and even abortions against their parents will and often enough without their knowledge, they are breaking the Fifth Commandment, "Honor Your Father and Mother."

Our Sages taught us to put a fence around the Torah. In a God-fearing society there is no premarital sex. Children are protected from the horrible effects of the media and even study in schools the are gender segregated. They grow up with an emphasis on their studies and are introduced to prospective partners when they are ready. Eighty-three percent of the Jewish Orthodox individuals marry before the age of thirty. The absolute majority of this sector build beautiful families with mutual trust. They have no fear of infidelity. These religious couples have the peace of mind to rear their children to help each other and to teach them to follow the Torah.

Loyalty

The best way to ensure full commitment and loyalty is in the form of a marriage contract. Without it the person you love stays in emotional limbo, waiting for your commitment. Women are sometimes so desperate for that commitment that they have children out of wedlock, hoping that a baby will tie the knot. Some people try to be cool and sustain an uncommitted relationship, but this affects them as a whole. American individualism has been so overvalued that it has encouraged many people to being very cold and self-centered. Many women make-believe that they don't mind being single, while crying inside their hearts. A marriage contract takes away boundaries between each other as individuals and places them around each other as a couple. That's the way it should be.

In the chapter, "Honor Your Father and Mother," I mentioned that loyalty to one's spouse takes priority over loyalty to one's parents and even loyalty to one's fiancé takes priority over loyalty to anyone else in the world. Like it says in Genesis 2:24, "Therefore a man should leave his mother and father and cling to his wife."

Sexual loyalty is of course a basic necessity for an honorable and healthy marriage. In addition to sexual fidelity, we have to be loyal to our spouse in many other ways too. The easiest way to make sure that you remain loyal is to prohibit secrets between each other. If you always stay open and tell the truth to each other and you maintain emotional honesty, you will never approach the point of infidelity. Here too, we have to remember the passage in Leviticus 18:1, "Be holy, for I am holy."

Everything that Happens is from Hashem

The American value is that you work and get results. If something goes wrong; tough luck. I feel sorry for people who have to live like that. If you live with a feeling that God is with you and everything that happens is because it was His will, then why get angry at people? Hashem would rather that we got angry at Him than at our family or friends. He can take the heat. If you get angry at Him, at least it shows that you know whose "fault" it really is! Hashem does everything for our benefit and he reproves those He loves.

> Proverbs 3:11-12, "My son, do not despise the LORD's discipline and do not resent his rebuke, because the LORD disciplines those he loves, as a father the son he delights in."

Are you going to get angry at God because your wife spilled coffee on your new tie? Then how can you get angry with your spouse? Unless she or he does something really wrong, a definite transgression against the Ten commandments, you should cling to each other. As it says in Genesis 2:24, "Therefore a man should leave his father and mother and cling to his wife and they shall be one flesh."

> Malachi 2:15 says, "Has not the one God made you? You belong to him in body and spirit. And what does the one God seek? Godly offspring. So be on your guard, and do not be unfaithful to the wife of your youth."

Here the scripture mentions the husband's duty to be loyal, just in case someone might think that since there is no death penalty on the husband who cheats with an unmarried woman, or that such cheating is all right. It is only forgivable if the man leaves his mistress and repents with all his heart. His wife can forgive him, but if she doesn't, she has a right to divorce with full alimony.

> The NIV translation of Malachi 2:16 says, "The man who hates and divorces his wife," says the Lord, the God of Israel, "does violence to the one he should protect," says the Lord Almighty. So be on your guard, and do not be unfaithful."
>
> The above translation is in error. The following is the correct translation of the Hebrew: Malachi 2:16, "He who hates her must divorce her said the Lord of hosts, and cover the wickedness on his clothing, and protect your spirit and do not cheat on her."

We also know from other sources that the Torah permits divorce, for example: ...

> Deuteronomy 24:1, "If a man marries a woman who becomes displeasing to him because he finds something indecent about her, and he writes her a certificate of divorce, gives it to her and sends her from his house..."

The true meaning of the words of Malachi are "If you hate your wife, then divorce her." Malachi encourages divorce rather than betrayal; alimony is a continuation of that loyalty. Sex is an act that can be very spiritual or very impure. Hashem does not want people who hate each other to have sex. Therefore, the prophet says He would rather they got divorced.

Even if you are not planning divorce but you are at odds with each other or there is tension in the air, you shouldn't have sex with your spouse. Hashem doesn't like it. You must have a meeting of the minds and hearts before you have a meeting of the bodies.

A marriage contract is a holy contract; we must do everything in our power to have a good healthy marriage. However, we don't have to sacrifice our health or the health of our children for any mitzvah. Therefore, if you've tried your best to have peace in the home and you've exhausted all other possibilities, divorce may be the only way for you to have a happy and healthy life. Hashem wants us to be happy. He will be proud of you if you do the right thing for yourself and your children. Here too the red line should be the Ten Commandments. Aside from infidelity, if your spouse defies God, steals, lies in court or hurts others in a dangerous way, count yourself out.

Homosexuality

The Hebrew words for the seventh commandments is *Lo Tinaf.* The exact translation of those words is "Do not commit a sexual abomination." This would include any prohibited sex that is mentioned in the Bible. The Torah prohibits sex between two men.

> Leviticus 18:22
> Do not have sexual relations with a man as one does with a woman; that is detestable.

Homosexuality is considered "*Lo Tinaf*" and transgresses the seventh commandment. Sex between females is not specifically prohibited; however, any sexual relationship that is out of wedlock is considered promiscuous activity.

Indulgence in sex is one of the things that pushes God away. From the 1960s, America's young adults started a movement to free up emotionally as well as sexually. The emotional freedom was very good for the world, but sexual liberty actually prevents emotional growth. When you pursue physical pleasures, you become a slave to your desires. You then don't do what's right for your soul; you do what your body wants. Freud called this the id ruling over the ego and the superego, which is normal and appropriate for immature children but not mature adults.

Homosexuality and heterosexual licentiousness start with discontent from indulgence in premarital sex for pleasure. If people don't find sufficient satisfaction from excessive hedonism with the opposite sex, they may look for sexual fulfillment with the same sex. Subsequent discontent may lead to bisexual experimentation and orientation. With still further unhappiness from failing to achieve sexual ecstasy, the disgruntled may progress to threesomes and then advance to orgies and illicit drugs.

We are not created to have sex for our own selfish indulgence. Sex is a very spiritual act and is not to be taken lightly. Sex can heal, and sex can destroy. Children, teenagers, and adults young and old must respect themselves and their holy souls. If there were no thought of having sex out of wedlock, there surely would be no sexual experimentation or ensuing searches to find one's own sexual orientation.

Teenagers should be busy with their schoolwork and should not be bothered with any kind of sexual behavior until they are married. This is the case in Orthodox Jewish schools. The boys are in different schools than the girls. When they are anywhere between eighteen and twenty-four, they start to date for the sole purpose of marriage. They then develop beautiful marriages and families. These couples have no fear that their spouse will look at others, let alone cheat.

According to medical science, our brains keep developing with their most significant advancement from birth until age twenty-four. In these years, you can train yourself to be who you want to be. You can train yourself to be needy of love or sensual pleasure from the same sex or even from people who are much younger or older than you. Indulging in sexual thoughts is detrimental to a young person's mind and can alter the personality and even sexual orientation. Sexually explicit X or even suggestive R rated films, let alone harder pornography, damage a person's spiritual advancement and can even damage one's character.

Even though as I mentioned earlier that the Torah does not prohibit lesbian relationships, it does not condone it. A woman can only be truly happy if she has a husband and a family. That is the way Hashem created her. The reason why Hashem didn't write a specific prohibition against lesbianism is because women like to hug and kiss. They even enjoy cuddling up in bed together. This is natural and harmless. If lesbianism was forbidden, then there would be rabbis who would not even allow girls to touch each other just as they prohibit boys from cuddling up with each other or sleeping in the same bed. For girls cuddling and hugging is natural. It would be stifling to normal girl to girl friendships if any boundaries were forced. It could even cause irreparable damage if girls in orphanages were not allowed to cuddle.

Don't Worship Your Man

There are a few secrets that Hashem would like to share with you about the relationship between husband and wife. Sometimes we are so close to our spouse that we forget Hashem. In this case Hashem can cause a rift between husband and wife in order that we seek help from Him.

In a book *Women in the Nineteenth Century* by Margaret Fuller, she describes the relationship between husband and wife at the time as being like idolatry. She was beginning a movement toward woman's liberation, and she observed how women look up to their husbands too much.

The fear that some women have toward their husbands takes away from fear of God. We should fear no man; the fear of God will free you from all other fears.

> Leviticus 25:17, " Do not take advantage of each other, but fear your God. I am the LORD your God."

The words "take advantage" here is a translation from the word *tonu* which means to hurt one another with words. If you say what you like with no regard to what impact it will have on your spouse, you surely do not fear God. On the other hand, if you work on yourself to be close to Hashem before trouble starts up between you and your spouse, you will certainly avoid a lot of stress.

Peace in the home is a spiritual gift. We should pray to have this gift which in turn brings health, wealth and happiness. Writing love letters may seem old fashioned but they still work. What works even better is a poem or a song for your beloved. The following poem is a letter to my husband that I wrote while he was on a trip away from home:

To My Dear Husband

I when I'm alone,
My heart is always
With you.
I can feel your thoughts
Your feeling and your needs.
I long so much,
not only just to see you,
But to hear your voice
To feel your energy.

Listen Hashem,
Take care, of the
Ones we love.
Instill in them a trust
For the one above.
How our lives depend
Upon each other.
Give us help to get along
With one another.

A man was created not
To be on his own.
A woman really doesn't
Like to be alone.
We thank Hashem for
Bringing us together.
And helping us to make
Our lives always better.

Even though,
You're not always with me
I know that in your heart

I'm always near
When we join,
Our forces together.
There will be no one that
We will fear.

Listen Hashem
Take care,
Of the ones we love.
Instill in them a trust
For the one above.
How our lives depend
Upon each other.
Give us help to get along
With one another.

Sexual Prohibitions

In Leviticus 18 and 20, the scripture mentions different prohibitions against incest. Surprisingly enough the prohibition on sleeping with your uncle's wife, your relative through marriage, is just as bad as sleeping with your own genetically related aunt (Leviticus 20:20). Even if the uncle passed away the prohibition holds. If your uncle divorced his wife, she is still your aunt, and therefore it is forbidden for you to marry her. The same goes for your father's wife, even if your father is no longer alive. Leviticus 18:8 says, "Don't reveal your father's wife's nudity, it is your father's nudity."

The Torah is teaching us that when two people are married, they become part of your family, not only in a friendly way but also in a spiritual way. Your father's wife is your father's other half, and therefore she is your close relative. Sleeping with her is considered incest.

Your Own Flesh and Blood

> Isaiah 58:7
> "Is it not to share your food with the hungry and to provide the poor wanderer with shelter—when you see the naked, to clothe them, and not to turn away from your own flesh and blood?"

The reason there is a question mark here is because the prophet Isaiah is giving reproof to the people for fasting on holy fast days without any repentance to change oneself for the better. Isaiah is asking the people, "Isn't one of the reasons that we fast is in order to know what it is to be hungry?" If we know what it feels like to be hungry then when we see a hungry person we will feel sorry for him and share our food. Scripture says that if our own flesh and blood is in need, we may not ignore them. Our sages teach us that your own flesh and blood is anyone from your family including your divorcee and her children, even if they are not your biological children.

It says in Genesis 2:24, "And they will be one flesh." The Bible doesn't say one flesh about any other relationship. Therefore, if your ex-wife or ex-husband is in need, it is more important for you to help her or him, than to give charity to a friend in the same situation. Even after divorce, she remains your relative.

If a man or woman has the means to help out others who are lacking food shelter and clothing, the first responsibility is to your spouse and your children. The second responsibility is to your parents and your parents-in-law. The third responsibility is to your ex-husband or ex-wife and their families. The fourth is to your siblings and their families and then to your good friends.

This is where premarital sex causes a complication. If you have intercourse with someone, he or she becomes your flesh and blood. You can't just make that bond go away. If you do not know the whereabouts of your many sex partners and you wish to repent, then Hashem says you should pray for them and pray for the old bonds to be broken and reattached to your one and only beloved. This is very distressing for our poor neshama. Our neshama is the very innocent part of our soul, it is also the vessel for our speech and wisdom. Think of your neshama as a little child. It needs tender loving care without exposing it to illicit sexual practices. Your neshama feels love and bonds very quickly. The damage that endures is immeasurable. On the other hand, Hashem doesn't want us to be celibate, He wants us to have one spouse because then we can feel whole and we each can teach the other half of our soul to know Hashem.

Who Is Your Closest Relative?

Most marital problems stem from the fact that the couple does not realize that they have a very special relationship that is closer than blood relatives. As a matter of fact, as mentioned previously, your spouse is closer to you than your parents.

> Genesis 2:24 says, "Therefore a man should leave his mother and father and cling to his wife."

If we would consider our spouse as our relative, we wouldn't ridicule her about her relatives or strange mannerisms. It's all in the family.

When couples marry for a second time, the stepchildren are true children of their stepparent. They may not be related genetically but their souls are related. If those families would realize this, there would be much more peace in their homes. The word *stepmother* has a very bad connotation because of the story of Cinderella. If you must tell that story, don't use the word *stepsister* or *stepmother*.

Donor Eggs

In today's modern times, there is a possibility of becoming pregnant through an egg donor. A younger woman can donate her eggs to someone who cannot otherwise get pregnant. If a woman takes a donor egg in order to get pregnant and the sperm is her husband's, the child is hers without a doubt. If she has other children from a previous relationship, the donor child is their sibling. Even if the child was born through a surrogate mother, the child of the biological father is also the child of his wife. Family is a straight plane, no steps.

Jewish law does not allow donor sperm unless the woman who wants to become pregnant is single. Because a woman is forbidden to have two husbands. It wouldn't be right to use donor sperm for a married woman. Nevertheless, if children were born through a donor sperm they cannot be considered bastards as they would be if the father of the children were an illicit lover. A mamzer or a bastard is the product of forbidden sex, not just a genetic mix.

We have friends who were sure they would not be able to have children because the doctors found no sperm in the husband's medical tests. However, with a closer look, experts were able to find some sperm in his testes and the couple had a beautiful baby boy. Modern medicine is doing wonders to help fertility, it's amazing!

The genes are given by the parents, but the soul is given by Hashem. When Hashem gives you a child through surrogacy, donor egg, or adoption, He gives the child a soul from your soul's family, just as he does for a biological child. Every adoptive parent knows that this is true. They have similarities with their adopted children that are uncanny.

The Song of Songs

The Song of Songs is a book in the Bible that is very often questioned. Why did our sages include the Song of Songs in the Bible at all? At face value it seems like a love story. Our rabbis teach us that this book is a parable between God and the people of Israel. Hashem doesn't want us to be in love with Him like the love between a man and a woman. He loves us like a father and a mother both combined, but not like a lover.

The Song of Songs opens with the words, "Let him kiss me with the kisses of his mouth—for your love is more delightful than wine." (Song of Songs 1:2) The word for love here is *Dodecha,* which really means your uncle or relative. The woman calls the man my beloved *"Dodi,"* which means my uncle in the Torah. The first time that the word *Dodim* has any other meaning is in Ezekiel 16:3 and

23:17, where it means lovers. The woman in the Song of Songs is not related to her beloved genetically, and that's why all the translations translate Dodi as my beloved. She is a relative to her beloved because her beloved is her husband.

Here are a few examples illustrating my assertion, that Song of Songs is speaking about a married couple.

> Song of Songs 4:3, "Your cheek is like a slice of pomegranate behind your kerchief." Jewish women only cover their hair after marriage.
>
> Song of Songs 4:12, "The garden is closed my sister my bride ..." The man calls the woman, "My sister my bride." This is because she feels as close as a sister but she is his bride.
>
> Song of Songs 8:7, "Many waters cannot quench love; rivers cannot sweep it away. If one were to give all the wealth of one's house for love, it would be utterly scorned."

In the last passage the Bible is trying to say that real love cannot be extinguished by the cold, unromantic waters of life and if someone wants to buy real love with money, that means he doesn't know what love is. Those who have love will make fun of him for wanting to buy love.

This allegory relates to the ancient custom of paying a father for his daughter. If someone thinks he can get a girl to love him just because he "owns" her, he should be ridiculed.

This paragraph alone shows true divine wisdom centuries ahead of its time. The Song of Songs is a song of love between a man and his wife and should be studied in order to know how important romance between husband and wife is, in this world and the next. If a couple is really close in this world they may merit to be in heaven together.

In the last chapter of Song of Songs, the couple is settled and is looking out for their sister. Song of Songs 8:8 says, "What shall we do for our sister on the day that she is spoken for?" She is *our* sister because your sister-in-law is your sister. "The day that she is spoken for" means that someone is looking to date her for the purpose of marriage. This couple is not going to worry about their little sister finding a mate if they themselves are not married.

The Song of Songs was put into the Bible because it puts marriage into a different perspective. Your spouse is your beloved; your beloved is closer than your closest relative. Your beloved's sister is your sister too. True love that includes true loyalty is the exact opposite of adultery.

The Blessing of Peace

The worst kind of sex is sexual idol worship. Idolaters used to have sex with harlots in front of the idols as part of a ceremony. Phinehas the grandson of Aaron was blessed with eternal peace for killing the leader of the tribe of Simeon while having sex with a gentile harlot from the enemy camp. He killed the two idolaters by stabbing a sword through their bodies.

> Numbers 25:7–8, "When Phinehas son of Elazar, the son of Aaron, the priest, saw this, he left the assembly, took a spear in his hand and followed the Israelite into the tent. He drove the spear into both of them, right through the Israelite man and into the woman's stomach. Then the plague against the Israelites was stopped."

> Numbers 25:10–12, "And Hashem said to Moses: "Phinehas the son of Elazar, son of Aaron the priest, has turned back my wrath from the people of Israel, in that he was zealous with my zealousness among them, so that I did not consume the people of Israel in my zealousness." Therefore, say, "Behold, I give to him my covenant of peace."

Phinehas, a sixteen-year-old boy, was so zealous for God that he felt as if he was personally insulted by the impudence of the Israelites. Phinehas speared Zimri, an Israelite leader of the tribe of Simeon, who coupled with one of many harlots for idol worshipers, from the people of Midian. Hashem promised Phinehas a covenant of peace. A few chapters earlier, Hashem commands Aaron and his sons to bless the children of Israel with peace:

> Numbers 6:22-27
> The LORD said to Moses, "Tell Aaron and his sons, 'This is how you are to bless the Israelites.' Say to them: 'The LORD bless you and keep you; the LORD make his face shine on you and be gracious to you; the LORD turn his face toward you and give you peace.' So they will put my name on the Israelites, and I will bless them."

This is the famous priestly blessing that was said in the Holy Temple and is still recited today in every Jewish synagogue by descendants of the children of Aaron whom we call Cohanim (priests). This is God's covenant of peace and the following is God's interpretation:

- *"Hashem will bless you."* Before you are born, God blesses you with talents, intelligence, character, beauty, and everything else with which you are born.

- *"And keep you"* the exact translation is, "He will watch over you and protect you." When you are a child, He keeps you alive. Children are always doing dangerous things, and Hashem is always there to save them.
- *"Hashem will make His face shine on you."* Hashem doesn't have a face. How can His face shine?

When you see the face of your soul mate, you can see the light of your own soul in his or her face. Our soul is a breath of Hashem and is compared to a candle. Like a candle, your soul shines on your face and on the face of your soul mate. When you are blessed, you will be able to see that light.

- *"And He will be gracious to you."* In Hebrew there is an idiom "to find grace in her eyes." It means that she will like you. It's not enough to see the light. The guy or gal has to like you too!
- *"Hashem will turn his face toward you."* The exact translation is *"Hashem will lift his face towards you"* In Hebrew the word for marriage is from the root to lift, *"Nisuin."* If a man wants to get married he says that he wants to "lift" a woman, *"Laset isha."* At a Jewish wedding, the bride's face is covered with a veil. She walks to the canopy with the accompaniment of her mother, the bridegroom's mother and scores of female guests. They all proceed toward the canopy to meet the male guests and the bridegroom. Under the canopy the bridegroom announces, "I sanctify you with this ring" and places it on her finger. After the rabbi and other honored guests bless the couple with seven blessings, the groom lifts the veil of his bride to give her a sip of wine. That is when they look at each

other for the first time as husband and wife. The groom then smashes the glass on the floor with his foot as a remembrance of the destroyed temples that stood in Jerusalem. Following the sound of the shattered glass, everyone begins to sing and dance with lively music.

- *"And he will give you peace."* The priestly blessing, that Hashem will lift His face toward you and give you peace, is a blessing of peace in the home.
- *"And they shall place My name on the children of Israel and I will bless them."* If you teach your children to love Hashem and mention His name in daily speech, He will bless them with the same blessing that the children of Aaron bless you.

Hashem wants us to teach our children to have faith in God. That faith should be so strong that Hashem is in their hearts and minds all the time. When we teach children about God, we place His name on their hearts. God blessed Phinehas with a blessing to find his soul mate, true peace in his home and children that have faith in the One above.

The exact opposite of illicit sex is the holy union of matrimony. Phinehas later inherited the position of high priest. He was one of the few people that saw the Exodus from Egypt and lived to enter the Land of Israel. The children of Phinehas would be the ones to continue the line of high priests. He would lead the other priests in this holy blessing and bless the children of Israel.

By striving for true peace with your spouse, you can fulfill the seventh commandment to its fullest.

Chapter 11

Do Not Steal

> Leviticus 19:11-13
> "Do not steal. Do not lie. Do not deceive one another. Do not swear falsely by my name and so profane the name of your God. I am the Lord. Do not defraud or rob your neighbor. Do not hold back the wages of a hired worker overnight."

In Leviticus the Torah spells out some examples of how strict we must be to avoid stealing. If we lie or swear falsely it can cause someone to lose money unjustly. Even if we don't pay a hired worker the wages on time it can be considered stealing. If you cause someone to wait for their money or merchandise too long, it can cause them to have to pay interest and that is another Torah prohibition. Even if it doesn't cause them to pay interest it is still forbidden. As a matter of fact, conning someone into giving you money or free merchandise is also stealing.

Every one of the Ten Commandments has something to do with the prohibition against stealing. In the next few pages, I will explain how each commandment teaches us not to steal.

1) "I am the Lord your God who took you out of the land of Egypt." (Exodus 20:1).

When the Israelites left Egypt they took riches from the Egyptians. Did they take advantage of them because the Egyptians were afraid? Were they defrauding their neighbors? Was that considered stealing?

To answer that question, let's go back to Joseph. Joseph was sold into slavery when he was seventeen years old. He was sold to Potiphar and served him until he was 28 when he went to prison for two years. Joseph was miraculously released at thirty years old and was appointed the viceroy by Pharaoh.

Joseph's position gave him great wealth and he shared it with his brothers. He built them homes and farms in the land of Goshen. Joseph lived until the ripe old age of one hundred and ten. He survived four Pharaohs. During his lifetime Joseph kept helping his people financially and he even advanced them politically. After Joseph's death, his sons Menashe and Ephraim must have received an inheritance that would be equivalent to the inheritance of the Pharaoh himself. Menashe and Ephraim were very wealthy and benevolent. They distributed their wealth to the poor people of the Israelites and the Egyptians by creating the first welfare system.

Bless the Children

Every Friday night we have a custom to bless our children before the Sabbath meal. The girls are blessed to be like our foremothers: Sarah, Rebecca, Rachel and Leah. You would imagine that the boys would be blessed to be like their forefathers, Abraham, Isaac and Jacob. Instead, the father blesses his sons to be just like Ephraim and Menashe.

When Menashe and Ephraim died, the Pharaoh didn't want to continue in their ways of giving to the poor. He taxed the people and took away their government benefits. The wealthy Israelites joined the simple Egyptians and began to make political rallies and riots all over the country. That is when the establishment began to fear that the Israelites would take over.

> Exodus 1:8-10
> "Then a new king, to whom Joseph meant nothing, came to power in Egypt. "Look," he said to his people, "the Israelites have become far too numerous for us. Come, we must deal shrewdly with them or they will become even more numerous and, if war breaks out, will join our enemies, fight against us and leave the country."

The Egyptian government was afraid of the Israelites because of their wealth. With wealth they could buy ammunition and conquer them. More than that, they could take the reins of power and control within the Egyptian government. Because of their superior social system of helping the poor, they already had the support of the majority of the nation.

When Pharaoh and his advisors realized the danger that the kingdom was in, they started arresting Israelites on any excuse. When the jails got too full they put them to work as slaves. That stirred up more violence and the Egyptians in turn incarcerated more Israelites and stripped them of their wealth. The slaves were assigned the building of two new cities of storage in order to store all the valuables that the government stole from them.

> Exodus 1:11, "So they put slave masters over them to oppress them with forced labor, and they built Pithom and Rameses as store cities for Pharaoh."

How did they get the general population to agree to such a plan? The government began a rumor that the Israelites were very rich and they were just taking advantage of them by giving them a little welfare. They would allow the Egyptians to come to the storage houses to receive jewels and gold. Of course we all know that a bit of jewelry and clothing as a one-time deal is nothing compared to a monthly stipend of food, but the Egyptians were fooled and stopped rebelling against their officials. They also revealed hiding places of Israelites and ratted out their Hebrew friends.

Many years passed. The Israelites were enslaved as well as their children, grandchildren and great-grandchildren. A son of a slave is also a slave. When it came time to leave Egypt the Israelites didn't steal, they asked nicely to have their wealth returned to them. The Egyptians had some gold and jewelry that they inherited from their ancestors but they knew that it was stolen from the Hebrews long ago. After the Egyptians were sufficiently traumatized by ten plagues, they were happy to give back anything that rightfully belonged to the Israelite nation and more.

> Exodus 12:35, "The Israelites did as Moses instructed and asked the Egyptians for articles of silver and gold and for clothing. The LORD had made the Egyptians favorably disposed toward the people, and they gave them what they asked for; so they plundered the Egyptians."

Our sages tell us that the people of the tribe of Levi were not enslaved. This makes sense because Aaron, Moses' brother, was free to go meet him at Mount Sinai after the revelation of the burning bush. Aaron was sent to Moses through his own prophetic vision. There is no mention of him having any fear of returning. I now understand why. Aaron wasn't a slave so he could come and go as he pleased.

> Exodus 4:14-17
> "What about your brother, Aaron the Levite? I know he can speak well. He is already on his way to meet you, and he will be glad to see you. You shall speak to him and put words in his mouth; I will help both of you speak and will teach you what to do. He will speak to the people for you, and it will be as if he were your mouth and as if you were God to him. But take this staff in your hand so you can perform the signs with it."

The reason that the Levites were never enslaved is because they never rioted against the government. They were the teachers, the counselors. and the peaceful clergymen. Because they never fought the government they were not arrested and taken into slavery in those early years, so they were not labeled as slaves. The Levites also did not worship idols so they didn't deserve the punishment of becoming slaves. When the Israelites worshipped the Golden Calf, the Levites did not participate:

> Exodus 31:25-29
> Moses saw that the people were running wild and that Aaron had let them get out of control and so become a laughingstock to their enemies. So he stood at the entrance to the camp and said, "Whoever is for the LORD, come to me." And all the Levites rallied to him.

> Then he said to them, "This is what the LORD, the God of Israel, says: 'Each man strap a sword to his side. Go back and forth through the camp from one end to the other, each killing his brother and friend and neighbor.'" The Levites did as Moses commanded, and that day about three thousand of the people died. Then Moses said, "You have been set apart to the LORD today, for you were against your own sons and brothers, and he has blessed you this day."

Stealing Humans

The worst kind of theft is the stealing of human life. Kidnapping is one example. Selling people into slavery is another. The first commandment is to remember that we were slaves in Egypt, and Hashem took us out of bondage.

In ancient times slavery was commonplace. Judaism has a totally different perspective on slavery. The Torah teaches us to give a slave the day off on the Sabbath. If there aren't enough pillows in the house, the slave gets one before the master of the house does.

The verse an eye for and eye in Exodus 21:24 is referring to a Hebrew slave owner that wounded a slave. In Exodus 21:26–27 there are specific instructions to free a slave, if his master injures his eye or his tooth. The master must give his slave monetary compensation according to the value of the damage that was done and grant him freedom.

In the Bible it says that slaves must be freed after six years of labor and sent off with presents and money to help them start a new life, unless they want to stay. Exodus 21:5 says, "I love my master and my wife, I don't want to go free." Then the slave may remain until the year of Jubilee, which happens every fifty years.

Why Does the Torah Allow Slavery?

In Biblical times if a man stole money and he had no way to repay it, he would sell himself into slavery. Torah law provides the possibility. If someone stole, the Torah law is that he must pay back at least double of what he took. What if the robber doesn't have the money? What if the robber had other debts that he didn't pay?

A rich landowner would agree to take the convict into his home, to provide a residence and put him to work on his property in exchange for his debts, whether they were unpaid because of his own poverty, or because of theft.

Thus, the slave had to work in order to pay back his debt. The slaves weren't kidnapped. They sold themselves for their own debt. The slave or the court may decide to do so, because otherwise he would not be able to pay his debt and still have enough money to have food and shelter for himself and his family. The slave was allowed to bring his family with him to the home or plantation of his new boss.

If a slave was married, his wife could stay with him to help her husband with his work. A married slave had more value than an unmarried one. The maximum time a man could be indentured would be six years. If he chose to, he could stay on until the Jubilee year, but that was not recommended. (Read Leviticus chapter 25 to learn more about the year of Jubilee.)

> Leviticus 25:28-40
> I am the LORD your God, who brought you out of Egypt to give you the land of Canaan and to be your God. If any of your fellow Israelites become poor and sell themselves to you, do not make them work as slaves. They are to be treated as hired workers or temporary residents among you; they are to work for you until the Year of Jubilee.

This is a far cry from the way the black slaves were treated in the South. Even today there are so many women who are sold into sexual slavery to be prostitutes all over the world.

That is stealing at its worst. Jewish law considers kidnapping a crime as serious as murder. Even though there was slavery in the time of the Bible, women were not allowed to be slaves over the age of puberty unless they were married and their husbands were also slaves. This protected them from any kind of prostitution. If a woman stole, it would be her husband's responsibility to pay her debt. If she wasn't married, the responsibility falls on her father or guardian. If a slave and his wife had children, the boys could work for the master, but the girls were not to work for the master of the house past the age of puberty.

In modern society, people who steal are punished, but the punishment is not productive and doesn't help the one who stole, or pay back anything to the one who was robbed. We have all seen movies where the thieves figure that they will sit in jail for a few years for robbery, but when they are released they will be so rich that they felt that it was worth it. The punishment for stealing in the Torah is to return double of what was stolen (Exodus 22:4). In the case of stolen livestock, the thief may have to pay up to five times the value of what he stole (Exodus 22:1). That would deter many first-time thieves from taking a chance!

Thus, the Torah gives a person a chance to repent and to work out his debt. In today's day and age that would mean that the thief is given a job and every month an automatic payment that will be deducted from his salary and pay the person that he owes. The difference between this and a regular debt is that the thief must pay back double of what he stole.

Many people might be reluctant to hire a thief, so there must be a factory or other place of work designated for these convicts to work with supervision. Woman cannot be a part of the men's work force. They would have to be in a separate facility, unless their father or husband is willing to pay or work for them.

If someone stole an amount of money that cannot be returned in a lifetime, efforts must be put in to find that money and the thief will pay for the investigation. If he is willing to tell the police where the money is, he still has to pay as much as he can in addition to the money that was found. However, according to Torah law he cannot be forced to work for more than six years. Stealing does not deserve a death penalty, therefore the Torah provided a limit to how long a person can be forced to work as a penalty.

Kidnapping

Some people might be forgiven for killing; for example, war, self-defense or accidents, but there is no excuse for kidnapping, even if the kidnapper is doing it "legally." Vicious custody battles that take children away from their parents is a form of kidnapping. If you poison children against one or both parents, it is slander and can lead to kidnapping. Removing children because of child protection laws is still kidnapping, unless there is sexual or extreme physical abuse. There is no excuse for removing children due to neglect. Are you allowed to steal someone's belongings just because they can't take care of them?

What should be done in the case of drug addicts who clearly cannot fend for their young?

In order to avoid stealing, social workers should get the parent's permission to take the children to a home of their choice on a temporary basis. During this time the parents should be taken to a rehabilitation facility. The parents should be able to choose a preferred home for their children where they can visit or stay with them in a sheltered environment. If the children are old enough to voice their opinion, they should have the right to choose where they want to be.

If the parents are not dangerous to the children, there should be no reason to take them away. Some parents need help in rearing their children, but separation is not the answer. The money that is spent on a foster home should be spent on a nurse or nanny to help the parents in their own home. Abandoning the children hurts them much more than it hurts the parents.

In very severe cases of abuse children might need another home to go to. Children need love more than anything else, especially abused children. The best is for them to go to the home of a close relative or good friend who can really give them the love they need. Many more children have been abused and even died in foster homes than in their own homes. If a parent is violent, the parent should be incarcerated, not the child! Some parents might need a hospital, in that case the other parent or a close relative should take the responsibility, not a foster home full of strangers.

Child protection laws started out with good intentions, but today many children are kidnapped from their homes to their own detriment with little or no proof of neglect or abuse. The Torah punishment for kidnapping is death and should be taken very seriously.

> Exodus 21:16, "Anyone who kidnaps someone is to be put to death, whether the victim has been sold or is still in the kidnapper's possession."

In a world run by Torah law children cannot be separated from their mother if they are under six years old. If they are older than six they get to say what they want and with whom they want to live. If a government agency is worried about the mother's ability to care for her child, it should take the child and the mother and take care of both.

Jail Time

Incarcerating an adult is also kidnapping, unless the person gives himself in willingly. But here's the good news: Because kidnapping a person is like killing them, if someone transgresses a commandment that is punishable by death, putting them in jail can absolve them. Just the pain of being incarcerated is enough to atone for their sin. So if someone did their time, they should be forgiven. When someone goes to jail he loses his life, he doesn't need any other punishments.

On the other hand, stealing is not a capital crime. The Torah wants the thief to pay back double of what he stole, that's it. If you stole and you didn't get caught, find a way to pay back double of what you stole, or of that is impossible, give that amount to a charity that the person you stole from would have chosen. This would be a way to have Hashem forgive you. If you don't pay back what you've stolen and you were over twenty years old when you took something without permission, you might have to pay in other ways. That will be Hashem's decision.

If someone was involved in illegal drugs, they should go to jail, because dispensing these drugs is likened to murder, and taking them is like suicide. Maybe after the jail sentence, the convict will feel reborn and will start a new life.

If someone is a drug addict, they cannot really be blamed for anything they do because they are really to be considered temporarily insane. It's a mitzvah to get them into rehab before they get very sick.

2) "You shall not have any gods before me" (Exodus 20:3).

If someone goes to other gods, they are taking from the Creator of the World without acknowledgment of the one true God. The second commandment is the only one that says that Hashem is jealous. He is jealous that we are using the energy He gave us and instead of thanking Him, we pray to other gods. Idol worshippers are, in a sense, taking advantage of God's gift and using it for nothingness.

Jewish law has a blessing before and after anything we eat. We even have a blessing to say after using the toilet. We thank Hashem that we can use our bodily functions. By educating our children to thank Hashem for every little thing, we teach them that nothing belongs to us. If they are taught to ask permission from Hashem to eat an apple, they certainly will not take a cellphone without permission.

The Prayer of a Thief

There is a question in the Talmud, "Does Hashem answer the prayer of a thief to succeed in his plans?" Hashem says that He definitely hears his prayer and if He really loves him, He may cause him to get caught or to fail, so that he will learn not to do it again. When Hashem doesn't give us what we ask for, it does not necessarily mean that He didn't hear our prayers.

Before his first move, a thief may contemplate, "*If I will take this money, I will be able to solve my problems.*" That statement itself is blasphemy. How can things be better if God doesn't help you? How can the solution to your problems be something that is clearly against the will of the Creator? If you believe in God and not in the power of money, you won't steal, because you know there will be absolutely no blessing in that money.

As we mentioned in the chapter on idol worship, money can be an idol in and of itself. Some people think that money will give them happiness or protection. Some people might even fear that they will lose their job if they don't cooperate with the boss's corrupt demands. If cooperation means doing something wrong legally or morally, then cooperating would be considered idol worship—fear of man above fear of God. When given that choice, we must choose to do what's right and trust that Hashem will provide.

Why are people so sure that they will be healthy enough to eat but they are afraid that they won't have money to buy the food they need. The one who gives life gives sustenance. It is much more complicated to give energy for your heart to pump than to give you money. However, because we fear the consequences of money problems more, Hashem gives us more tests with money. The following verse in Psalms is a saying that I say to myself and to others. It helps me keep my focus off my worries and let Hashem take care of everything.

> Psalm 55:22,
> Cast your cares on the LORD and he will sustain you; he will never let the righteous be shaken.

3) "Do not take the Lord's name in vain, because He will not cleanse the one who says his name in vain" (Exodus 20:6).

Sometimes the Torah court would demand that a person take an oath that he didn't steal. When someone is suspected of stealing and there are no witnesses, the Torah accepts an oath in God's name as the truth. On the other hand, in a murder trial, one cannot testify for oneself. If a person can kill, he may be mentally ill. There are countless people who admitted guilt to serious crimes even though they were innocent.

However, in the case of theft or on suspicion of theft, an oath in the name of God is enough to free you in a Torah court of law. If the plaintiff swore falsely, Hashem doesn't forgive him. That's worse than stealing, it's not worth it.

4) "Remember the Sabbath to keep it holy." (Exodus 20:8)

When I was in fifth grade, I had a big argument with some of girls in my class. They were Jewish and even traditional, but their fathers worked on Shabbat. One girl said, "A man has to make a living!" I was way ahead of my years, and I was screaming that you couldn't work on Shabbat for any excuse. Today I believe that any money you make on Shabbat has no blessing in it, and you will not enjoy that money. Observing Shabbat teaches children from a very young age that you don't do everything or anything for money. We don't even talk about money on Shabbat.

Every week we have to stop thinking about money for twenty-four hours. How can one become a thief if one doesn't think about money every day? We become angel-like every week. We look forward to the next Shabbat all week long. When we shop for food, we have in mind that the food or clothing will be in honor of Shabbat. If you look forward to the day that is disconnected from money, you will never have the desire to have money that doesn't belong to you. How can you buy food or clothing for the Holy Day with stolen money?

In the 1980s the Israeli Airline El Al was in a financial crisis. They were on the verge of bankruptcy. New elections brought religious parties into the Parliament that insisted that El Al stop working on the Sabbath. They were an already failing business and the staff was sure that if they stop working one day a week they will go totally bankrupt. What happened was the exact opposite. To the amazement of their personnel, once El Al stopped flying on Shabbat, the luck of the business turned around. Until this day El

Al is a strong international airline that has no flights from Friday night until Saturday night.

5) "Honor your father and mother." (Exodus 20:12)

In the Chapter "Honor Your Father and Mother" I explained that one way to observe this commandment is by honoring other parents. The most important parent to honor is the parent of your own kin.

Many parents try to steal their children from their ex-spouse by reporting false accusations to authorities, by fighting viciously in divorce court and even by lying to the child himself. Taking a parent away physically or emotionally from a child is robbing his or her inborn right to have two parents to love.

On the other hand, authorities sometimes force children to go to visit a parent that they don't want to visit. That is also stealing because they are treating the child like a slave; merchandise that can be transferred from one place to the next forcefully.

The treatment of children was very bad in different times and places throughout world history. However, for Jewish children there were times that it was unbearable. In 19th century Russia during the reigns of Czar Alexander I and Czar Nicholas I, Jewish boys were taken away from their parents and recruited into the army at six years of age. In prewar Europe Jewish children were taken from their homes and put in institutions against their will. In New York city many Jewish children died because of the harsh conditions of child labor in the 20th century sweat shops.

Today in Israel children cannot be forced to go to a parent or family that they don't want to visit.

When my daughter Gila was nine years old and her father and I were divorced, the Jerusalem police came to our house looking for her. They said that she did not show up for the visit with her father. Gila was in school at the time, but when she came home we told her that the police came. She was very upset and wrote a letter to the police in her fourth grade handwriting:

> Dear Policeman,
> I don't want to go to my father's house. There is not enough food there and it is not clean. If you force me to go I will run away.
>
> Thank you,
> Gila

Gila and I brought the letter to the local precinct. A policeman took her aside and spoke to her in person. Believe it or not, the police did not come back to our home. The next week Gila and my son Jonathan met with their father and went for a ride. They didn't like his house so he did not oblige them to go there.

A few weeks later their father insisted that he would take both children to his house to sleepover for Shabbat. They actually ran away! There are no buses in Jerusalem on Shabbat so they walked for two hours until they arrived at home. They were strong-willed kids. The Israeli police are instructed to give the child's will top priority even against a court ruling. The father eventually took us back to court and he was granted two visits a week, but no overnights.

This is a far cry from the American justice system that forces children to obey the court's decision against their will. Hashem loves children. They are considered innocent from sin but are rewarded for their good deeds. The Israeli government has special respect for children, they look up to them as their future leaders.

Jewish law obliges boys to keep the Torah law from thirteen years old for boys and from twelve years old for girls. However, total responsibility for everything a person does begins at age twenty. That is why Hashem instructs Moses and Aaron to recruit men to the army from twenty years of age.

> Numbers 1:3, "You and Aaron are to count according to their divisions all the men in Israel who are twenty years old or more and able to serve in the army."

The idea that an eighteen-year-old is an adult, has no basis whatsoever in medicine, psychology, sociology or Torah. The Torah says that at twenty years old boys should be drafted because that is the age that we become adults.

Inheritance

Many elderly people get their estates stolen by lawyers, old-age homes, or anyone else who can get their hands on the money. This is not only stealing, it is disrespectful to the deceased mother or father who earned the money and saved it for their family, their rightful heirs.

Somehow, when it comes to inheritance, people who were honest their whole life, change. Many parents who have passed away see their children fighting over their estate and are in so much pain that they regret even saving that money. Whether your parents are dead or alive, you mustn't use their money in a way that would anger them. This money is not a gift; it's a responsibility.

6) "You shall not murder" (Exodus 20:13).

The Torah teaches us not to murder a thief:

> Exodus 22:1–2
> "If a thief is caught breaking in at night and is struck a fatal blow, the defender is not guilty of bloodshed; but if it happens after sunrise, the defender is guilty of bloodshed."

This is one of the proofs that the Torah was written way ahead of its time. Even as recent as two hundred years ago, who would think twice before killing a thief? Stealing is not punishable by death. The only time a person is absolved from killing a thief is, if a thief enters his house at night. Since it's dark the sudden fear can cause a person to react with all his adrenaline. If you don't know whether the intruder is dangerous or not, you cannot be blamed from protecting yourself.

Believe it or not but the Torah has a law that you must put a fence around your rooftop in order to protect even a thief from falling off and getting hurt.

> Deuteronomy 22:8, When you build a new house, make a parapet around your roof so that you may not bring the guilt of bloodshed on your house if someone falls from the roof.

This shows that Hashem wants us to have mercy even on those who are bad to us, unless they do something that is a capital crime in Torah law. We can learn from this law that if someone transgresses a law that does not deserve a death penalty he should be protected and even helped.

Of all the transgressions in the Torah stealing is the easiest one to repent. A person who steals usually feels guilty even as he is doing it. That's why they don't have to be punished so severely. All that he has to do is ask forgiveness from his Creator and pay back double to the one he stole from. In the Middle Ages people were punished and tortured severely for theft and even for debts.

Stealing Food

Jewish law rules that if someone is caught stealing food, he may not be convicted. In the famous story *Les Miserables*, the main character was put in prison for stealing a loaf of bread for his sister's hungry family. In Jewish law, if people steal food, their situation must be investigated, and if they really stole because of lack of bare necessities, the community is blamed for the theft. They must collect money to pay back the storekeeper and to buy food for thief and his family. Of course the family is to be reprimanded and told that they must tell the leaders of the community if they are lacking anything.

Jewish law states that if someone asks for food, you are not allowed to check out the truth of his claim. First feed him, and then ask questions. If someone asks for money or for a future commitment, then you have the responsibility to investigate. Charity is the opposite of theft. In a society where people help each other financially theft is very rare.

Our body is not a gift from God; it is a loan. When we have a child, we are given a body and a soul to take care of until it is grown. As adults we still have the responsibility to take care of our own body and soul. The first thing is to take care not to let our body get so weak that our soul cannot complete its mission on earth. If you abuse your health with unhealthy habits like smoking, drinking alcohol, taking drugs, or even eating unhealthy food, you are damaging a body that was given to you on loan. If you borrow your friend's car, do you have permission to trash it? Do we have permission to trash our bodies and cause ourselves to be ill?

When we give our children unhealthy food, we our giving them something that can harm them without asking their permission. We are tricking them into thinking it's good for them. If cake or candy is given as a prize, the message is that it is a fantastic thing to eat! If we don't let them know that it isn't healthy, who will? If they are too young to make the choice, we cannot abuse their total trust.

If a food is even questionable as far as freshness is concerned would you give it to your toddler? Of course not.

Is it any different if you give that same toddler ice cream that can give him a sore throat or holes in his teeth? Did you explain to your child that this food is not healthy?

Children have a right to know if what they are eating is good for them. I realized this only after I learned it from my son Jonathan:

When Jonathan was six years old, his father would buy him popsicles every day after school, sometimes even two or three—you know, the kind with sugar and food coloring. I spoke to my son in very adult like voice and explained him that there was a disease called diabetes that is caused by eating too much sugar. He looked at me with blaming eyes and said, "Why didn't you tell me that there was a disease that comes from eating sugar?"

I felt so guilty. Jonathan was complaining that he did not have informed consent! Your children are innocent; they are not born with knowledge about nutrition or life. It's up to you to provide him with that information. Without informed consent we cannot give our children anything that may not healthy for them. It's actually deceiving. Once we have children it is our moral responsibility to provide them with healthy nourishing food. Even when you give them food that is somewhat healthy, you are robbing them of their right to fully healthy nutrition. In my book *Choose Life*, I delve into the medicinal qualities of different foods and their life giving qualities while I teach you all about God's view on nutrition.

7) "You shall not commit adultery or incest "(Exodus 20:14).

Adultery is stealing someone's wife or husband. Incest is stealing a relative's body and innocence and even destroying their life.

> Leviticus 29:17 says, "If a man takes his sister the daughter of his mother or the daughter of his father and he saw her private parts and she saw his it is an abomination."

The word that is translated as an abomination in Hebrew is *chesed*. *Chesed* does not mean abomination. *Chesed* means benevolence, doing good, giving. In Israel charitable organizations are called *Irgunai Chesed*. This word is used in the Bible very often with that meaning. For example, Genesis 24:12 says, "Then he prayed, 'LORD, God of my master Abraham, make me successful today, and show kindness to my master Abraham.'" The word kindness is *chesed* in the original text. There are 245 places in the Bible where the word *chesed* is used denoting kindness and benevolence.

The connection between close family members is that of benevolence. If a father, God forbid, told his daughter to have mercy on him and have sex with him, then the sexual act would be one of giving a favor. Naturally there is no lust between close family members, so the only way a sister or daughter would consent to having sex is because she is helping her brother or father. This is taking advantage of her; it is stealing her privacy, stealing her heart. So the Torah really says that if a father seduces his daughter, "It would be taking advantage of her kindness." Even if the incest is rape it is still caused by the father taking advantage of the child's kindness because he trusts that the child won't call the police. It's scary to report a family member to the authorities, even if you know that it is the right thing to do. Likewise, any sexual act that is based on helping your partner without real passion is not permissible. You can be good to people, but there must be a limit.

This prohibition is not only sexual. If you allow a friend to take advantage of your goodness in a way that hurts you or hurts your family, it is forbidden in the eyes of Hashem. If you allow a friend or a guest to take you away from your family, you are actually allowing him to steal you from those to whom you owe your loyalty the most.

I would like to tell you a story about a family of five. The father was being overly kind to his gym instructor. He started spending more time with him than with his wife and three children. The relationship between the two men got so close that it became homosexual, even though this father had no prior homosexual tendencies. The couple divorced and the wife was devastated.

Once you have a spouse and/or children, you owe them quality time. You are not free to do as you please. Your devotion or lack of it, will certainly have consequences in the not so distant future, when you get older and really need them. Giving attention to your family is an obligation. Failing to commit to that obligation is in essence, stealing.

8) "You shall not steal" (Exodus 20:15).

When you first hear the words *do not steal,* you think, "money." Money mean investments, investments mean interest. If the Torah was observed, there would be no interest allowed.

> Deuteronomy 23:20, "Do not take from your brother interest, money interest or any other kind of interest that you might take."

Observing this mitzvah would solve most of the money problems of the world. No interest on loans means that there would be no mortgages from private banks. You either have the money or you get a loan from a friend or relative free of interest. All the finances of the world would have to work differently. Housing would be very inexpensive. There would be much more public transportation, and everyone would be calmer. It was like that when we first came to Israel in 1976. Everything was simple, even though people had mortgages, they were government loans and they weren't linked to the cost of living, the interest was lower than the rate of inflation, so they were really free loans.

Today Israel has copied America, giving loans with high interest to people who can't afford it. Everyone is busting from tension and lack of funds for basic necessities. The prices of housing skyrocketed.

Lending money with interest has caused unbelievable damage to the world. We have seen the devastating results in the past years. Without high interest mortgages the price of houses would stay low, and there would we lots of cheap rentals. My parents bought their first house in 1971, and it cost $25,000 for a big house, with four bedrooms, a backyard and a basement in the big city. In a few years the price almost doubled, and now it is worth ten times that price. It's all because the banks give higher mortgages with more and more interest.

If the interest on the loan is low and there is some kind of financial benefit in taking that loan, like tax deductions, then it would be permissible. Lending money to help someone start a business is permissible even with interest, as part of partnership agreement. Interest for a loan used in a business deal can be considered dividends. However, high interest that takes money from the poor and gives to the rich is against Torah law.

In the Middle Ages the Christians were aware of this prohibition. They didn't want to transgress the law of the Bible, so they appointed the Jews to be the money lenders. The Jews of Europe agreed to take the job of being money lenders, because that was all they were allowed to do. Anti-Semitic rules prohibited the Jews from owning land or private businesses. Of course this caused the anti-Semitism to escalate. Everyone was hoping that their money lender would die or be expelled so that they wouldn't have to pay him back.

The Jews should have refused to lend money with interest. If this would have forced them to leave the country, that would be Hashem's will. Maybe it would have led to many more Jews arriving in Palestine before the Holocaust. Torah law is eternal. Choosing God's way is the best way.

The excuse that the Jews used in order to agree to be money lenders is the verse in Deuteronomy 28:12.

> "The Lord will open the heavens, the storehouse of his bounty, to send rain on your land in season and to bless all the work of your hands. You will lend to many nations but will borrow from none."

This verse is a blessing that we will be so rich that we will be able to lend to others. That doesn't mean that we will lend with interest. Maybe we will lend out of the goodness of our hearts. A general rule for understanding the Bible is that we cannot cancel an explicit Torah law with another verse or Biblical prophecy.

Gambling

We are commanded to work six days and rest on the Sabbath. This means that besides resting on the Sabbath, we also are commanded to work for a living. The work we have to do must be work that helps build the world or helps people and other living things. Gambling as a way to make a living is not permissible because you are not working at advancing the world. In actuality many families have been totally destroyed because of gambling. Gambling is also a form of stealing because the winner is taking money from someone without his sincere will to give.

When people play a game for money, they are hoping to win but don't pray to win. Hashem likes when athletes openly pray to win. Even though winning a competitive sport is not a life-threatening situation, professional athletes have a desperate hope to win. If you hope to win, then you should pray to win. No wish is too small or too big in the eyes of the Creator.

9) "You shall not give false testimony against your neighbor" (Exodus 20:16).

If someone is bribed into being a false witness, that's definitely stealing. You are also stealing if your false testimony causes your friend to have a loss of money or freedom. The other way around, you must do everything in your power to give a truthful testimony. If you don't go to testify on your friend's behalf, you may cause him to go to jail or suffer penalties. That would be stealing his time and his happiness. You are not obligated to testify if your testimony will hurt your friend, unless it is a murder trial and you were an eyewitness. However, if you are subpoenaed, you may not lie.

10) You shall not covet.

> Exodus 20:17
> "You shall not covet your neighbor's house. You shall not covet your neighbor's wife, or his male or female servant, his ox or donkey, or anything that belongs to your neighbor."

There is a lot to write about a prohibition against emotions. All stealing can be avoided if no one would covet, or have any feelings of jealousy or desire for the belongings of others. You can never have true wealth if you covet the belongings of your friends or neighbors. Psalm chapter 24 brings the whole subject of honesty to a different level:

> Psalm 24:3-6, "Who will ascend into the mountain of Hashem and who will stand in his holy place? One with clean hands and a pure heart; who has not sworn in vain, and has not sworn deceitfully. He will receive a blessing from Hashem, and righteousness from the God of his salvation. This is the generation of those that seek him, those who strive for Your Presence, O God of Jacob, Selah.

This psalm teaches us that it isn't enough just not to steal; you have to have clean hands and a pure heart. This means that you do not covet. Having a pure heart means, that even secretly you do not feel jealous. Then you will receive true blessings from Hashem.

The modern world is so corrupt that the definition of stealing has been blurred. Entire governments and companies do things for the sole purpose of having more money in their own personal bank accounts. The movie *The Inside Job* shows a little glimpse of the power of people to manipulate the stock market and the general market at will. The source of the problem is people's lust for money.

As children we are taught to wish for presents. We come to believe that objects, things that cost money, will bring us happiness. When we run out of things to buy, then just having money in the bank will somehow protect us. Many people save money their whole lives, not sharing it even with their own family. They say that the money is to be saved for emergencies. When the emergency comes, they still don't spend, lest they will need it for an even bigger emergency.

> Psalm 49:16-17, "Do not be overawed when others grow rich, when the splendor of their houses increases; for they will take nothing with them when they die, their splendor will not descend with them."

"Do not covet" is a sin relating to jealously over wealth. As the above psalms says, we don't take the wealth with us. Our whole sense of priorities has to change. We must save our good deeds and not our cash. After a person dies, he comes to heaven with his bank account of good deeds. If he has more than he needs, he gets to give out his extra points to his loved ones.

Keeping the Torah, observing the Sabbath, putting Hashem's will before yours, and other mitzvoth of the Torah will give you true wealth. You will become a better person, and stealing is not even an option. Our goal in life isn't money; our goal is to make Hashem happy.

In order to really be honest, you must love God more than you love money. True honesty comes when our main goal is to do God's will and not our own. Hashem will bless you and your money much more if you are honest. It says in the Ethics of the Fathers, "Everyone that has God's spirit in him will be loved by others." If you are really a good person, people will give you. They'll hire you, or they'll buy from your store and they'll send you more business because they feel your goodness and honesty.

The Hollywood musical Oliver was a very big hit in the 1960's. The song *You Gotta Pick a Pocket or Two*, always gave me the shivers. This was a musical for children. Why are they encouraging pickpocketing? We came up with a better version:

You Got to Make a Mitzvah or Two

In the next life, one thing counts,
In your mitzvah bank, large amounts.
I'm afraid these don't grow on trees,
You got to make a mitzvah or two.
You got to make a mitzvah or two boys,
You got to make a mitzvah or two.
Good deeds just don't grow on trees,
You got to make a mitzvah or two.
Why should you turn your back?
If you give, you won't lack.
Better give to your fellow man,
It's a precept to understand.
You got to do a good deed or two girls,
You got to do a good deed or two.
Better invest in charity,
You got to make a mitzvah or two.
Pharaoh was an evil King,
He stole souls not just things.
Charity saves, once we were slaves.
Go out and pick a mitzvah or two.
You got pick a mitzvah or two now,
You got pick a mitzvah or two. P
haraoh was a lowly crook.
Get out and make a mitzvah or two.
Take a tip from David the King,
Honor and riches don't mean a thing.
I recall he started small,

He had to make a mitzvah or two.
You got to make a mitzvah or two boys,
You got to make a mitzvah or two.
Money you can't take with you,
You got to make a mitzvah or two.
If Hashem, makes you rich,
Remember that there is a hitch.
You will find some peace of mind,
When you make a mitzvah or two.
You've got to make a mitzvah or two girls,
You've got to make a mitzvah or two.
You will find some peace of mind,
When you make a mitzvah or two.

Chapter 12

Do Not Bear False Witness

Exodus 20:16, "You shall not give false testimony against your neighbor." This commandment and the third commandment, "Do not carry God's name in vain" both prohibit lying. The third commandment prohibits swearing in God's name, in court or out of court. The ninth commandment prohibits lying in court or in any type of official setting even if you do not swear.

There are some religious people, Jewish and Christians, who try to avoid going to court because they are afraid to swear in God's name even to the truth. This is very wrong. If you have evidence that can help someone or save his life, you may not be silent. As it says in Leviticus 19:16, "Don't be a gossiper in your nation and don't stand over your friend's blood." A gossiper tells stories about other people for no good reason. It's a juxtaposition, as if to say, don't gossip idly. If you have something to say, then say it where it will make a difference!

Joseph Meets Pharaoh

Pharaoh had a team of dream interpreters. It was a prominent profession in Joseph's day. The cupbearer was a witness to Joseph's talent and he said nothing until Pharaoh was suffering sleepless nights worrying about his dreams. Then he came to Pharaoh in all honesty and declared, "Today I am reminded of my sins" (Genesis 41:9). He told Pharaoh about Joseph and his amazing ability to know the meaning of dreams. In Modern Hebrew the verse, "Today I am reminded of my sins" has become an idiom and is used when a person wants to apologize poetically.

Pharaoh's cupbearer told Pharaoh that he and his friend had dreams when they were in jail and Joseph interpreted them. When he heard that Pharaoh needed an interpreter for his dreams, he remembered Joseph from two years prior. He felt extremely guilty for not mentioning him earlier. Of what was he guilty?

> Exodus 23:7
> Have nothing to do with a false charge and do not put an innocent or honest person to death, for I will not acquit the guilty.

In this verse the "guilty" that Hashem will not acquit is the one who caused the death of an innocent person, either by witnessing falsely or by not witnessing at all. We mentioned in the chapter "Do not steal," that incarcerating a person is like killing them. If that is the case today, imagine how the jail conditions were in ancient Egypt.

The cupbearer felt guilty because he didn't try to get Joseph out of jail sooner, by telling the Pharaoh about his ability to interpret dreams. The failure of the cupbearer to report to Pharaoh anything about this super talented convict was a transgression of the commandment, "Do not bear false witness." It is so interesting to see how the Bible stories are actually built around the theme of the Ten Commandments. I am sure that there were many events that occurred in Egypt in Joseph's eighty-year reign that were not mentioned in the Torah. Hashem didn't want us to have a Torah that would be too long, so he chose the stories that can teach the importance of the Ten Commandments to all ages.

Finally, Joseph, the son of Jacob, was called to speak to Pharaoh. He had an opportunity to show off his talents and maybe get out of prison. Despite the grave situation he was in, Joseph did not want to take the credit. In Genesis 41:16 he said, "I cannot do it," Joseph replied to Pharaoh, "but God will give Pharaoh the answer he desires." Joseph told Pharaoh the truth—that his ability to interpret dreams is a holy intuition from God and not his own expertise. He took the opportunity not only to tell the truth, but also to teach Pharaoh and the entire Egypt all about the God of Abraham. Just like Joseph in Egypt, I would like to take this opportunity to say that everything that I write is from Hashem. God has given me a gift to be able to hear his messages and comprehend. He also is helping me understand the Bible and its grammatical perfection in detail. Thank you Hashem for giving me the education that I needed in order learn and teach your holy books. Amen.

Gossip

> Leviticus 19:16 says, "Do not go about spreading slander among your people. Do not do anything that endangers your neighbor's life. I am the Lord."

Gossiping is another form of false witnessing. Even if what you are saying is true, it is the perspective that changes the meaning of the story.

Leaving out details can give a person a bad name, and then you may cause them real damage. For example, if your colleague at work has scheduled an interview for a new job and you tell the old boss. Even though it is true, it is false witnessing. Your friend might not get the job and your boss already painted a black picture of her, thinking that she wants to quit. If your friend doesn't get the job and she loses the old job, then you are guilty of "standing over your friend's blood." You promoted the loss of her livelihood because of a few words that were really unnecessary.

There are people who take tremendous pleasure out of gossip. They waste hours talking about others. These people are wasting their lives at best. Sometimes, gossip can even kill a person.

The first chapter of Psalms talks about these people, calling them mockers. If your neighbors, your relatives, or even your colleagues are scoffers you must avoid listening to them. These deriders are dangerous and have been known to put people in prison on false charges. Any idle talk leads to gossip and is very damaging to the brain. As a teenager I had the guts to walk out of a room full of friends because I did not want to listen to hearsay. Just hearing it is a sin; imagine talking and spreading rumors.

> Psalm 1:1–2, "Blessed is the one who does not walk in step with the wicked or stand in the way that sinners take or sit in the company of mockers, but whose delight is in the law of the LORD, and who meditates on his law day and night."

The remedy that the Psalms offers for avoiding these mockers is to study the Torah. Studying the Bible regularly, can enrich your life and give you lots of things to talk about with your friends and family. In my experience, learning anything productive will help you avoid gossip, because it gives you something interesting to talk about. My mother used to talk to people about all kinds of interesting things. Education, needlework, arts and crafts and cooking. She said, "People gossip because they are bored. Taking up hobbies will give you something to talk about instead of other people's business."

The Real Judgment

This world is only temporary. After we pass away we go to another world where we will be judged. We go with all of our ethics, our manners, and everything we believe in. Then we get to see ourselves in a big 3D movie. We don't necessarily know that we are watching our own life events, but we make comments and judge ourselves. If we were in the habit of being merciful, then we will be merciful on ourselves. If we were strict with others, we will be strict on ourselves. Our own judgment is a major factor in deciding the final verdict.

One of the biggest lessons that we must learn in life is to judge people favorably. If you get into the habit of giving people the benefit of the doubt, you will have a better chance on being less judgmental on yourself.

We have to keep practicing to be objective when judging people. Try not to come to conclusions too fast. Don't interrupt when your friend is explaining himself. Even if you are sure that you're right, don't say so. You may be sorry. If you give your opinion gently after they have a chance to talk it out, people will take you more seriously.

To Speak or not to Speak?

I once had a client who came to me because he wanted a remedy for a sexual disease that he contracted from a woman that was not his wife. I knew his wife very well but I didn't tell her. She was a very innocent woman and slightly deaf. If I would have told her she might have gotten very, very ill.

A couple of years later he came back with the same problem. He was cheating again! I told him that I will give him the remedy he needs but if it happens again I will tell his wife. A few months later he got a heart attack and his wife lovingly took care of him. If I had told his wife she would have not even visited him in the hospital and he probably would have died in sorrow. Now they are a loving couple. The man saw how good his wife was and how Hashem really punished him severely. He never cheated on his wife again. Just in case you are wondering what medicine I gave this man, it was lysine, an amino acid that can kill herpes and other serious infections.

There was another story where I reacted quite differently. I was speaking to and old friend and she was complaining that her husband is talking to his secretary all day long. Even at home she calls him up and they chat. The wife didn't think that he was cheating on her but she was hurt that her husband was conversing to another woman instead of spending time with his family. As providence may have it, I met the secretary on the bus one day. She knew me as a well-known healer, and sat down right next to me. Slowly we got into a conversation and she said that she works for my friend's husband. Now was my chance! I told her that his wife was suffering because of her and she better fix it before it's too late. She did not hesitate to quit her job the next day.

In this case I was not a gossiper. I didn't speak behind the secretary's back. I told her straight and to the point that she is playing with fire. I was an observer, telling her about the wife of her boss. I talked about my friend's plight to a person who can really do something about it.

I was pretty proud of myself for that incident but the husband was steaming at me. He forbade his wife to invite me to their house ever again. The peace in his home was restored temporarily, but years later I met my friend and she had gotten divorced. Her ex had stooped to new depths, as the years went on so she had no choice but to leave him.

Don't Be a Hypocrite

In the chapter *"Do Not Take God's Name in Vain,"* a point was made that a religious person shouldn't do things that are not befitting to a someone who is carrying Hashem's name. This ninth commandment is not necessarily meant for a religious person but for any person who has ethics.

This commandment prohibits us from going against our own principles.

For example, a doctor cannot ignore his family's health while healing others. He certainly can't smoke in secret, if he tells others not to smoke. This sounds ridiculous, but you would be surprised how commonplace it is. I have also seen how a judge, who preaches human rights, makes a prejudiced ruling.

Hashem knows people's hearts. He knows our secrets. He knows if a psychologist is helping couples get along and he himself doesn't get along with his own spouse. Practicing what you preach is a basic principle that Hashem uses in order to judge us. Even if people don't believe in God, they must be steadfast in their own principles.

If someone has good values in life but goes against what he believes in, Hashem becomes very angry with him even more than if he transgresses a Torah law.

A person might be forgiven for not having enough faith. People are judged differently depending on their upbringing. If a person is consistent with his ethics and honest to the core, Hashem loves him, even if he never gets chance to learn about God. However, if you can't practice what you preach, it is distasteful in Hashem's eyes, to say the least.

Lying

False witnessing also includes lying. If you tell a lie that is damaging to someone else, it is definitely prohibited. If you are not in a courtroom or in a political office, it is permissible to lie for the sake of peace, or to prevent someone from getting hurt emotionally or physically. For example, if your fellow worker cursed the boss, you shouldn't tell, and you can even deny that he cursed in order to save your friend's job. If you tell it is called gossip. Depending on the results of your gossiping, you can be blamed for the consequences. Here's where, "Love you friend as you love yourself" (Leviticus 19:18) can be your guide.

Hashem Changes His Words

Sarah was shocked when she heard the blessing of the visitor in Genesis 18:10-12:

> Then one of them said, "I will surely return to you about this time next year, and Sarah your wife will have a son."
> Now Sarah was listening at the entrance to the tent, which was behind him. Abraham and Sarah were already very old, and Sarah was past the age of childbearing. So Sarah laughed to herself as she thought, "After I am worn out and my lord is old, will I now have this pleasure?"

When Hashem repeated the words of Sarah to Abraham He said:

Genesis 18:13
> Then the LORD said to Abraham, "Why did Sarah laugh and say, 'Will I really have a child, now that I am old?'

The Creator of the Universe changed the words of Sarah who said, "My Lord is old" and said "I am old," in order not to insult Abraham. From this we learn that it is permitted to lie in order to keep the peace.

This law does not apply when it comes to presenting yourself in a court of law. Then you may not lie or twist the truth. No protecting friends. It is a mitzvah to go up to the witness stand and say everything you know. The exception is, of course, if you are a spy or a soldier for your country, you are allowed to lie to the enemy of your country especially if telling the truth would put others in life threatening danger.

The Worst Transgression of All

In order to be a false witness in court it takes premeditation. You have to agree to be on a list of witnesses, travel to the court and wait your turn. Even at the last minute when you are offered the Holy Bible on which to place your hand, you can still change your mind and just say the truth. If you still lie, then you are also transgressing the second commandment, "Do not take Hashem's name in vain."

Therefore, there is no excuse for this transgression. It is against all moral, legal and religious standards. What will you say to the Holy One Blessed Be He, when you are faced with your own judgement?

Some might give the excuse that they obeyed the orders of their lawyers or boss. Are you so weak that you have no values at all? If you give a false testimony that convicts a person of murder, you are in a sense a murderer yourself. If you give a false testimony that takes a child away from his or her mother or father, you are no better than a kidnapper. It's even worse, because you are doing it in a setting of a court of law that stands for justice, especially if you have lived by the ethics of truth and justice your whole life.

Hashem can have a lot of patience for our mistakes. If you say a lie it may be forgiven, but if you lie in a court of law and it has the potential to damage an innocent person, you are in trouble. Hashem might not even want to look at you unless you make amends to the person you lied about.

Hashem wants us to have values upon which to live. On the other hand, if someone lied in court in order to save his friend and it doesn't cause the court to punish another suspect, that is forgivable. For example, in a custody case a witness says that the father is very good father and he never hits his children. Really, he once saw the father give the child a slap on the wrist. He doesn't have to reveal that to the court because it will be misinterpreted. The father in question is known to the witness as a loving father and his son is very close to him. Saying the whole truth might cause the whole picture to be deceiving and it will ultimately cause injustice. This is why the wording of the Commandment is, "You shall not give false testimony against your neighbor." and not just, "You shall not give false testimony."

Conspiracy

Jewish law does not prosecute anyone for a capital crime unless there are two witnesses (Deuteronomy 17:6). So even though the Torah seems to have very strict laws and corporal punishment, these were hardly ever enacted.

The Torah warns of two witnesses who plan to invent a false story together in order to hurt someone else. If two witnesses have stories that are identical, their testimonies are not accepted because it may have been planned. If there is proof that they planned their scheme and lies, their punishment is the punishment they were planning for the accused.

> Deuteronomy 19:19
> The judges must make a thorough investigation, and if the witness proves to be a liar, giving false testimony against a fellow Israelite, then do to the false witness as that witness intended to do to the other party. You must purge the evil from among you.

This is very comforting news. Even if you have suffered from a conspiracy against you, Hashem, the Judge of all judges, will punish them. Whatever they planned against you will boomerang. It may take time, but justice will prevail.

Spouses often go against each other in court. Someone who loved you and shared everything with you, all of a sudden may turn on you. The only time that this is permissible is if you have to protect someone who is in danger—for example, your children or yourself. You must love your friend as much as yourself, not more than yourself. Your children are your responsibility and are considered your own flesh and blood, even if they are adopted. If you must take your spouse to court in order to protect any of your children, it is mandatory. Nevertheless, you still cannot lie or exaggerate.

If your spouse is not endangering you or your children in any way, you have to be careful to be very peaceful and honest in any divorce settlement. As much as possible, don't reveal any secrets to the court that are not necessary. If your spouse is viciously plotting against you, don't take revenge. If you stand up for yourself in a respectful way, God will surely be on your side, and He will protect you.

During my own divorce case, the social workers were against me having custody of my son. They wanted to divide the children. My ex knew very well that Jonathan was better off with me and his sister. With the help of a mediator, we were able to get to an agreement and I got custody of both children. If I would have fought my ex, I would have lost custody of my son.

In the world of souls, your spouse, even your ex-spouse is your relative. Try to get along. If you need help, get it from friends or clergymen. Show the court that you are mature adults, especially when there are children involved.

One of the reasons it is best to stay out of court, is because some people are not strong enough to say the truth in court. Sometimes even lawyers will tell you to lie. I had that experience myself. I almost was willing to obey my lawyer and fib, but when it came to swearing on the stand, I told the truth. It didn't hurt in the long run, because it was a civil suit and we ended up making a compromise. If I had lied, I would have still felt guilty years later.

Can You Be Your Own Witness?

We mentioned previously that Torah law does not accept a guilty plea in a murder case. The testimony of a killer cannot be accepted because there is a real chance that he is mentally ill. However, you can be your own witness in other cases. The question is, are you allowed to make a plea agreement in order to get a compromise even though your plea is false? In this case your lawyer is the one to decide. Hashem does not want you to suffer for Him. If your lawyer is really on your side and he is wise and experienced, you should listen to him. Hashem will forgive you, and punish those who force you to admit to a crime that you didn't commit.

Judges, lawyers, policemen and social workers who are deceitful in ways that hurt people, will be punished in heaven. After they arrive at the heavenly courts, the angels fault them for something that they didn't do.

The accused will start screaming about their own innocence. While this is transpiring, all his relatives discuss what he did. Suddenly, while the accused is going out of his mind because of the lack of justice, Hashem's voice will come out from above and say, "Now you know what it feels like to be falsely accused." Hashem will then show this soul movies of all the different people that he or she misjudged, misrepresented or cause harm to through false testimony. The humiliation will be very great, while all the soul's deceased relatives and close friends watch his transgressions.

Torah is a Witness

The word *witness* is used in the Bible many times not only for people, but the earth, the sky and even a book can be a witness. My favorite is:

> Deuteronomy 31:26, "Take this book of the law and place it beside the ark of the covenant of the Lord your God. There it will remain as a witness against you."

The Torah is a witness that the miracles of the Exodus from Egypt really happened. It is also a testimony that Hashem gave the Ten Commandments on Mount Sinai and we accepted them as our mutual covenant.

If Hashem calls the Torah a witness, then written or photographed evidence is considered a witness. Since the Torah askes for two witnesses you would need two pieces of evidence or a witness and other evidence that give the same testimony. Circumstantial evidence only works for non-capital crimes. For any capital offense, there must be at least two eyewitnesses over the age of twenty, because they must be questioned.

God is a Witness

The Torah is God's testimony. There really was an Exodus from Egypt, and He really gave the Ten Commandments on Mount Sinai. Sometimes He even swears by saying, "I am God." I found at least forty times in the Torah that God says, "I am God" in the context of an oath. Usually it is after a very important statement. Any time you see such a verse in the Bible, you have to know that it is serious.

Hashem swears to the truth and He detests those who swear falsely even more than those who worship idols. This commandment is not a religious one. It is a crime even for an atheist. If a person can't even adhere to a national, moral and ethical law Hashem has no hope for that person.

If someone is brought to justice in a country that has no justice, all bets are off. You have to do everything to save your life. A court of law that tortures people or puts them to death with little or no evidence, is not considered a court of law in Hashem's view. Let's say a prayer for any good people who fell into such horrific circumstances, "May God be with all the innocent people in the world and save them from the clutches of evil." Amen.

Chapter 13

Do Not Covet

Covet is the English translation to "*Tachmode.*" This word means to have an desire for something that some else has. When the desire is fierce, it causes jealousy. When you have no hope to realize your own aspirations in life and you just are angry that someone else has more than you, the result is jealousy.

Cain killed Abel because he was jealous. Esau wanted to kill Jacob out of jealousy. The brothers of Joseph also planned to murder Joseph because they were jealous. It seems like jealousy is the number one motive for murder in the Bible. That is why this prohibition is important enough to be in the Ten Commandments.

> Exodus 20:17, "You shall not covet your neighbor's house. You shall not covet your neighbor's wife, or his male or female servant, his ox or donkey, or anything that belongs to your neighbor."

How can Hashem command a person what to feel or not to feel? In order to answer that question, I would like to explore other laws of the heart.

> Leviticus 19:18, "Do not seek revenge or bear a grudge against anyone among your people, but love your neighbor as yourself. I am the Lord."

In the chapter *"Do Not Murder,"* we explored the possibility of changing your faith outwardly in order to save lives. God sees our heart as no one else does. He can command you to have a change of heart because that is what you will be judged on in heaven. Hashem will reward you for your good intentions even though you didn't fully succeed. If we are very angry or jealous in our heart, we may act politely, but we will not give a good feeling to the recipient of our favor.

The best way to change our heart is to learn the Bible. The Old Testament will enter your heart and give you good pure energy. Reading my books will also give you a change of heart. I have seen how some of my readers have transformed by reading my work and internalizing my messages.

"Do unto Others"

One of the great sayings of our sages is, "Don't do unto others what you don't want others to do unto you. That is the first step in fulfilling the Torah laws." If we are careful never to hurt other people, including our spouse and children, we can begin to feel love towards them and get rid of envy and revenge.

If you help your friend study for a test, are you jealous if he succeeds? It's not possible! If you help your friend shop for new clothing, are you jealous of how well it fits? Not at all—you feel happy for your friend and proud of yourself, for helping her choose the right fit.

The commandment not to covet is also a commandment for the fortunate person to share. You should allow friends to participate in your good fortune. Coveting comes from keeping distant and from showing off.

If you buy a new car, take your friends for a drive let them enjoy themselves. Instead of being jealous, they will feel lucky that they have you as a friend. If your friend shows off that he just bought a big yacht, you can be jealous, but what if he invites you for a ride? Instead of feeling jealous, you will feel lucky and proud to have him as a friend. The rich yacht owner gets the reward for not causing you to covet.

This commandment specifies the problem of one man being jealous of another man's wife. If you help your friend, encourage him and give emotional support, he won't feel jealous that you are married. He'll respect you as a married man. By asking him for detailed information in order to understand what he needs in a mate, he will realize that your spouse is special for you and he has different needs. Of course you should remind him that matches are made in heaven.

This touches on the next point of this commandment: We must believe that whatever we have is what Hashem wants us to have. What your friend has is what Hashem wants him to have, unless it came to him through theft or any other transgression in the Torah. In that case you certainly shouldn't be jealous.

When you start helping people and sharing with them, Hashem will bless you with a good heart. He will bless you with the ability to love people and to love Him. When you "serve Hashem with all you heart and all your soul," you take advantage of this gift of love and you use it to pass it on to others.

Be Happy with Your Lot

Ethics of the Fathers is an ancient book on good ethics and values. It was written in the first century CE by the first Rabbis and is still applicable today. *Ethics of the Fathers* asks a question and answers: "Who is happy? The one who is happy with his lot." Would you want to change your whole life with all of your problems, with the lives of your friends? Most people would rather keep their lot in life, than forfeit the gifts that God gave them for the gifts He gave to others. If you get to know all about your friend's life in minute detail, you will probably stop being jealous. Just pray to Hashem with all your heart for what you really need, He will take care of you.

Healthy Jealousy

> Exodus 20:17, "You shall not covet your neighbor's house. You shall not covet your neighbor's wife, or his male or female servant, his ox or donkey, or anything that belongs to your neighbor."

The law "Do not covet" includes material things like wealth and physical pleasures. When I was growing up, I was jealous at times that my friends had a normal, peaceful, non-abusive family. Being jealous of peace and happiness in the home when it is absent, is normal and healthy. I didn't realize it, but this jealousy motivated me to spend more time at my friends' homes to learn what happy home environment felt like. You are also allowed to be jealous of your friend's ability to learn and do good deeds.

Healthy jealousy is also helpful in getting us to try harder. I remember when I was fourteen years old, one of my friend's sisters spent a year in Israel. She was able to speak Hebrew fluently. I was so jealous! It wasn't a burning jealousy; it was a dream. *"Maybe I will someday be fluent in Hebrew."* Two years later I was in Israel working very hard on learning the language. I became fluent in the "Holy Tongue" and even got my diploma as a Hebrew teacher for Israelis.

When you share with your friend, you may or may not be performing the mitzvah of charity because he may not necessarily need assistance. However, you are still performing the mitzvah not to covet. This is a general rule for all the Commandments. If you help someone perform the commandment successfully, you get the credit.

When I was a very young mother, we were not well to do. However, the neighborhood in which I was living was a very poor one, and we had a car, a little Fiat. In Jerusalem in the 1980's, any car was something to envy. We had a name of being well to do, even though we were living very simply for American standards. One day, a neighbor of mine came knocking at my door. She asked to borrow twenty-five dollars until the end of the month, when her child support came in. She was divorced with three children. I told her that I had no money to spare, but I would like to help her out. She needed bread, milk, and eggs. I took my charity box and shook it out, and we both counted together enough money for the milk and bread. I told her that my husband had bought lots of eggs and I could give her one dozen if she paid me back on time. I gave her the eggs and the small change, and she left satisfied. Even though I had no money, I felt even happier to help than she was to receive. I didn't realize at the time, but I was not only giving charity. I was also performing the mitzvah not to covet. Hashem rewarded me for that deed. A week later my husband bought a few cases of fresh eggs from a neighboring farm. I sold them and earned some money. It was a couple of weeks before Passover. With the money I earned, I bought plenty of food for the holiday.

Generous people are not overly attached to their money or envious of other people's money or belongings. When you die, you can't take your belongings or your money with you and get compensated or credited for them. You do take your good deeds and your good character traits with you; your true wealth.

True Wealth

We can't close a chapter on the subject of jealousy without mentioning the very rich. Many actors and famous singers went into drugs and died young. Others just struggle with alcohol, divorce, emotional stress and health problems, much more than in the average population. So no matter how much money and fame, they were still not happy. They have nothing of which you should be jealous. Happiness comes from within. Only spiritual happiness is everlasting. The only desires that are truly positive, are the wholesome desires you can take with you to the next world. Strive to take your healthy longings as you can't take your belongings with you! If you accomplish the ability to learn from life's mishaps, to give, to share, and to grow emotionally and spiritually, you have true wealth. Of course if you have a good marital relationship as well as good children, you are the richest of all.

When I was a young adult struggling for every cent, I felt jealous of friends of mine who had rich and generous parents. One day, when I needed money for a real emergency, my own mother refused to help me. She even attacked and blamed me for wasting my money. So I called up one friend whose father-in-law was a millionaire to borrow $5,000. She said, "That's a lot of money. I go through major calculations and criticism for every penny that we need. This is something that my parents won't agree to."

Then I asked another friend whose father was a multimillionaire, and she said, "I have to ask for money for myself. Everything I need goes under examination."

I said, "Maybe your father will agree for a loan of just a few months."

She said, "No, he would never agree." She was really afraid to even ask.

I wasn't angry with my friends. I was just sad. For decades I was jealous of these friends who had their families' support. I went to their homes seeing all the luxury and burned with jealousy. Now I found out that they were prisoners of their parents' wishes. I'd rather have my own place even though it's rented, but I am free. I am free to decide what I want to do with the money that I earn. Even better than that, I have a spouse with whom to share that freedom. This lesson was beautifully taught in a motion picture called *Arthur* starring Russell Brand. It is a lovely comedy about a multimillionaire's son who wanted to be a free man.

Sometimes God uses money as a vehicle to wake us up; to change our behavior and our lives. He would rather take away our money than take away our health. Hashem loves us and doesn't want to hurt us, so if you lose money, think of it as a sign that Hashem is giving you second chance. He wants you to improve without going through a major catastrophe.

What happened at the end? Did we get the money we needed? Another friend's husband, who had no extra money of his own was so grateful to me for helping his wife that he signed as a guarantor for a low interest bank loan. Sometimes poor people are much more generous than the rich ones. They don't idolize their money.

This World Is Temporary

Your friends' worldly possessions are only temporary. They can't take them to heaven. It is not worth being jealous of others for their temporary ownership of impermanent objects and fleeting substances.

In this world we have courthouses, banks, loans, tape recorders, videotapes, and DVD movies. All these inventions are Hashem's way of revealing to us how things are in the world to come. Every soul who reaches heaven does not have the same experience.

When you go to the next world, you may have your judgment day in the heavenly court. Some souls may watch a review of their lives as a movie. The result of this judgement is not a simple guilty or innocent verdict. It is an exact accounting of the pluses and the minuses, the good deeds and the sins. There is absolute overall justice.

God will reward you for the good things you have done, even if no one knew about them in this world. You will also get paid for enduring challenges and tests of faith and character in this world. Nothing goes unnoticed in the heavenly review of your life. You leave the judgement hall with a bank account. If you are in plus, you can use it to help your children and grandchildren on earth. If you are in minus you might have to return to earth as a newborn baby and attempt to improve the next time around.

I was a natural healer for twenty-six years, helping people day and night. Even though we were very popular and helped thousands of people, we didn't make much money. The Jews of Jerusalem are very poor. Many asked for discounts, and we rarely denied anyone our help. Our success wasn't in money; it was in mitzvot. I met many former patients who praised me for their miraculous recovery, years after they have been cured by my advice, and they are still healthy. One day, after we die, we will be judged in heaven. We will have lots of witnesses to speak on our behalf.

Judgment Day

A man goes to the next world,
Without belongings for his needs.
He takes with him an enormous sack,
With bundles of his deeds.
He will face the judgment day,
Trembling with fears.
His relatives who passed away,
Will wipe away his tears.

> *They can see a movie screen,*
> *The most modern of its kind.*
> *They see a man doing things,*
> *And going out of his mind.*
> *To his surprise he did OK,*
> *Despite his terrible sins.*
>
> *His transgressions were outweighed,*
> *When he helped his neighbor and her kids.*
> *The true size of a good deed,*
>
> *You won't know at all.*
> *Until that very fateful day.*
> *Meanwhile you're on call.*

****

Thus, you basically have three things to work on in this world:

1) To accumulate mitzvoth—or good deeds
2) to improve your character
3) to teach your loved ones to do the same

Many people worry about whether they are going to have enough money to survive this world. If you start feeling spiritually wealthy, your worries will vanish and God will bless your belongings and your money in this world as well as in heaven.

Chapter 14
The Eternal Laws

Now that you've learned the basics, do we really have to observe them? Are the Ten Commandments ancient rules that were limited to a particular period of time?

Hashem said that the Ten Commandments would all be eternal. In the following passage Moses reminds the Israelites of the importance of the Ten Commandments:

> Deuteronomy 5:9-13, "Only be careful, and watch yourselves closely so that you do not forget the things your eyes have seen or let them fade from your heart as long as you live. Teach them to your children and to their children after them. Remember the day you stood before the LORD your God at Horeb, when he said to me, "Assemble the people before me to hear my words so that they may learn to revere me as long as they live in the land and may teach them to their children." You came near and stood at the foot of the mountain while it blazed with fire to the very heavens, with black clouds and deep darkness. Then the LORD spoke to you out of the fire. You heard the sound of words but saw no form; there was only a voice. He declared to you his covenant, the Ten

> Commandments, which he commanded you to follow and then wrote them on two stone tablets."

Hours before his death Moses reminded the Israelites about that fateful day on Mount Sinai. He knew that in the future the Israelites would sin and worship other gods, but he also knew that God's words would not be in vain. In the future the nation of Israel would keep Hashem's Torah in heart and in action and the words He uttered on Mount Sinai would be a message to the whole world forever.

> Ecclesiastes 3:14
> I know that everything God does will endure forever; nothing can be added to it and nothing taken from it. God does it so that people will fear him.

Hashem has been waiting patiently for someone to convey that message. I am touched in my heart as I realize that Hashem chose me to write this book. Hashem's dream is that His message from 3500 years ago gets around. I am overwhelmed by the thought that I can help God fulfill His dream.

Alive here Today

> Deuteronomy 5:1-5
> "Hear, Israel, the decrees and laws I declare in your hearing today. Learn them and be sure to follow them. The LORD our God made a covenant with us at Horeb. It was not with our ancestors that the LORD made this covenant, but with us, with all of us who are alive here today. The LORD spoke to you face to face out of the fire on the mountain. At that time, I stood between the LORD and you to declare to you the word

of the LORD, because you were afraid of the fire and did not go up the mountain."

When Moses said that the Lord made this covenant, "with all of us who are alive here today," He meant you and me. The Torah is eternal and it was written for every generation. Today, more than ever before, millions of people, young and old are literate enough to study the Torah. The Internet and the multi-media facilitate the proliferation of Hashem's words to the world.

In Deuteronomy chapters 31-32, Moses prophesized that the children of Israel would sin and forget God and His Torah. The stone slates of the Torah were put in a safe place in the Holy of Holies in the Tabernacle. They would be a witness.

> Deuteronomy 31:24-26
> After Moses finished writing in a book the words of this law from beginning to end, he gave this command to the Levites who carried the ark of the covenant of the LORD: "Take this Book of the Law and place it beside the ark of the covenant of the LORD your God. There it will remain as a witness against you."

The Ark of the Covenant was placed in the Holy of Holies. No one was allowed into this area except the high priest once a year. He entered in order to pray on the holiest day of the year. He was not allowed to touch anything inside. The Torah and the Ark were kept in the Holy of Holies until the Holy Temple was destroyed in the year 586 BCE.

Today the Torah is a witness for us. It is a witness that the Exodus from Egypt really happened and God made miracles that broke the laws of nature. The mere fact that the Torah survived until today and is even more famous than it ever was, gives witness that its words are divine.

Thus, the Torah was hidden for over a thousand years. From Moses' death until Ezra the scribe, the Old Testament was not in circulation. How did it survive? How can we be sure that we have the original words as God told Moses? How did the Israelites repent from their sin of idol worship? Hashem promised the Land of Canaan to twelve tribes of Israel, so why are the Ten Lost Tribes not with us to inherit the land?

In my next book, *God's Hidden Treasure* you will learn just how the Torah survived physically and spiritually. The book will give answers to the above questions and many more. The answers that I discovered are surprising but the evidence that I give is undeniable. I also explain why Hashem revealed Himself in a burning bush that wouldn't be consumed. The important but undocumented role that woman had in Jewish history is also revealed.

May God bless you with the pleasure of learning the Bible, the strength to carry out the laws of the Ten Commandments, and the wisdom to discern truth from fiction, especially when you read my next book. Amen.

Epilogue: God's Way

After completing this book, you must feel like we have gone through a long journey together, a journey of the soul. Everyone goes through many treks in life be they good and bad, funny and miserable. Without faith, people tend to make their own rules and regulations. Sometimes the rules are good and sometimes they are not so good. The main thing is that they are to be followed. No one is free. People may feel free, unencumbered to do things their way, but after many years, their way becomes the only way.

For example, when you walk into a home of an older woman, you must put your coat where she says and eat where she permits you to dine. She herself may have made herself dietary rules and is very strict about what she can or cannot eat and when. She also has a set calendar and set rules of when she can go out in the sun or out in the cold. She may have established self-made regulations as to how to talk and how to dress. The rules are endless. Do you know what? God's rules are easier!

If I'm going to end up with a long list of rules and a particular way of life, why not make it God's way? His laws are a lot better that any mortal can create and chances are we will make a lot less mistakes if we just do things the way the Torah teaches.

We are under the illusion that in this day and age everyone is allowed to make their own rules. This is so far from the truth. Modern life dictates rules and regulations endlessly. You must obey the rules of every government office religiously. You must adhere to your doctor's orders even if you don't feel like it. All these rules and regulations can become quite confusing and sometimes they seem unfair or unjust.

In this crazy world that we live in, it is comforting to have the Torah and the Ten Commandments so we know what Hashem's rules are. Unlike the government officials, Hashem didn't make rules for His own advantage. When you have a doubt in life, always think about what God would like you to do. That will be the best choice that you can make. When you follow God's way you are really doing it your way, because God's way is the best way to get the results that you want and need. I hope this book can be your guide in understanding God's way.

The following song is my finale. I didn't write this book my way, I did it "God's Way."

God's Way

And now, the end is near,

And so I face the final pages.
You've learned, the words are clear,
They're from Hashem and from our sages.
To write a book that's full,
I gave the quotes, not just what I say,
And more, much more than this,
I gave you God's way.

Troubles, we've had a few
We've made mistakes, some that I've mentioned
I wrote what we could do,
To see it through despite the tension.
God planned each charted course,
Until He said He's guiding my way.
And when, He told me this, I did it God's way

Yes, there are times, I'll tell you now,
I asked Hashem just why and how.
But after all, there is no doubt,
I had a lot to write about
I faced it all 'cuz I'm on call, to teach you God's way.

You sang, you laughed and cried,
You've been impressed, but it's confusing.
And now, we say good-bye,
I hope you found this song amusing.
To see all that I've done,
And may I say it, in a shy way?
"Oh, no; no it's not me,
It's only God's way"

For what's a woman, what's she got?
If not Hashem, then she has naught.
I say the things He truly feels,
These are His words not to appeal.
My story shows just how it goes,
So do it God's way.

Glossary

Aliyah: Immigration to Israel

Ashkenazic: Descendants of Jews who formed communities in central and eastern Europe, traditionally speaking Yiddish.

Baal Teshuva: A secular person who commits himself to observing the Torah and keeping the commandments.

Bris (or Brit): Circumcision ceremonially performed on an eight-day-old male Jewish baby in observance of the covenant established between God and Abraham where God promises to multiply the descendants of Abraham and give them the Land of Canaan.

Canonization: The sealing of a religious book or set of books and declaring them holy. After canonization, the book cannot be revised or edited. The Old Testament was canonized in 200 CE. The New Testament was canonized in 400 CE.

Chassidic: The adjective of Chassidism. It is a branch of Orthodox Judaism that began in the eighteenth century. The first rabbi that started Chassidism was called the Baal Shem Tov. The Chassidim, his followers, are much stricter than others about dress and separation between the genders. They are also emphasizing music, dance, and doing kindness to others. They wear clothing that was worn in Europe before WWII.

Chesed: Loving kindness. An act of benevolence. Giving without anticipation for reward.

Cholent: A stew made from beans, barley, potatoes, and usually meat which is left to cook slowly all Friday night to be eaten for the Sabbath meal on Saturday.

Cohen: Israelite priest, a descendant of Aaron the brother of Moses.

Cohanim: Plural of Cohen. Israelite or Jewish priests

Dead Sea Scrolls: Scrolls from over two thousand years ago found from 1946 till 1956 that were preserved in caves near the shore of the Dead Sea. The texts include the earliest known surviving manuscripts of works later included in the Hebrew Bible.

Diaspora: The dispersion or scattering of a nation from its homeland.

Eilat: A city at the southern tip of Israel at the shore of the Red Sea. Eilat is known internationally for its tourist attractions.

Elul: The month of repentance before Rosh Hashanah, usually falling in September. Corresponds to the astrological sign of Virgo.

Ethics of the Fathers: This is a book of sayings and morals of rabbis that lived before the destruction of the Holy Temple. In Hebrew it is called Pirkei Avoth. This book of faith and ethical behavior is a compilation of sayings that were learned by heart until the second century, when it they were written down.

Essenes: A Jewish cult of the first century BCE to the first century CE. The Essenes lived in the area of the Dead Sea. They were a group of celibate men who worked all day copying the Bible and preserving it. The Dead Sea Scrolls were found in caves in Qumran near the Dead Sea between 1946 and 1956. Their writings also include their rules and customs. The holy writings are identical to the Bible that we have today. All the books of the Bible were found there with the exception of the scroll of Esther. This is true evidence that the Bible hasn't changed for two thousand years.

Gaavah: Haughty pride

Gematria: A Jewish system of numerology that assigns a numerical value for each Hebrew letter. The numerical value of a Hebrew word or phrase and the identical numerical value of those words and phrases suggests a relationship between them.

Gentile: Anyone who isn't Jewish

Haggadah: A prayer book used on Passover evening at the dinner table to recite the story of Exodus and prayers of thankfulness for our freedom from slavery.

Halacha: Jewish law as instructed by the rabbis since the year 1570 CE.

Halachically: A conjugation of the word *Halacha* meaning "according to Halacha."

Hashem: Literally "the Name." A nickname for God. This word is the most common name that Orthodox Jews use for God, even when they are speaking in other languages.

Hasmonean: See Maccabees

Havdalah: Literally, division. A prayer said at the end of Sabbath on Saturday night to divide the holiness of Sabbath from the secular week which begins Saturday night, considered to be a weekday when all work is permitted.

Hay: The fifth letter of the Hebrew alphabet. It has a consonant sound like the letter H, or it can be silent at the end of a word, as in the name Sarah.

High Priest: There were many priests in the holy temple to do the work of the sacrifices but just one high priest who led the ceremonies. He entered the Holy of Holies of the Holy Temple, where the tablets of the Ten Commandments were kept along with the Torah, once a year on Yom Kippur, the Day of Atonement. The first high priest was Aaron the brother of Moses.

Israelites: The descendants of Jacob, who was also called Israel. He acquired that name from an angel who fought with him all night until Jacob won. Israel in Hebrew is *Yisrael*, a combination of the two words, *Yashar*, meaning straight and also means honest, and *El*, meaning God. Thus, Yisrael is the Hebrew word for Israel. It means straight to God and no one intervenes between man and God. The faith of the Israelite must be honest, with no extraneous or sacrilegious motives.

Jubilee: In the ancient Hebrew calendar every seven years there was a sabbatical year and a Jubilee year every fifty years (see Shmittah in Glossary).
Leviticus 25:8-13 states:
"Count off seven sabbath years—seven times seven years—so that the seven sabbath years amount to a period of forty-nine years. Then have the trumpet

sounded everywhere on the tenth day of the seventh month; on the Day of Atonement sound the trumpet throughout your land. Consecrate the fiftieth year and proclaim liberty throughout the land to all its inhabitants. It shall be a jubilee for you; each of you is to return to your family property and to your own clan. The fiftieth year shall be a jubilee for you; do not sow and do not reap what grows of itself or harvest the untended vines. For it is a jubilee and is to be holy for you; eat only what is taken directly from the fields. In this Year of Jubilee everyone is to return to their own property." The Hebrew term is *Yoval*. On the Jubilee year all slaves are freed and all debts are absolved. Any land that once belonged to a family of a tribe of Israel returns to its owners. Nowadays the Jubilee is not observed as we are not sure exactly when it is. The Sabbatical is still observed in Israel by orthodox Jews.

Kabbalah: A body of mystical teachings of rabbinical origin, often based on an esoteric interpretation of the Hebrew scriptures.

Kabbalist: An expert who is highly skilled in obscure or difficult or esoteric matters as a student of the Jewish Kabbalah

Kasher: To make utensils or meat kosher. The laws for koshering meat include soaking it half an hour in water and then an hour covered in coarse salt before it is finally rinsed. Broiling the meat over a flame to remove the blood also makes it kosher.

Ketuba: A Jewish marriage contract written on a scroll. The rabbi writes a handwritten contract on a leather parchment. It lists the man's obligations to his new wife and a large sum of money offered by the groom as compensation in case of divorce. Sometimes women waive their rights to that money in order to speed up the divorce process, but some women insist on it, especially if there is a case of infidelity. The *Ketuba* is signed by the groom and two witnesses but not by the bride. It is read aloud, right before the marriage ceremony under the canopy.

Kiddush: A prayer said over wine on Friday night and Saturday morning in honor of the Sabbath.

Kinneret: The Sea of Galilee. It is Israel's largest lake. It is in the northeast section of Israel surrounded by hills, mountains, and beautiful landscapes.

Kotel: The western wall surrounding the Holy Temple in Jerusalem. Also known as the Wailing Wall, the remaining wall left standing from the time of the Holy Temple, where Jews today assemble to pray.

Kumran: An ancient city near the Dead Sea. Today an archeological site of the Essenes culture. This is the site where the Dead Sea Scrolls were discovered.

Levite: A man who belongs to the tribe of Levi, the third son of Jacob. The Levites served in the holy temple, singing and playing musical instruments. They washed the hands and feet of the priests (Cohanim) and assisted in the maintenance of the Holy Temple and the Tabernacle in the wilderness. They were responsible for teaching Torah to the Jewish people. They did not receive an inheritance of land so they could spread out in the land to instruct the people in the laws of the Torah.

Maccabees: In 167 BCE, Matthias and his five sons formed a small army to fight the Assyrians and the Hellenists.

They called themselves Maccabees for the initials of their motto, "Who is like you, Hashem, among the gods?" They conquered the Holy Temple, purified the temple, and restored the temple service. They were also known as the Hasmoneans. The Hasmonean Dynasty held rule in Israel from 142 BCE to 63 BCE.

Marranos: In the year 1492 the Spanish kingdom declared that all Jews must leave their country with only minimum belongings. If they don't leave within the first year they must either convert or die. Many Jews left and many stayed and converted. The converts were called Marranos. Some of the Marranos continued their faith secretly, but if they were caught they were persecuted and tortured to death. Many Jews were burned at the stake in a public arena. This period of history was called the Spanish Inquisition. It lasted until the 17th century. Most of the Jews forgot their heritage but remembered they were Jewish. They were very careful to marry within the nation. Nowadays, there is a movement of some Marranos to return to the faith of their ancestors and live in Israel.

Megilla: A scroll constructed from animal skin intended for writing.

Melacha: Usually translated as work, it is activity that is prohibited on Shabbat and or on festivals.

Midrash: A story that helps in the understanding of biblical contents. Midrashim (plural of Midrash) were originally passed on orally and originated in the second century CE.

Mikvah: Also spelled mikveh. A ritual bath connected to a direct source of rain or well water. A mikvah must have enough water to cover the entire body of an average-sized person. A mikvah must hold a minimum of approximately 575 liters. Immersion purifies ritual impurity. A natural source of water like a pond, lake, river, sea, or ocean may also serve as a mikvah.

Mitzvah: Literally and biblically a commandment from God. In modern colloquial Hebrew, the word mitzvah is used as a merit that you receive for keeping one of the commandments. For example, "You'll get a big mitzvah if you help me get this loan." Mitzvah is also used as a way of defining an act as being a favorable deed to do according to the Bible. For example, "It's a mitzvah to help that girl."

Mitzvot: Also can be spelled mitzvoth, it is the plural of mitzvah.

Moshav: Farming village

Nefesh: The part of the soul that gives life.

Neshama: The part of the soul that gives human understanding and especially speech.

Noachide Laws: Laws that were given to Noah.

Oneg: Delight

Orah: Spiritual light

Ordinances: Statues, laws, or decrees

Passover: The Torah ordains the observance of a seven-day holiday when eating leavened bread and baked goods are forbidden and it is a commandment to eat matzot, or unleavened bread. Passover commemorates the story of the Exodus as described in the book of Exodus, in which the Israelites were freed from slavery in Egypt. Pesach is the Hebrew term for Passover. On the first night of Pesach, Jews read the *Haggadah*, a booklet which tells the account of the Exodus. A festive meal called the *seder* is prepared. An order of different blessings on foods, stories and songs is arranged in the Haggadah. Pesach is a time when Jews traditionally give charity so everyone can participate in a seder of their own or in a community seder.

Pekuach Nefesh: Life-threatening emergency

Pentateuch: The first five books of the Bible, also known as the Torah

Phylacteries: They are a Jewish prayer ornament called tefillin in Hebrew. They consist of two leather boxes with leather straps. One is tied onto the arm and one to the head. They contain four paragraphs from the Torah that are written on parchment. Jewish men put them on for their daily prayers. Below is a diagram of a man wearing Phylacteries.

The source of this mitzvah comes from Deuteronomy 6:8 "Tie them as symbols on your hands and bind them on your foreheads."

Rabbinate: A group of Rabbis that form a legal organization. The Israeli Rabbinate is in charge of marriage, divorce, inheritance and kosher food. Their guideline is Torah Law.

Rashi: An acronym for Rabbi Shlomo Yitzchaki. He was the first rabbi to write a clear, word-for-word commentary on the entire Bible and Talmud including grammar and vocabulary explanations. Rashi lived in the eleventh century, but his commentaries are still the most popular and the most widely studied within the Orthodox Jewish community. It is the first commentary to be studied in school. In Jewish day schools the children start learning this commentary in the fourth grade.

Rebbe: A Yiddish word derived from the Hebrew word for rabbi. He is a personal mentor and teacher, as well as a spiritual leader, but unlike a rabbi, he is not necessarily an authority on Jewish law. A rebbe blesses his congregants and is sometimes considered a holy man. His followers are called Chassidim, and Chasidism is the name of the movement. The first rebbe was the Baal Shem Tov in the eighteenth century.

Reincarnation: The rebirth of a soul in a new body. Jews believe in reincarnation for any person who was not perfect in their lifetime. Every lifetime the soul has new challenges in order to further grow and develop.

Righteous: Morally good. Someone who excels in goodness and who acts in virtuous ways for God, not for his own pride.

Rosh Hashanah: The beginning of the Jewish New Year. A two-day holiday when no work is done. Considered as the Day of Judgment for the actions in the past year. It is a day of blowing the shofar or ram's horn and of prayer to God for a favorable decree in the coming year.

Sanhedrin: An assembly of twenty-three appointed judges in every city in the Land of Israel. The Supreme Jewish Court or Sanhedrin consisted of a body of seventy-one judges. The court had an odd number of judges to prevent deadlocks. These judges were God fearing Bible scholars, who were also knowledgeable in secular studies. They made their decisions in accordance with Jewish law.

Shabbat: Sabbath in Hebrew with Israeli pronunciation.

Shabbos: Sabbath in Yiddish, or in Hebrew with Ashkenazic pronunciation.

Safed: A city in northern Israel situated on high mountains. In Hebrew it is called Tzfat. The city has ancient history and today is still a vibrant town full of historical sites and tourist interest.

Seminary: A post high school institute for religious studies. In Jewish girls' seminaries, there are also secular studies for occupational options, mostly careers in education.

Sephardic: Descendants of Jews who lived in the Iberian Peninsula, predominantly from Spain as well as a minority from Portugal before the late fifteenth century. The Spanish and Portuguese Inquisitions forced many Sephardic Jews to convert to Christianity or maintain their Jewish faith in secret as Crypto-Jews. Sephardic Jews under persecution emigrated to North Africa, Asia Minor, the Middle East, and elsewhere around the world. They also escaped from Spain to South America with Columbus in 1942. Some of the descendants of Crypto-Jews converted outwardly and remained in Iberia, they were called Marranos. Sephardic Jews are unified in their prayer book and traditional customs that differ from the Ashkenazic Jewish customs and liturgy.

Shalom Bayit: Peace in the home between husband and wife and among family members.

Shavuot: The holiday known as the Feast of Weeks, which falls fifty days after the start of the second day of the holiday of Passover. Traditionally, Jews celebrate the giving of the Torah on Mount Sinai on Shavuot.

Shmittah: A sabbatical year for the land in Israel following the Torah prohibition not to work the land every seven years

Sukkah: A temporary shed constructed specially for the eight-day holiday of Succoth (Tabernacles) where meals are eaten and holiday prayers and songs are recited and sung.

Sukkoth: Also spelled Succot, plural of Sukkah, known in English as the Feast of Booths or Tabernacles. It occurs in September or October, depending upon the Hebrew calendar. On this holiday, meals are eaten inside the sukkah, a hut made of wood or cloth. It is a celebration of the exodus of the Israelites from Egypt and the wandering for forty years in the Sinai wilderness, dwelling in huts. In ancient Israel it was also a day to celebrate the end of harvest season.

Tabernacles: See Succoth

Talmud: A compilation of discussions of the Rabbis of the first half of the first millennia CE. It is the central book of Rabbinic Judaism, written in the year 500 CE and revised many times until the invention of the printing press.

Tanaim: The rabbis living in Israel from the year 70 CE until 200 CE.

Ten Lost Tribes: The tribes of the kingdom of Israel that were exiled after they were conquered during the Holy Temple period.

Torah: The first five books of the Bible known as the Pentateuch. Torah literally means teaching or instruction.

Tractate: A portion of the Talmud. There are sixty-three tractates in the Talmud.

Tribes of Israel: The Israelites were divided into tribes according to their ancestors, the twelve sons of Jacob. Joseph is not counted as one of the tribes. Instead his two sons are enumerated as leaders of tribes, Menashe and Ephraim. The tribe of Levi did not receive land because they were destined to be the teachers of Israel and spread all over.

Yeshiva: A school for religious studies, for males over thirteen years old. The young women attend seminary while the boys and men go to Yeshiva.

Yiddish: A language that Jews spoke in Eastern Europe and Russia. It is a German dialect laced with Hebrew words and written in Hebrew letters. Today the language remains alive in some Chassidic towns in America Europe and in Israel.

Yom Kippur: The Day of Atonement. The single most important day of the Hebrew calendar. It is a fast day and also a day of prayer for repentance.

Index

A

abortion 9, 10, 82, 211, 212, 213
Abraham (Hebrew patriarch) 20, 21, 22, 23, 24, 25, 27, 28, 29, 32, 33, 38, 41, 43, 59, 60, 61, 82, 83, 84, 85, 96, 97, 98, 112, 113, 141, 156, 162, 199, 211, 257, 277, 289, 295, 296, 321
accounting 8, 9, 12, 13, 16, 229, 310
animals 6, 7, 13, 14, 16, 17, 67, 73, 78, 136, 150, 169, 171
atheism 76, 92, 93

B

Bible stories xi, 10, 289

C

child sacrifices 81
cities of refuge 201, 203
Courtrooms of the Mind (Teller) 129
covenant xxii, 5, 17, 18, 19, 27, 28, 29, 32, 35, 36, 38, 41, 66, 70, 71, 95, 140, 151, 161, 170, 227, 252, 301, 313, 314, 315, 321
covenant of peace 252

creation,
    days of 1, 2, 151
creation story 146

D

Dead Sea 53, 114, 322, 323, 326
death xix, 23, 24, 30, 31, 70, 83, 88, 109, 121, 127, 129, 147, 167, 168, 169, 170, 171, 175, 176, 179, 180, 198, 199, 200, 202, 204, 212, 213, 214, 221, 225, 227, 228, 229, 230, 238, 256, 263, 265, 273, 274, 288, 302, 314, 316, 327
death penalty 30, 167, 168, 169, 171, 175, 176, 180, 200, 225, 227, 228, 229, 238, 263, 274
descendants 8, 17, 23, 28, 32, 95, 252, 321, 324, 331
disease 107, 108, 179, 209, 210, 213, 276, 292
divorce 110, 195, 227, 228, 229, 231, 232, 233, 239, 240, 246, 270, 299, 308, 326, 329

E

Egypt xiv, 28, 31, 32, 35, 37, 38, 43, 52, 56, 57, 64, 65, 69, 71, 77, 78, 86, 97, 99, 105, 136, 137, 138, 139, 167, 173, 254, 256, 257, 258, 260, 262, 288, 289, 301, 315, 328, 332
Egyptians 31, 58, 78, 97, 256, 257, 258
Elijah (prophet) 59
Exodus Case (Moller) 22, 34, 35, 54

F

false prophets xxi, 59, 83, 89, 121
false testimony 281, 287, 296, 297, 298, 300
false witness 12, 31, 117, 129, 281, 289, 296, 298
free will 13, 75, 77, 88, 89, 101
Friday 92, 132, 133, 134, 135, 155, 157, 158, 159, 164, 165, 171, 256, 270, 322, 326

G

Genesis
    book of 85
    stories of 20, 33
God, image of 2, 7, 9, 11, 29, 210, 211
gods xiv, xvii, xviii, xxi, 20, 21, 31, 32, 43, 58, 59, 61, 66, 67, 68, 69, 70, 71, 72, 73, 75, 76, 79, 83, 86, 93, 94, 95, 111, 120, 121, 161, 205, 207, 266, 314, 327
gossip 287, 290, 291, 295
government xi, 19, 62, 92, 257, 258, 259, 265, 272, 279, 318

H

Hashem
    children of 115, 189
    name of 140
Hashem command 106, 303
holidays xvi, 56, 57, 58, 157, 191
Holy of Holies 315, 324
honesty 128, 194
honor 24, 134, 151, 155, 156, 157, 169, 175, 178, 192, 209, 269, 270, 326

I

idolatry 68, 71, 75, 106, 107, 243
idols,
    worship of 72
incest 4, 5, 8, 12, 31, 180, 205, 224, 225, 245, 246, 276, 277
infidelity 8, 225, 228, 229, 230, 237, 240, 326
inheritance 27, 32, 129, 156, 198, 199, 219, 256, 272, 326, 329
Intelligent Design 91, 93, 148
Isaac (son of Abraham) 23, 25, 27, 29, 33, 38, 43, 60, 82, 84, 95, 96, 198, 224, 257
Isaiah xvii, 77, 86, 93, 94, 95, 140, 155, 156, 158, 159, 172, 220, 226, 246
Israel xiv, xvi, xvii, xxii, 4, 14, 15, 19, 22, 27, 28, 31, 32, 33, 35, 36, 37, 38, 39, 42, 52, 53, 56, 59, 60, 62, 63, 64, 65, 69, 70, 71, 72, 75, 76, 80, 89, 92, 96, 99, 104, 106, 114, 118, 132, 133, 134, 136, 138, 139, 140, 143, 147, 151, 153, 160, 169, 170, 172, 173, 179, 184, 199, 201, 216, 217, 220, 222, 225, 226, 230, 239,

249, 252, 254, 260, 270, 272, 276, 279, 307, 314, 315, 316, 321, 322, 324, 325, 326, 327, 330, 331, 332, 333
Israelite nation 141, 258
Israelites xiv, xvi, xxii, 13, 15, 16, 20, 32, 33, 35, 36, 37, 38, 42, 45, 46, 47, 50, 52, 54, 55, 56, 58, 59, 61, 64, 69, 70, 77, 78, 80, 81, 83, 86, 87, 96, 97, 99, 105, 106, 113, 121, 133, 135, 137, 158, 161, 167, 173, 225, 251, 252, 256, 257, 258, 259, 262, 313, 314, 316, 324, 328, 332, 333

J

Jacob 29, 30, 31, 33, 38, 43, 60, 96, 156, 198, 199, 257, 282, 289, 303, 324, 326, 333
jealousy 30, 229, 282, 303, 306, 307, 308, 309
Jeremiah (prophet) 71, 81, 83, 84, 86, 225, 226
Jewish Bibles 156, 158
Jews xv, xvi, 4, 13, 14, 32, 37, 47, 48, 54, 56, 57, 90, 92, 97, 107, 113, 114, 133, 137, 139, 140, 144, 145, 158, 160, 168, 169, 170, 174, 206, 207, 216, 217, 222, 224, 279, 280, 311, 321, 323, 325, 326, 327, 328, 329, 330, 331, 333
Jews, Orthodox xv, 224, 323
Jews, religious 133, 145
Jews, Sephardic 158, 331
Joseph (Hebrew patriarch) 29, 30, 31, 256, 257, 288, 289, 303, 333
Joshua (Israelite leader) 69, 70, 71, 89, 90, 97, 100
Jubilee 261, 262, 324, 325
judgment day 310, 311

justice system 5, 16, 17, 271

K

kidnapping 29, 30, 31, 262, 263, 264, 265

L

laws
    child protection 264
    court of 16, 49, 168, 169, 199, 229, 268, 296, 297, 302
    world 18
Levites 117, 201, 202, 259, 260, 315, 326
loyalty 93, 183, 189, 226, 237, 239, 251, 277

M

Maimonides (Torah scholar) xix, xx, xxii, 113, 149, 169
Malachi (prophet) 63, 238, 239
Marranos 96, 206, 327, 331
marriage contract 227, 228, 233, 234, 237, 240, 325
marriage, laws of 230, 231
medicine 11, 26, 76, 106, 107, 108, 110, 194, 249, 272, 292
miracles xiv, xxi, 56, 62, 65, 77, 78, 106, 120, 146, 147, 148, 167, 301, 315
mitzvah 25, 32, 56, 101, 110, 120, 121, 123, 128, 130, 162, 165, 167, 177, 179, 189, 191, 192, 193, 205, 208, 214, 218, 222, 240, 266, 278, 285, 286, 296, 307, 308, 328, 329
Moller, Lennart 22, 54
money,
    lending 279
Moses (Hebrew prophet) tablets xiv

Mount Sinai x, xxii, 20, 29, 34, 35, 37, 39, 40, 41, 45, 47, 49, 50, 52, 54, 55, 56, 63, 64, 69, 71, 136, 161, 259, 301, 314, 331

murder 5, 8, 9, 12, 30, 82, 98, 99, 126, 198, 199, 200, 201, 202, 204, 205, 207, 208, 209, 211, 212, 213, 215, 219, 222, 262, 266, 268, 273, 281, 296, 299, 303

N

nature, laws of 25, 110, 315

Noah (Hebrew patriarch) 1, 2, 4, 5, 7, 8, 14, 16, 17, 18, 21, 25, 27, 28, 29, 35, 149, 211, 328

non-Jews xvi, 13, 137, 139, 169, 216, 217

P

Pharaoh 32, 33, 37, 54, 78, 87, 256, 257, 258, 285, 288, 289

prayers xviii, xix, 15, 32, 33, 46, 57, 61, 63, 72, 84, 95, 115, 124, 160, 165, 166, 173, 174, 196, 267, 323, 329, 332

priests 35, 36, 73, 75, 89, 95, 120, 201, 202, 252, 254, 322, 324, 326

prophecy x, xix, xxii, 40, 49, 121, 226, 280

prophet xviii, xix, xx, xxi, xxii, 14, 20, 39, 49, 59, 60, 63, 80, 82, 93, 96, 121, 138, 156, 157, 159, 239, 246

Psalms, book of 124

punishment x, 13, 30, 72, 168, 169, 172, 180, 183, 229, 230, 233, 259, 262, 265, 297, 298

R

Rashi (commentator) 45, 46, 329

religions xix, xxii, 37, 58, 61, 62, 77, 87, 161, 162, 193, 204, 205

respect xii, xiii, xiv, 6, 31, 44, 74, 93, 106, 110, 111, 125, 127, 128, 169, 177, 178, 180, 181, 182, 183, 184, 185, 190, 192, 193, 195, 207, 217, 241, 272, 305

responsibility 192, 193, 246, 247, 262, 265, 272, 273, 274, 275, 276, 298

revenge 203, 299, 304

S

Sabbath ix, xvi, 23, 24, 29, 44, 57, 92, 124, 132, 133, 134, 136, 137, 139, 140, 141, 142, 145, 146, 150, 151, 152, 155, 156, 158, 159, 160, 161, 162, 164, 166, 167, 169, 170, 171, 172, 174, 175, 181, 191, 218, 223, 256, 260, 269, 280, 283, 322, 324, 326, 331

sacrifices 6, 14, 15, 16, 20, 69, 81, 86, 87, 88, 103, 140, 324

Saturday ix, xvi, 133, 134, 137, 138, 139, 171, 172, 174, 175, 181, 270, 322, 324, 326

science xi, 62, 65, 76, 89, 90, 242

scientists xi, 91, 139, 148

sex
    premarital 230, 231, 232, 233, 241, 247

Shabbat food 158

Shabbat violator 168

Shabbos xvi, 134, 135, 137, 164, 165, 166, 331

Shabbos Candles 164

sinner 179, 180, 200, 225

slavery 29, 32, 37, 38, 52, 56, 57, 138, 139, 173, 256, 259, 260, 261, 262, 323, 328
slaves 28, 38, 43, 56, 65, 124, 125, 136, 137, 138, 139, 167, 168, 199, 257, 259, 260, 261, 262, 285, 325
Song of Songs 249, 250, 251
stealing 30, 190, 255, 256, 260, 262, 264, 266, 268, 270, 272, 274, 276, 277, 278, 281, 282, 283
suicide 9, 98, 207, 208, 209, 210, 266
Sunday xi, 133, 134, 172, 174, 175

T

Ten commandment
    first 52, 53, 66, 67, 260
    second 31, 67, 99, 111, 176, 266, 296
    seventh 240, 254
    third 131, 287
Torah v, ix, x, xiv, xv, xvi, xviii, xix, xx, xxi, 2, 8, 15, 16, 20, 24, 36, 46, 47, 48, 53, 55, 57, 62, 63, 65, 66, 67, 70, 71, 75, 77, 81, 82, 84, 85, 87, 88, 89, 90, 94, 97, 98, 99, 104, 113, 114, 115, 117, 118, 121, 123, 128, 133, 138, 142, 143, 146, 147, 153, 159, 162, 163, 164, 165, 167, 169, 174, 175, 177, 180, 181, 183, 184, 189, 190, 200, 201, 202, 203, 204, 205, 211, 213, 215, 219, 223, 224, 225, 226, 227, 228, 229, 230, 231, 232, 233, 239, 240, 242, 245, 249, 255, 260, 261, 262, 263, 265, 266, 268, 272, 273, 274, 277, 278, 279, 280, 283, 289, 291, 294, 297, 298, 299, 300, 301, 304, 305, 314, 315, 316, 318, 321, 324, 326, 328, 329, 331, 332
Torah law 82, 147, 181, 225, 261, 263, 265, 272, 274, 279, 280, 294, 299

W

waters 17, 67, 112, 148, 149, 150, 250
Who is God? (Shemesh) x, 2, 38, 89, 116, 148, 199
wife 76, 92, 203, 224, 225, 226, 227, 228, 229, 231, 237, 238, 239, 243, 245, 246, 247, 248, 250, 254, 260, 261, 262, 276, 278, 282, 292, 293, 295, 303, 305, 306, 310, 326, 331
witnesses xxii, 94, 168, 200, 204, 234, 268, 296, 297, 298, 301, 311, 326

www.ingramcontent.com/pod-product-compliance
Lightning Source LLC
LaVergne TN
LVHW091528060526
838200LV00036B/530